Date Due

DIPLOMACY AT THE HIGHEST LEVEL

STUDIES IN DIPLOMACY
General Editors: G. R. Berridge and John W. Young, Centre for the
Study of Diplomacy, University of Leicester

David H. Dunn (*editor*)
DIPLOMACY AT THE HIGHEST LEVEL: The Evolution of
International Summitry

Michael Hughes
DIPLOMATS IN A TIME OF CHANGE: The British and Russian
Diplomatic Establishments, 1894–1917

M. J. Peterson
RECOGNITION OF GOVERNMENTS: Legal Doctrine and State
Practice, 1850–1995

Gary Rawnsley
RADIO DIPLOMACY AND PROPAGANDA: The BBC and Voice of
America in International Politics, 1954–64

Diplomacy at the Highest Level

The Evolution of International Summitry

Edited by

David H. Dunn

Lecturer in International Studies
University of Birmingham

First published in Great Britain 1996 by
MACMILLAN PRESS LTD
Houndmills, Basingstoke, Hampshire RG21 6XS
and London
Companies and representatives
throughout the world

This book is published in the *Studies in Diplomacy* series
General Editors: G. R. Berridge and John W. Young

A catalogue record for this book is available
from the British Library.

ISBN 0–333–64941–9

First published in the United States of America 1996 by
ST. MARTIN'S PRESS, INC.,
Scholarly and Reference Division,
175 Fifth Avenue,
New York, N.Y. 10010

ISBN 0–312–16273–1

Library of Congress Cataloging-in-Publication Data
Diplomacy at the highest level : the evolution of international
summitry / edited by David H. Dunn.
p.   cm. — (Studies in diplomacy)
Includes bibliographical references and index.
ISBN 0–312–16273–1 (cloth)
1. Diplomacy.   2. Summit meetings.   I. Dunn, David H.
II. Series.
JX1662.D535   1996
327.2—dc20   96–2976
                                                CIP

Selection, editorial matter and chapters 1 and 15 © David H. Dunn 1996
Chapters 2–14 © Macmillan Press Ltd 1996

10   9   8   7   6   5   4   3   2   1
05   04   03   02   01   00   99   98   97   96

Printed and bound in Great Britain by
Antony Rowe Ltd, Chippenham, Wiltshire

For Jayne

Contents

Acknowledgements

This project is in part the product of a seminar series of the Graduate School of International Studies at the University of Birmingham which took place in the autumn of 1994. As such a debt of gratitude is owed to the Graduate School for funding this seminar programme and to Elizabeth Bradley for help in its organization. I would like to thank Shahin P. Malik and Rob Shaw for their research assistance in the preparation of my contributions to this volume. Various sections of this work have been discussed at length and read throughout its preparation. Accordingly, I would like to thank Stuart Croft, Peter Wilson, Peter Willets, David Nicholls and David Malone for their efforts in this regard. I am also grateful to Gráinne Twomey of Macmillan for her tolerance over deadlines and to Geoff Berridge and John Young for their interest and encouragement as series editors. My thanks to Longman Group publishers for permission to reprint an amended version of John Young's chapter. Finally, I would like to thank my wife, Jayne, for her encouragement and support throughout this project.

Notes on the Contributors

Michael Andersen is a research student in the Department of Politics at the University of Exeter. His work is currently funded by a NATO Research Fellowship.

J. D. Armstrong is Professor of Politics at the University of Durham.

G. R. Berridge is Professor of International Politics and Director of the Centre for the Study of Diplomacy at the University of Leicester.

David H. Dunn is Lecturer in the Department of Political Science and International Studies at the University of Birmingham.

Theo Farrell is Lecturer in Security Studies in the Department of Politics at the University of Exeter.

Erik Goldstein is Reader in the Department of Byzantine, Ottoman and Modern Greek Studies at the University of Birmingham.

Richard Hodder-Williams is Professor of Politics at the University of Bristol.

John Lanchberry is Director of Environmental Projects at the Verification Technology Information Centre (VERTIC) in London and Research Scholar with the Implementation and Effectiveness of International Environmental Commitments Project at the International Institute for Applied Systems Analysis, Laxenburg, Austria.

James Mayall is Professor of International Relations at the London School of Economics and Political Science.

Sally Morphet is a civil servant in the Research and Analysis Department of the Foreign and Commonwealth Office, London.

Bill Park is Senior Lecturer in the Department of History and International Affairs at the Royal Naval College, Greenwich, and is also Visiting Lecturer at the City University, London.

John Redmond is Senior Lecturer in the Department of Political Science and International Studies at the University of Birmingham.

Mark Smith is a research student in the Department of International Politics at the University of Wales, Aberystwyth.

Edmund Yorke is Senior Lecturer in the Department of Defence and International Affairs at the Royal Military Academy, Sandhurst.

John Young is Professor of Politics at the University of Leicester.

Introduction
David H. Dunn

In the huge literature that has been written on the politics of the twentieth century about the relationship between domestic and international elements, there has been surprisingly little attention devoted to the institution of the summit meeting. The aim of this book is to fill that gap in the literature, and consider the changing role of the summit within international diplomacy. While there have been articles and books which deal with specific types of summitry, there has been in recent times no systematic attempt to address the subject as a whole at length.* Accordingly, this study traces the development of what has become an international institution. It elucidates a working definition of summitry, examines its evolution, and explains the different functions served by various types of summit.

The volume consists of fifteen chapters split into four parts. Part I sets the scene for the more specific studies of particular summit institutions in Part II, while Part III looks at specific *ad hoc* meetings. Part IV concludes the book with a more general examination of the advantages and disadvantages of summit meetings.

Part I analyses the evolution of summitry in two chapters. The first of these takes a thematic approach to explain the factors which have promoted the growth of summit meetings in the twentieth century. It also examines the various ways in which the term 'summitry' has been used in the post-war period, and sets out a working definition for the volume. Chapter 2 takes a historical approach, revealing the long history of this activity, and relating how modern summitry has evolved from conference diplomacy.

In Parts II and III various incarnations of international summitry are analysed in order to illustrate different environments and circumstances in

---

* See especially R. Schaetzel and H. B. Malmgren, 'Talking Heads', *Foreign Policy*, 1980; R. D. Putnum and N. Bayne, *Hanging Together: The Seven-Power Summits* (Cambridge, Mass., Harvard University Press, 1987); A. D. Clift, *With Presidents to the Summit* (Fairfax, Vir., George Mason University Press, 1993), and G. R. Weihmiller and D. Doder, *US–Soviet Summits* (London, University Press of America, 1986).

which summit meetings have been employed. While an attempt has been made to assemble a balanced set of case studies, any collection of essays on such a global activity can only strive to be representative. The choice of case studies, however, does span a broad range of summit activity. Part II looks at regular 'institutionalized' summits, and in each chapter the nature of the meetings is described. Who meets where, for how long, how often and for what purpose? Key turning-points in the relationships of the individuals, of the countries and in the development of the summit itself are also set out. Part III examines one-off or *ad hoc* summit meetings in order to show how important these diplomatic episodes were and how summitry has evolved over time. In Part II the authors address five questions in approaching their case studies:

1.   To what extent are summits mainly symbolic and to what extent are they substantive? Are they just an opportunity for a photo-call, or are they more often than not the venue and opportunity for substantial dialogue?

2.   To what extent is the substance of the summit negotiations largely concluded before the meeting takes place? Are they 'pre-cooked' or free-ranging? How much scope is there for individual participants to make a difference to the result of the summit meetings?

3.   To what extent is the format of a summit meeting best suited to high as opposed to low politics? How practical are summits as fora to influence and shape international events? Are they a useful institution, and are they more successful for certain subjects under certain circumstances than for others?

4.   To what extent do summits serve domestic as well as foreign policy goals? Has the relationship between these two functions evolved in a particular direction and if it has, what factors have driven this trend?

5.   To what extent are these particular summits now firmly institutionalized as part of a fixed regime? Are they still evolving, or are they unlikely to change substantially? Is their importance being diminished by the increasing frequency of less formal personal diplomacy (for instance, telephone calls between heads of government), or by the growing number of specialist advisers who are in more regular diplomatic contact?

While some authors have addressed these questions more explicitly than others, this framework allows the case studies to contribute in a focused way to our understanding of the ways in which the use of summit meetings has evolved to suit different circumstances. In Part II, the main institutionalized summits are analysed. The studies of the G-7 Western Economic Summit, the European Council, and NATO summits offer particularly revealing insights into the way in which these different institutions, which involve many of the same countries, produce very different styles of summit meeting. While NATO summits are mostly bland affairs where the conclusions have largely been worked out beforehand, European Council meetings are often the venue for truly substantive dialogue and negotiations. G-7 summits by contrast, which are usually informal in nature, can be wide-ranging in subject matter but tend to be of much less consequence than the other two fora. Farrell and Andersen's study of superpower summits illustrates how these meetings acted as a mechanism for the regulation of the US–Soviet relationship during the cold war. These summits were important, they argue, in providing a means for the leaders to take each other's measure, for allowing a non-violent means of asserting status and for providing an impetus for arms control and disarmament. Similarly, Morphet's study of the Non-Aligned Movement illustrates how its summit meetings have provided new regimes with an opportunity to learn about global politics, assert their collective standing, and promote a distinctive international policy agenda. Hodder-Williams' study of summitry among African states also shows the importance of this type of meeting to these newly independent states. The lack of an alternative diplomatic structure in many post-colonial African states, together with the trend towards centralized rule, established summitry as the main forum for substantive international dialogue on this continent. Another legacy of the decolonization process is the Commonwealth Heads of Government Meeting (CHOGM), analysed by Mayall, who describes it as an 'association of states which are not necessarily like-minded but which find the historical accident that has brought them together useful for a wide variety of continuing reasons'. Berridge's analysis of funeral summits illustrates the more general trend of the growth of summit meetings as a consequence of advances in technology and the increased informality of international dialogue.

In Part III specific 'one-off' or *ad hoc* summit meetings are analysed in more detail. These four summits, which span the post-war period, illustrate the learning process which has taken place in the use of international meetings of this nature. Young's analysis of the Bermuda summit demonstrates the pitfalls of the lack of detailed preparation on several counts. The lack of an agreed agenda and the summiteers' inattention to the press coverage of the event contributed to the failure of this early summit. The controversy surrounding the role of the Nassau summit in securing the purchase of the Polaris missile system is analysed by Smith, who concludes, though less forcefully than others, that this summit was the venue for a dialogue between conflicting foreign policy priorities and that the act of meeting clearly affected Kennedy's decision over Polaris. A similar conclusion is reached by Yorke in his analysis of the Lancaster House Summit on the future of Rhodesia. Yorke describes the multiplicity of means used by the British goverment to exert influence on the delegates, including applying pressure at the preceding summits of the CHOGM at Lusaka and at the Non-Aligned Movement in Cuba, and exploiting the leverage of the Royal family in London. The role of the 1992 Earth Summit in Rio de Janeiro, attended by 183 countries, is examined by Lanchberry. He explains that having such a large group of world leaders gathered together in some circumstances effectively prevents meaningful dialogue, since the number of individuals involved is simply too great. He concludes, however, that without the political profile which the summit gave to the environmental agenda, it is doubtful whether any of the agreements reached would have been concluded, let alone implemented, with such speed.

Part IV of the book seeks to draw some general conclusions about the advantages and disadvantages of summitry. It does so by offering, where possible, different examples from the summits analysed within the preceding chapters in an effort to illustrate further the points being made. Although not specifically addressing the five questions set out above, it does cover the issues they raise.

The development of summit diplomacy in the twentieth century has had a significant impact on the way in which the dialogue between states is conducted. Its development as a new institution of diplomacy has been controversial since its contribution to international politics has been both positive and negative. It is a subject area, however, which has remained surprisingly under-studied. It is intended that the essays in this book will provoke further interest and debate in this important area of international relations.

Part I
The Evolution of Summitry

1 What is Summitry?
David H. Dunn

INTRODUCTION

Summitry has become an established part of the political interactions of states in the twentieth century. Not only has 'summitry' become an established term, but so too has the panoply of associated language, such as 'pre-summit' 'base camp' meetings prepared and supported by staff known as 'sherpas'.[1] Neither the activity of this type of diplomacy, however, nor the level at which these interactions take place are new. Indeed the practice of sovereigns meeting to discuss their affairs is one which pre-dates the establishment of resident embassies in the fifteenth century, and was also a commonplace of court weddings and funerals. Meetings were also arranged for specific purposes, such as the conference arranged by King Vortigen of Kent with the Jutish chieftains of Horsa and Hengist in AD 449 in order to solicit support against the Picts and the Scots.[2] A further example is provided by the meeting of Napoleon and Alexander I of Russia on a raft in the middle of the river Niemen near Tilset in East Prussia in 1807 to discuss relations between their two states. What is unique to the present age, however, is the frequency with which these meetings take place, and the extent to which they have replaced more established and traditional methods of diplomatic discourse.[3] Huge periods of time each year in the diaries of world leaders are now blocked off for pre-scheduled meetings of various international organizations. Further time is also consumed by meetings at short notice, either in bilateral or multilateral settings. This chapter sets out to explain the origins and the evolution of this development in international politics. Firstly it will explain various factors which have promoted the development of meetings at this level. It will then analyse the various ways in which the concept has been broadened in its usage to reflect a much wider type of high-level meeting. The pitfalls of such usage will be examined in an attempt to construct a more useful and durable definition.

THE DEVELOPMENT OF SUMMITRY

The term 'summit' comes from Winston Churchill's constant calls during the 1950s for meetings at the highest levels of government to resolve international differences. Addressing the House of Commons in 1953, for instance, Churchill asked: 'If there is not at the summit of the nations the wish to win the greatest prize of peace, where can men look for hope?'[4] It was a concept linked in its initial incarnation to both the issues and situation of a world gripped by the affairs of the Great Powers. Implicit in its initial definition was also the idea of a meeting of rivals, if not antagonists, to discuss issues of high politics of global consequence. As the number and purpose of high-level meetings increased in the post-war period, however, this definition of summitry has been relaxed as the term has been broadened to include a variety of different high-level contacts, a theme that will be returned to below.

As old as it is, summitry has been consistently resented by professional diplomats, who have constantly warned of the dangers of amateurism. In the fifteenth century Philippe de Commynes was among the first to urge caution in this regard, advising that 'two great princes who wish to establish good personal relations should never meet each other face to face, but ought to communicate through good and wise emissaries'.[5] Writing in the eighteenth century, François de Callières warned that 'the passions of princes and of their ministers often overrule their interests'. Similarly the English diplomatist Harold Nicolson, writing in 1939, was equally convinced that

> repeated personal visits ... should not be encouraged. Such visits arouse public expectation, lead to misunderstandings and create confusion. The time at the disposal of these visitors is not always sufficient to allow for patience and calm deliberation. The honours which are paid to a minister in a foreign capital may tire his physique, excite his vanity or bewilder his judgement. His desire not to offend his host may lead him with lamentable result to avoid raising unpalatable questions or to be imprecise regarding acute points of controversy.[6]

Such comments, while commonly expressed by career diplomats, are not confined to that profession. Former Secretary of State Dean Rusk also cautioned against this expediency, warning that 'summit diplomacy is to be approached with the wariness with which a prudent physician prescribes a habit-forming drug – a technique to be employed rarely and under the most exceptional circumstances with rigorous safeguards against its becoming a debilitating or dangerous habit'. He went on to add that 'the experienced diplomat will usually counsel against the direct confrontation of those with final authority'.[7] Similarly, academic Keith Eubank concluded his study of the summit meetings which took place between 1919 and 1960 with the view that 'none of these summit conferences proved that the heads of governments performed better, quicker, more accurately, or more efficiently than their foreign ministers or their professional diplomats. There is no proof that their presence made the agreement any better or any more durable; often the reverse was true.'[8]

Given such hostility to this development within international statecraft it is necessary to ask why this practice has grown, for despite constant opposition, as Schaetzel and Malmgren explain, 'casually and without plans summitry has transmogrified from a spontaneous event into a new international institution'.[9] A number of features of twentieth-century political life can be used to explain this development. Not least of these has been the ferocity, duration and magnitude of both the physical and political conflicts which have characterized twentieth-century international politics.

CRISIS DIPLOMACY

Summitry grew initially out of political crisis where the speedy conclusion of grave international questions was at a premium. As Abba Eban wrote of the wartime gatherings of the Big Three, 'only the emergency of war could have impelled these elderly men and their associates to accept such frequent toil and risk'.[10] With the war ended no superpower summit meetings took place until 1955, when the cold war had deepened to such an extent that the extraordinary nature of this form of diplomacy was once again considered necessary. As the cold war continued the feeling developed among politicians that diplomacy in the nuclear age was too important to be left to the diplomatists. Thus developed the trend for greater involvement by political leaders in the detailed process of international dialogue. The development of the idea of 'crisis management' as a discrete activity, separate from more regular diplomatic dialogue, accentuated this trend at the emissary level, with the 'shuttle diplomacy' of US Secretary of State John Foster Dulles an early example of this art.

TECHNOLOGICAL DEVELOPMENTS

The technological developments of the twentieth century have also been responsible for the development of summitry. After all, the establishment of resident embassies and ambassadors with plenipotentiary powers were acts of necessity rather than choice in the first instance. Nor was this system such an unparalleled success as the professional diplomatists would have us believe. Not all emissaries were willing to act on their own initiative in the way that Americans Robert Livingston and James Monroe were over the Louisiana purchase. When ordered to purchase New Orleans and West Florida from the French for $10 million, Livingston and Monroe exceeded their instructions considerably in order to buy 820 000 square miles between the Mississippi River and the Rocky Mountains for $15 million. For many others, however, the inability to communicate with their political masters resulted only in caution and inactivity.[11] As Roetter explains, 'the vast majority [of ambassadors] asked for instructions from home in every instance, knowing that it would be weeks or months before a reply could arrive and that the conditions and circumstances with which the instructions were supposed to deal would almost certainly have changed in the meantime. It was all a splendid excuse for doing nothing.'[12]

Without the need to rely on the judgement of ambassadors operating without the means for consultation, it is only natural that political principals want a more direct role in the resolution of their foreign policy concerns. With the advent of travel by jet aircraft, on some routes at supersonic speeds, it is not surprising that politicians seek to present their arguments firsthand, especially in matters of high politics where an atmosphere of crisis prevails. Thus, during the crisis following the invasion of the Falkland Islands in 1982, the British Foreign Minister was able to leave London at eight in the morning in order to attend a crisis meeting in New York at the same time on the same day.

Travel by jet aircraft has not only meant that political principals can meet at short notice and with a minimum of inconvenience, it also means that the loss of contact with a negotiating partner who is in transit can be substantially reduced if not eliminated. The absence of contact with the Japanese delegates to the 1935 Naval Conference during their five-week journey by sea to London stands in marked contrast to the thirteen hours that the journey takes today.[13]

In addition to their impact on the means of travel, technological developments have also influenced the development of summitry in other ways. The ease with which heads of government can now communicate by telephone, facsimile, video-link and other electronic means has increased both the contact between political principals and their involvement in foreign policy matters. This familiarity with both the issues and the personalities of their opposite numbers has also led to a greater willingness to meet in person in order to resolve outstanding issues rather than to rely on the regular diplomatic channels. Here the growth in the number of summit meetings is part of a more general trend of heads of government bypassing the regular diplomatic channels in order to get an immediate and authoritative response. As President Carter's National Security Adviser Brzezinski explains, 'I was many times in the Oval office when the President would reach for the telephone and phone the Prime Minister of the United Kingdom or the Chancellor of Germany. The chances were that we probably wouldn't even bother to tell our ambassador that such a conversation took place because it was so frequent.'[14] Improvements in communications have also made it much easier to actually arrange summit meetings at short notice and with minimum disruption to other business.

FUNERAL SUMMITS

Although this is a practice with a long history, the improvements in the speed, safety and comfort of air travel which were introduced in the 1960s have led to the gradual development of funeral diplomacy.[15] Although necessarily brief in nature, and varying in the preparation time involved, these peculiar opportunities for high-level meetings provide a valuable point of contact between the new leadership and foreign politicians. They are relatively risk-free for the participants, since paying respects to the dead is unlikely to be regarded as a political concession, even when these respects are to the leader of an antagonistic regime. The deaths and state funerals in quick succession of Brezhnev, Andropov and Chernenko, for example, provided good opportunities for various side meetings between the 'mourners'. The latter two funerals provided the occasion for fruitful meetings between West German Chancellor Helmut Kohl and East German leader Erich Honecker, the first meeting of the two leaders of divided Germany.[16] Former British Foreign Secretary Geoffrey Howe also described how Andropov's funeral 'gave opportunities for Margaret [Thatcher] and myself to meet foreign leaders, with whom bilateral meetings had not, until then, been easy to arrange, from Spain's Prime Minister Felipe Gonzalez to Pakistan's President Zia'.[17]

The growth of the 'working funeral' has also been facilitated by other twentieth-century developments. Technological improvements in embalmment and refrigeration have aided this diplomatic practice since quick burials are no longer required for reasons of public hygiene. The increasing secularization of diplomacy has also reduced the taboo of conducting business on such occasions.

THE NEW DIPLOMACY

Summit diplomacy is also very much a product of the New Diplomacy, that is diplomacy in the democratic age between open and accountable governments. It is in this context that a meeting between heads of government can be seen by domestic audiences as a good thing in its own right, irrespective of any more tangible benefits which might result. According to former American Under Secretary of State George Ball, this view is based on 'the widespread misperception as to what foreign policy is all about. It is too often assumed that nations have no opposing interests or objectives that are fundamental and that the world's peoples could all live happily together "if only they could understand one another".'[18] Increasing understanding, of course, will only result in a relaxation of tensions if the original antagonism was caused by misunderstanding. If the tension was caused by more fundamental disagreements then further clarification of the position, especially at the highest level, may actually worsen the relationship. Despite this fact, belief in the importance of the atmospherics of summitry is often fanned by the press coverage which attends such meetings and, indeed, by the statements of politicians themselves, keen to exploit such opportunities for domestic political gain. Thus although little that was tangible was gained from the meetings of the Great Powers in the 1950s, much was made of 'the spirit of Geneva' in 1955, and 'the spirit of Camp David' in 1959. Writing in 1985 on the importance of superpower summits, Nixon was dismissive of the importance of such factors in international politics, stating that

> Spirit and tone only matter when two leaders of nations with similar interests have a misunderstanding that can be resolved by their getting to know each other. Such factors are irrelevant when nations have irreconcilable differences, which is the case as far as the United States and the Soviet Union are concerned.[19]

Interestingly the same sentiment was expressed by Khrushchev in his memoirs, in which he asked,

> Do you think when two representatives holding diametrically opposing views get together to shake hands, the contradictions between our systems will simply melt away? What kind of daydream is this?

Not all politicians are so cynical, however, and as a consequence they too can believe that differences can be reconciled by reasoned dialogue. It was on this basis that Chamberlain tried to reason with Hitler at Munich, taking as his first principle that war would be so terrible that all reasonable men would wish to avoid it. President Reagan shared this utopian optimism believing that personal contact could dispel ideological differences which were the real substance of international conflict. His memoirs are replete with statements of his wish to 'get a top Soviet leader in a room alone and try to convince him we had no designs on the Soviet Union and Russians had nothing to fear from us'. Despite having no summit meetings with the Soviet leadership until 1985, Reagan wrote in his memoirs that

> Starting with Brezhnev, I'd dreamed of personally going one-on-one with a Soviet leader because I thought we might be able to accomplish things our countries' diplomats couldn't do because they didn't have the authority. Putting that another way, I felt that if you got the top people negotiating and talking at a summit and then the two of you came out arm in arm saying, 'We've agreed to this,' the bureaucrats wouldn't be able to louse up the agreement.[20]

It was this belief which informed Reagan's approach to the 1986 Reykjavik summit, at which unaccompanied negotiations between the two superpower leaders resulted in proposals and tentative agreements which caused great alarm within both the US bureaucracy and among America's NATO allies.[21] It was this approach to summit meetings which lead to heightened public expectations of these meetings. This was particularly true of superpower summits during the cold war when the press coverage of these events gave the impression that the prospects of war or peace could be materially influenced by these talks.

POLITICIANS' SUSPICIONS OF DIPLOMATS

An associated feature of both the proliferation of states and different regimes and the new diplomacy is the incumbency of politicians with very different personal, professional and educational backgrounds from the diplomats who serve them. One of the consequences of this trend is that politicians may not always trust and value the information and advice that the diplomats provide. Stalin, for instance, regarded the entire diplomatic profession as being intrinsically bourgeois and consequently untrustworthy. 'With a diplomat,' he wrote, 'words *must* diverge from acts.... Words are one thing and acts something different.... A sincere diplomat would equal dry water, wooden iron.'[22] As a consequence Stalin, and later Khrushchev, insisted on conducting their own negotiations. It was also for this reason that President Nixon justified his summit diplomacy with both the Soviet and Chinese regimes. Where power was vested in a single man, he insisted, it was necessary to deal on a one-to-one basis. Even critics of summitry, such as former diplomat Sir Geoffrey Jackson, who regarded the summit diplomacy of the Nixon administration as 'arbitrary, vulgar and tough', was willing to concede that this 'was probably the best way of eliciting quick decisions from tough and authoritarian men, whether as individuals or as collective dictatorships'.[23]

Such suspicions as Stalin's, however, are not restricted to revolutionary states. Writing on the British Foreign Office before the Second World War Gordon Craig lamented the fact that the expert advice of the diplomatic service was routinely ignored by its political masters, stating that

> There was a recurring tendency on the part of the political leaders of the state when matters of high moment were pending to believe that the professionals in the foreign office were incompetent to deal with them because of their narrowness of view, dependence on traditional concepts or lack of realism. Lloyd George believed this, Ramsey MacDonald believed this and it became dogma with Neville Chamberlain.[24]

More recently Prime Minister Thatcher, whether at home or abroad, displayed the same distrust of the British Foreign and Commonwealth Office by relying on her own personal advisers at the expense of the formal structures. As Geoffrey Howe notes, 'by the end of her time she was conducting herself abroad virtually with the sole support of two personal assistants. ... On occasion she was reluctant even for our local ambassador to accompany her to meetings with "his" head of government.'[25] Thatcher herself describes how she liked to keep 'tight personal control over decisions' she considered especially important, such as British reactions to President Reagan's Strategic Defence Initiative, arguing that 'irreparable harm could have been done to our relations with the United States had the wrong line or even tone been adopted'.[26]

Such distrust of the official foreign policy bureaucracy highlights the tension between two different conceptions of the right qualifications to represent the state abroad. On the one hand professional diplomats stress their linguistic expertise, diplomatic training and knowledge of the country in which they are serving, qualities not always found in politicians. Indeed in this regard Ernest Bevin once remarked that Foreign Secretary was the only job he could ever hold in the British Foreign Office since he could not have become even a fourth secretary not having passed examinations in history and French.[27] Political leaders, on the other hand, stress the importance of their electoral mandate as evidence that they are more in tune with the wishes and interests of the electorate than the diplomat, who may have spent 20 years away from the home country. Though these things need not necessarily be in conflict, with the ideal being a blend of professional knowledge guided by political directives, in practice there are tensions which have contributed both to the growth of summitry and its resentment by the diplomatic service.

CONCENTRATION OF POLITICAL POWER AT THE CENTRE

The growth of executive power in both general terms and in foreign policy in particular is a feature of modern politics in many countries and has also led to the growth of summitry. In foreign policy this trend is at the expense of both the professional diplomatic service and the foreign minister. Whereas in previous ages political principals have been willing to delegate this area of responsibility, the modern trend is for this function to be jealously guarded. Former British Foreign Secretary Geoffrey Howe's comment that he came to dislike travelling abroad with Mrs Thatcher 'because of her unquenchable tendency to play second fiddle as well as first' captures this point beautifully.[28] Equally revealing is Thatcher's own comment with regard to Britain's relations with Washington that 'laid back generalists from the Foreign office – let alone the ministerial muddlers in charge of them – could not be relied upon'.[29] The tendency for presidents and prime ministers to try to be their own foreign secretaries has also resulted in less able ministers being appointed to these posts as the job itself is downgraded in the cabinet hierarchy to a position below finance and trade. It is also a trend which is self-reinforcing, since differences of position between leaders and their foreign secretaries lead to the discounting of the views of the latter, and a desire only to deal with the former.[30] An associative trend of the tendency of leaders to usurp the positions of their foreign secretaries is that trade and finance ministers are increasingly called upon to accompany or to represent the head of government in some meetings instead of foreign ministers, in recognition that they possess skills and knowledge appropriate to the agendas of such events. This trend is not universal, however, and where possible many leaders prefer the control and intimacy of one-to-one summit meetings.[31] This trend is particularly true in countries with constitutions which allow strong executive leadership. Such concentration of political power at the centre is also a feature of many of the newest states to gain their independence.

EXPANSION OF THE INTERNATIONAL COMMUNITY

Summitry has developed as an international institution in the twentieth century in part as a consequence of the expansion of the international community. As a result of the various waves of decolonization, including most recently the collapse of the Soviet Empire, the diversity and number of states has greatly increased. While most of these states have adopted the European model of diplomatic representation as part of the process of joining international society, not all have replicated it in all its forms. A country's embassies, for example, might be used as a place of exile for opponents of the regime, be manned by military personnel in order to ensure their loyalty, or staffed on the basis of political favours or family bonds.[32] In such circumstances the inability of these channels to provide a reliable service often results in their circumvention. Such situations reinforce the tendency for newer actors, both states and regimes, to conduct their foreign policy through the centre, thus leading to a growth in summitry by heads of government and their special envoys.[33] This trend is also a consequence of the limited resources of small or poor countries who are less able to provide the foreign exchange necessary for a comprehensive diplomatic service of resident embassies. Following the decolonization of the 1960s, many countries were also left with few trained diplomats and no established diplomatic machinery, since all foreign representation had been conducted through the metropolitan power. What started out as a necessity for these countries soon became an established custom, particularly among newly independent states.[34]

REGIONAL DIPLOMACY

The growth of regional diplomacy is another contributory factor in the development of summitry. The proliferation of groups of states within a regional setting for either joint economic development or for a defensive alliance has become a common feature of the second half of the twentieth century. The development of fast air travel has accelerated this process, bringing countries formerly considered remote into closer touch and understanding. As Satow observes, 'previous to 1945, an Organisation of African Unity was neither politically nor physically thinkable'.[35]

These groupings range in scale and scope from the comprehensive and well-established European Union (EU) to the embryonic and issue-specific Asia Pacific Economic Cooperation forum (APEC). While most such groupings are indeed primarily geographically linked, other groupings of states are formed around single issues, such as the Organisation of Petroleum Exporting Countries (OPEC), or specific identities, such as the Arab League. Such groupings have contributed greatly to the growth of summit meetings at which participation by heads of governments is politically necessary.

This development of regional and functional groupings of states in the twentieth century reflects the growth in the role of governments domestically and the interdependence of states internationally. In the post-war period, governments have become increasingly involved in economic, social and technical affairs which they had previously ignored or left to other agencies, such as central banks. With this burgeoning government agenda increasingly influenced by global or regional factors there has been a corresponding growth in the need for international contact on these questions. Indeed the degree to which states can provide for the needs of their citizens unilaterally while limiting their contact with foreigners to issues of high politics continues to decline as the century progresses. The growth of truly global issues such as environmental concerns and international terrorism has also created issue areas which political principals feel they ought to address directly.

WORLD TRADE AND COMMERCIAL DIPLOMACY

One such global issue which has provided another stimulus for the proliferation of summit meetings is the growing interdependence of the world economy, which has led to the expansion of commercial diplomacy. It was for this purpose that Prime Minister Thatcher utilized her visit to Asia in 1984 to sign the Joint Declaration on Hong Kong to promote British business in various capitals of the world en route to, and from, this meeting. The visit by President Bush to Japan in the run-up to the 1992 elections was a similar example of commercial diplomacy. Bush went primarily as the head of a delegation of industrialists rather than as a visiting head of state, but crucially he did meet the Japanese leadership in order to present his case for greater market access. As governments become increasingly involved in the promotion and management of bilateral trade on an intergovernmental basis, it seems likely that this trend in summitry will continue.

WHAT CONSTITUTES A SUMMIT?

As has been demonstrated above, in the twentieth century summit meetings have become more frequent and the purposes for which they have been utilized have been widened. The term 'summit' has been used to describe other high-level meetings and contact between leading politicians and, in some instances, officials. The way in which the term has been used by the news media has evolved considerably from Churchill's initial conception in which the 'highest level' not only implied the meetings of political leaders but also the meetings of leading states. Writing in 1963 in defence of this definition, Donald Watt argued that for a meeting to qualify as a summit it must be multilateral and be between 'the recognised leaders of the great powers'.[36] This overly restrictive definition of summitry, however, was wholly unconvincing even at the time, since it excluded Khrushchev's meetings with Eisenhower in 1959 and Kennedy in 1961.[37] More importantly this definition had already been abandoned in contemporary popular media usage in favour of one which included almost any gathering of heads of government. Thus, writing in 1976 Ball complained that

today the word 'summitry' is used, without discrimination to describe any occasion on which chiefs of state or heads of government get together bilaterally or in large meetings. It has, as a result, become so vague in meaning as to be not only useless but downright misleading.[38]

At its broadest level, the term is indeed, as Ball suggests, of little value in that it is indistinguishable from the activities of heads of government, their ministers and officials in the foreign policy arena. *Time*, for example, used the front page headline 'The Sisterhood Summit' to describe the UN's Fourth World Conference on Woman in Beijing.[39] A broad definition is also favoured by Elmer Plischke, who argues that the term 'has gradually been broadened to include less formal meetings, official visits, and communications among political leaders'. Addressing his remarks to the American political system, Plischke goes even further in arguing that the term is sufficiently broad to be able to encompass

the following distinguishable elements: (1) presidential foreign policy-making and enunciation, (2) personal presidential communications, (3) presidential personal representatives or special agents, (4) visits of world leaders to the United States, (5) presidential visits and tours abroad, and (6) summit meetings and conferences.[40]

While such a definition of summitry may well reflect the loose way in which the term is used journalistically, a more narrow interpretation is both possible and more desirable. A clearer definition of summitry can be gained by analysing the different ways in which the term has been used and the advantages and problems which those usages present. For this purpose it is useful to look in turn at two categories of usage: the actors or 'agents' involved in summits, and the activities which constitute such meetings.

Agency

As the discussion of Watt's notion of summitry above shows, the definition of agency at summits has clearly evolved since the first post-war meetings. How far this definition can usefully be expanded, however, while still remaining a term of conceptual clarity, is open to question. Plischke offers the following definition of summitry:

> Simply stated it is diplomacy engaged in by political principals above the cabinet or ministerial rank, including the participation of chiefs of state, heads of government, a few others who qualify by virtue of their official positions (such as presidents-elect, crown princes, and the ranking officers of international organizations), and certain agents of heads of government *who genuinely represent* them at their level.[41]

The key feature of this definition is the notion of executive agency. For Plischke, meetings may take place between heads of government or their special representatives which are summits, provided that they all act explicitly as or on behalf of the political principal of the state. The problem with this approach is that what constitutes executive agency is very difficult to identify and may be inconsistent between individuals at the same notional level. At any level executive agency may vary from issue to issue within negotiations and across time. As a result a foreign minister might have the authority to act on some issues but not to trade across the agenda, whereas his counterpart may have a similar level of authority, but in incompatible areas. There is also the question of how far down the chain of command this agency goes. Are ambassadors, or even second secretaries, who are genuinely acting on the explicit instructions of their head of government, engaged in summitry? If so then how does this function differ from the ancient diplomatic role of representation? A way around this problem, which is implicit in many critiques of summitry, is for the term to be applied only to those activities which involve politicians. Certainly many of the features, both positive and negative, attributed to summitry are more generally applicable to the involvement in diplomacy of professional politicians. Excluding officials from a definition of summitry in favour of politicians, however, is not problem-free, since the problem of definition arises again for those whose system does not maintain a clear distinction between career posts and politically appointed posts in the diplomatic service. The US Foreign Service, and the higher ranks of the State Department, as well as the diplomatic service of many developing countries are populated by individuals who owe their position to party or personal political contacts. As a result, it is not always easy to establish where precisely executive agency stops. If the definition is further restricted to cabinet members then some of these problems are eliminated, but others remain. As well as the inconsistency of executive agency among governments, within cabinets themselves the authority with which different individuals speak can also vary enormously. This is particularly true of cabinets of coalition governments, or where different factions are represented for the sake of party unity. The trend for the concentration of power in foreign affairs in the hands of those with executive authority also complicates the issue of executive agency. Where there is the perception that going over the head of a minister or an official may result in a different position or even nuance, the notion of executive agency is compromised.

Another problem with the notion of executive agency, which will be returned to below, is that even heads of government may lack the authority to interact on equal terms with their international counterparts. Political leaders possess different degrees of executive agency depending on the nature of their domestic political system and their own standing within it. Thus differences exist between the constitutional positions of presidents and prime ministers, and there are different levels of executive power between leaders of coalition governments and dominant party systems. Thus even President Carter was unable to deliver the ratification of the SALT II Treaty, despite his solemn undertaking to do so at his summit meeting with Brezhnev in 1979. Thus it could legitimately be asked whether this notion of executive agency is useful at all in describing diplomacy at the highest level, since ultimate authority is not guaranteed even by the commitments of heads of state. Certainly the amount of authority exercised by leaders, relative to their ministers, differs by a matter of degree, rather than of kind.

Thus the focus on executive agency in an attempt to broaden the definition of agency at summit meetings poses problems. If it is defined too broadly it can become indistinguishable from the process of foreign policy-making and implementation, as Plischke's definition implies. A more useful distinction which can meaningfully differentiate summit meetings from other diplomatic and political activity is the involvement of the head of government or state. Even if their participation coincides with other official and ministerial negotiations, taking place at the same time or in parallel discussions, the key element of summitry is executive participation, diplomacy at the highest possible level. Individual leaders may differ in their ability to deliver on the agreements reached, but by virtue of their position they are not able to be contradicted by any other individual.

Where the head of government is in dispute outside of the constitutional framework, such as in a civil war, then a meeting of the leaders of the various factions is also a summit meeting. Thus the Lancaster House Conference on the future of Rhodesia-Zimbabwe also qualifies as a summit, since the negotiations were conducted at the highest possible level. Indeed participation in summits is not totally confined to leaders of states. Leaders of international organizations such as NATO, the Commonwealth and the European Commission also attend summit meetings as do the heads of other non-state actors such as the PLO and, before post-apartheid South Africa, the ANC. As leaders of recognizable political entities their meetings with heads of government also qualify as summits. The activity which constitutes a summit, however, is another area of controversy.

Activity

While the activity required of a summit meeting seems somewhat self-evident when we consider the early post-war summit meetings, this has subsequently become much less clear. The early summits were exceptional, substantive, multi-issue affairs which offered the only opportunity for world leaders to conclude their business in a timely and secure manner. By contrast modern communications technology offers the opportunity for video-conferencing, whether live on CNN or privately on the various hot lines that now exist. Although Plischke is content to include 'summit communications' in his description of summit activity, the concept of 'summitry' thereby runs the risk of becoming indistinguishable from the routine communication which takes place between one chief executive's office and another's.[42] Even if this communication involves the active participation of the heads of government, to describe this activity as summitry is to move away from the idea that such meetings are exceptional and that they have a special value because of that. However, the act of sitting down together as opposed to talking on the telephone as a distinction between what is and what is not a summit is a fine line to draw. Yet the very act of visiting someone, because it is more difficult and because it usually involves a ceremonial dimension, does represent a greater commitment of time, energy and political risk than is present in a telephone call. The public diplomacy dimension of summitry is also important to the success of these meetings, since it is often the desire for an outcome which is a public success which enables previously intractable obstacles to be overcome. Similarly, the personal interaction of individuals in a one-to-one environment is often cited as being of value in itself and in the resolution of other issues. Clearly the psychological dimension of physically meeting does offer something quantifiably different from telephone diplomacy.

Thus a more useful and more discrete definition than that offered by Plischke would require that a high-level meeting actually takes place. In this sense summitry must be differentiated from diplomatic contact between political principals as part of the growing trend of 'personal diplomacy' where diplomatic communication is engaged in by remote means. As a result the exchange of long and detailed telegrams on matters of substance, such as those between Eisenhower and Khrushchev, and the frequent telephone conversations between heads of government, such as the lobbying of foreign powers by President Bush following the Iraqi invasion of Kuwait in 1990, would be excluded by this definition. While summitry is a part of personal diplomacy, then, the two are not identical.

This is not to say, however, that summit meetings are always more substantive and politically significant than less formal and remote communications between leaders. Summit meetings are distinguished by their form of personal contact and the level of the meetings that take place rather than the importance of the issues discussed or the results obtained. Whether bilateral or multilateral the purpose and nature of summit meetings varies greatly.

But are all meetings of political leaders summits? Hamilton and Langhorne argue that while the term 'summitry' has been widely applied to most meetings of heads of government 'many purely ceremonial and less formalized encounters have so far escaped the epithet'.[43] Excluding such meetings from a definition of summitry is not without its problems, however, not least because most visits (with the exception of private visits which can be omitted) combine ceremonial and substantive, formal and informal elements. More importantly even summit meetings which are primarily ceremonial or informal may be of great importance to one or more parties. There is no necessity for all parties to view a high-level meeting as equally important for it to be classified as diplomacy at the highest level, even if it is only high-level symbolism. That is not to say, however, that all summit meetings are equally important or that we should view them all in the same way.

One useful distinction in bilateral summitry, which involves the visit by one head of government to another, is that made between 'official' or 'State' visits with their full ceremonial accompaniments, and 'official working' visits which focus more on substantive dialogue. Here the nature of the programme indicates the purpose for which the visit has been conducted.[44] More conceptually, Berridge has identified three different kinds of summitry. First, the 'serial summit' conference, which is part of a regular series of meetings; second, the *ad hoc* summit, which is usually an issue-specific one-off affair but which may turn out to be the first of a series; and third, the high-level 'exchange of views'. The latter type of meeting is more often bilateral than multilateral, is most often low-key and may even be secret. In line with this, these meetings are often arranged for more modest purposes such as gaining intelligence, clarifying intentions or clearing the way for progress in negotiations at a lower level.[45] Thus different types of summit exist for different purposes without this affecting their status as a summit.

SUMMARY

Summitry has re-emerged in the post-war period as a significant diplomatic institution for a variety of reasons. The impact of communications technology and the processes of democratization and decolonization have been among the most significant influences on this development. Along with the increased frequency of summit meetings has gone a broadening of the activities to which the term has been applied. From a restricted usage in the early post-war period, applied only to the meetings of the leaders of the Great Powers to discuss issues of global consequence, the term has now been broadened in journalistic use to the point where it is almost meaningless. Accordingly, for the purposes of this study narrower definitions of summitry and the agents of summitry will be adopted. Foreign ministers or other envoys are excluded in favour of chief executives such as heads of governments and international organizations. For our purposes, the key element of summitry is executive participation, diplomacy at the highest possible level. As far as summit activity is concerned, a wider definition is advanced in order to encompass the many different purposes which are served by the meeting of political leaders. This definition excludes, however, those communications which do not involve the actual meeting of the parties, and visits of a purely private nature. In short then, the definition of summitry used for this study is the meeting of political leaders for official purposes, an activity which constitutes diplomacy at the highest level.

NOTES AND REFERENCES

1. The term 'sherpas' refers to the local bearers who assist mountaineers in the Himalayas. It was a name which entered the diplomatic lexicon at the same time as 'summits' as a result of the publicity surrounding the first successful ascent of Everest in 1953.

2. Charles Roetter, *The Diplomatic Art* (London, Sidgwick and Jackson, 1965), p. 199.

3. Abba Eban, *The New Diplomacy: International Affairs In The Modern Age* (New York, Random House, 1983), p. 359.

4. Churchill, cited by Eban, *The New Diplomacy*, p. 360.

5. Ibid., p. 358.

6. Sir Harold Nicolson, *Diplomacy* (Washington DC, Institute for the Study of Diplomacy, Georgetown University, 1988), p. 52. See also Charles Thayer, *Diplomat* (New York, Harper and Brothers, 1959).

7. Eban, *The New Diplomacy*, p. 359.

8. Keith Eubank, *The Summit Conferences, 1919–1960* (Norman, Oklahoma, University of Oklahoma Press, 1966), p. 196.

9. R. Schaetzel and H. B. Malmgren, 'Talking Heads', *Foreign Policy*, no. 39 (Summer 1980), p. 130.

10. Eban, *The New Diplomacy*, p. 361.

11. Ibid., p. 358.

12. Roetter, *The Diplomatic Art*, p. 208.

13. Sir Ernest Satow, *Guide to Diplomatic Practice*, ed. Lord Gore-Booth, 5th edn (London, Longman, 1979), p. 438.

14. S. Jenkins and A. Sloman, *With Respect, Ambassador: An Inquiry into the Foreign Office* (London, British Broadcasting Corporation, 1985), p. 129.

15. See G. R. Berridge, 'Diplomacy After Death: The Rise of the Working Funeral', *Diplomacy and Statecraft*, vol. 4, no. 2 (July 1993).

16. G. R. Berridge, *International Politics: States, Power, and Conflict Since 1945*, 2nd edn (London, Harvester Wheatsheaf, 1992), p. 200.

17. Geoffrey Howe, *Conflict of Loyalty* (London, Macmillan, 1994), p. 354.

18. George Ball, *Diplomacy for a Crowded World* (Boston, Little, Brown and Company, 1976), p. 31.

19. Richard Nixon, 'Superpower Summits', *Foreign Affairs*, vol. 64, no. 1 (1985), p. 1.

20. Ronald Reagan, *Ronald Reagan: An American Life* (London, Hutchinson, 1990), p. 634. See also Henry Kissinger, *Diplomacy* (New York, Simon and Schuster, 1994), chapter 30.

21. See Phil Williams, 'West European Security After Reykjavik', *The Washington Quarterly*, vol. 10, no. 2 (Spring 1987), and Margaret Thatcher, *The Downing Street Years* (London, Harper Collins, 1993), who observed,

'My own reaction when I heard how far the Americans had been prepared to go was as if there had been an earthquake beneath my feet' (p. 471).
22. Joseph Stalin, *Sochineniya* (Moscow: Gosudarstvennoe Izdatelstov Politicheskoi Literaturi, 1946) vol. 2, pp. 276–7, cited by Henry Kissinger, *Nuclear Weapons and Foreign Policy* (London, Norton & Company, 1969), p. 60.
23. Sir Geoffrey Jackson, *Concord Diplomacy: The Ambassador's Role in the World Today* (London, Hamish Hamilton, 1981), p. 17.
24. Gordon Craig, 'The Professional Diplomat and His Problems, 1919–1939', *World Politics* (January 1952), p. 151. Cited by Eban, *The New Diplomacy*, p. 360.
25. Howe, *Conflict of Loyalty*, p. 395.
26. Thatcher, *The Downing Street Years*, p. 463. Thatcher was particularly at odds with the established bureaucracy over SDI, she being more in sympathy with the US position on several issues. For her, 'neither the Foreign Office nor the Ministry of Defence took SDI sufficiently seriously' (p. 464).
27. Eban, *The New Diplomacy*, p. 366.
28. Howe, *Conflict of Loyalty*, p. 394.
29. Thatcher, *The Downing Street Years*, p. 464.
30. Howe recounts how US Secretary of State George Shultz had remarked that 'his perception of the gap between Margaret [Thatcher] and [Foreign Secretary] Francis Pym had prompted him to discount the latter'. Ibid.
31. Thatcher preferred one-to-one meetings as these comments on meetings with Gorbachev and Reagan illustrate: 'The atmosphere was more formal than at Chequers and the silent, sardonic presence of Mr Gromyko did not help'; and, 'I had brought Geoffrey Howe [Treasury] and Michael Heseltine [Defence] with me for my meeting and working lunch with the President, which made for a more stilted and less satisfactory conversation than on other occasions. (I did not bring them again).' Ibid., p. 469.
32. R. P. Barston, *Modern Diplomacy* (London, Longman, 1989), p. 95.
33. Ibid.
34. These themes are developed by Richard Hodder-Williams in chapter 9.
35. Satow, *Guide to Diplomatic Practice*, p. 439.
36. D. C. Watt, 'Summits and Summitry Reconsidered', *International Relations*, II (1963), pp. 493–504. See also Keith Hamilton and Richard Langhorne, *The Practice of Diplomacy* (London, Routledge, 1995), pp. 221–3.
37. Ibid.
38. Ball, *Diplomacy for a Crowded World*, p. 34.
39. *Time*, 11 September 1995.
40. Elmer Plischke, *Modern Diplomacy: The Art and the Artisans* (Washington DC, American Enterprise Institute, 1979), p. 171.
41. Ibid., p. 170. My italics.
42. Ibid., pp. 174–5.
43. Hamilton and Langhorne, *The Practice of Diplomacy*, p. 222.
44. As Manheim explains, in the US 'the choice offered to visiting chief executives is between ceremony and substance. The State and official visits offer more of the former, including ample photo/video opportunities, and appear

to carry more prestige. Working visits, on the other hand, command more "quality time" with the president.' Jarol B. Manheim, *Strategic Public Diplomacy and American Foreign Policy* (Oxford, Oxford University Press, 1994), p. 65.

45.   G. R. Berridge, *Diplomacy: Theory and Practice* (London, Prentice Hall/Harvester Wheatsheaf, 1995), p. 83.

2 The Origins of Summit Diplomacy
Erik Goldstein

Summit diplomacy is not a new device of international relations, and its origins are to be found in the earliest history of diplomacy. It was, however, a rare occurrence until the last century. The ancestry of summit diplomacy can be found in a number of earlier diplomatic developments, among them the infrequent meetings of sovereigns in medieval and early modern times, the occasional congresses which started to be held in the seventeenth century, and the meetings of the political leaders of the Great Powers in the nineteenth and first part of the twentieth centuries.[1]

EARLY SUMMITS: ROYAL MEETINGS

Personal meetings between rulers of powerful states were infrequent before the nineteenth century, the logistics of travelling making such meetings difficult. The problems associated with travel can be seen in the experience of the Anglo-Saxon kings of England of the seventh and eighth centuries; while four of them travelled to Rome, three of them died there.[2] King Canute had greater success with his trip to Rome in 1027 for the coronation of the Emperor Conrad. Canute took the opportunity created by this gathering of powerful figures to resolve some of the difficulties facing his subjects when travelling on the continent. In a remarkable personal account of these events Canute records, 'I therefore spoke with the emperor and the lord pope and the princes who were present, concerning the needs of all the people of my whole kingdom ...'. Canute goes on to proudly record his success in these negotiations.[3]

Mutual suspicion and fear often permeated these early meetings, not without justification. In 968 a Byzantine mission was sent to King Adalbert of Italy with orders to liaise with him 'if he proved to have the military capability which he had pledged. If he did not, he was to be seized and he, together with the money earmarked for him, was to be handed over to Otto I.'[4] When Edward IV of England met Louis XI of

France at Picquigny in 1475, in the aftermath of a botched English invasion, extraordinary precautions were taken. Louis, one of the most artful rulers of his day, allowed the English soldiery the free run of nearby Amiens, together with free drink. Within three days the English army was immobile.[5] Having thus insured himself against any danger of an English attack Louis then proceeded to meet Edward on a bridge, specially thrown across the Somme. 'In the midst of the bridge there was contrived a strong wooden lattice, such as the lions' cages are made with, the hole between every bar being no wider than to thrust in a man's arm ...' and the two powerful monarchs carefully '... embraced through the holes of the grate'.[6] On his way to this meeting Louis was still sufficiently suspicious to order his diplomat Philippe de Commynes, to whom we owe the account of this meeting, to wear identical clothing as a precaution against assassination. The famous meeting of Henry VIII of England and Francis I of France, immortalized as the Field of the Cloth of Gold (1520), though meant as a show of amity was draped in an air of suspicion and had to be held on the border between the English enclave of Calais and French territory.[7] Despite its grandeur this meeting of sovereigns had no tangible result.

Opinion as to the efficacy of meetings between leaders at the summit was as divided in the past as it is today. The Burgundian chronicler Georges Chastellain believed that Charles VI and Philip the Good of Burgundy, and Duke Charles the Bold and Louis XI did not understand each other because they never met.[8] On the other hand, Philippe de Commynes advised that great rulers who wished to enjoy good relations should never meet, but rather '[accommodate] their differences by the mediation of wise and faithful ministers'.[9]

The problem of venue was and remains an important aspect of summitry. The meeting of Edward IV and Louis XI on a bridge is symptomatic of the problems surrounding such meetings. In the Middle Ages bridges were popular venues, as indeed were border areas in general, allowing the participants to avoid travel through potentially hostile territory. In 1807 Napoleon and Tsar Alexander I met on a raft in the middle of the Niemen at Tilsit. During the Second World War Stalin in his three summit meetings with his fellow allied leaders refused to travel to any destination which would force him to leave territory he controlled. Even in the cold war American–Soviet summits it was some time before a meeting was held in either Moscow or Washington.

There were also linguistic difficulties at such meetings, and in diplomacy generally.[10] The English Ambassador Edward Lee, on meeting the Emperor Charles V in 1526, reported that 'the Emperor hath no pleasure to speak Latin, although he understand; and I can speak no French, ne well understand it.'[11] English was an almost unknown language for the purposes of diplomatic discourse. When Cardinal Wolsey went to meet the French King Francis I he instructed his entourage that 'the French would speak to them in French, as if they understood every word; the English should in that case, speak back in English "for if you understand not them, they shall no more understand you." He then summoned a gentleman from Wales: "Rice, speak thou Welsh to him and I am well assured that thy Welsh shall be more diffuse [obscure] to him than his French is to thee."'[12] Issues surrounding language, status and security all provided opportunities in these meetings not for the resolution of problems but rather the seeds of future disputes.

Meetings fraught with so many difficulties were therefore exceptional, rather than normal diplomatic activity until very recently. Louis XIV of France never met his great rivals, William III of Orange, Charles II of Spain or the Emperor Leopold I;[13] and no American president met a foreign head of state until 1919. Given such problems of travel and security most negotiations until the fifteenth century were conducted by correspondence. When viva voce negotiation was required an embassy could be dispatched, but these were occasional and quite grand affairs. When Thomas Beckett went to Paris in 1158 as the ambassador of Henry II he entered the city

> with a retinue in excess of 450, all richly dressed and singing as they went, bringing with them hounds, greyhounds, and hawks. There were eight great wagons, each drawn by five warhorses, each horse carrying a monkey on its back and each wagon guarded by a chained mastiff. Two wagons were loaded with the best English beer.[14]

Ambassadors were seen as the representative, indeed the personification, of their sovereign, hence the ostentation of their arrival. Consequently, these early embassies could be viewed as summit diplomacy by proxy.

By the fifteenth century the needs of international relations required a more regular basis than occasional missives and temporary embassies. The first great technical innovation of modern diplomacy was the invention of the resident embassy, which evolved in the early years of the Italian Renaissance amongst its city states, and by the end of the sixteenth century had spread across Europe. This was followed by the gradual establishment of specialized ministries of foreign affairs, as the machinery of state developed, and by the end of the eighteenth century all the major states possessed such ministries. It was this new bureaucracy, with its regular channels of communication, which dealt with most issues. In extraordinary circumstances, however, in particular the termination of a war, extraordinary methods were still required.

EARLY INTERNATIONAL CONGRESSES

In the seventeenth century there began to emerge a new mechanism of diplomacy, the congress, which can also claim to form part of the ancestry of the modern summit. Its origins can be found in the Great Councils of the Church, summoned to resolve issues which threatened not only spiritual but by implication political stability. Many of the princely summits of early modern history concerned religious issues. 'In 1517, the papal nuncio in England told ambassador Giustiniani that the popes were always against princely conferences, for the first thing that they discussed there was the reformation of the church which was to say of the pope and cardinals.'[15] However, such meetings provided the precedent for international gatherings to discuss other matters of common concern, particularly after the Reformation removed shared religious concerns from the European agenda.

Ten such congresses were held prior to the French Revolution. All were summoned to end particularly complex wars, but the opportunity was also frequently taken to settle other matters or to determine general issues of principle. The first of these congresses were the linked meetings held at Münster and Osnabrück (1643–8) which resulted in the Peace of Westphalia. Given the existing diplomatic methods the delegations, though in close proximity, negotiated mostly by exchange of correspondence. It was not until the Congress of Oliva (1660) that viva voce negotiation became accepted procedure. In particular these early congresses had to resolve questions of protocol, one of the problems which underlies the Westphalian agreement on the principle of sovereign equality. Until questions of precedence and procedure could be resolved, direct negotiation was difficult, if not impossible. The Congress of Ryswyck (1697) saw one of the great innovations of diplomatic procedure, the introduction of the round table. Increasingly though the real work of such gatherings was not taking place in the formality of official sessions, but in the private talks which occurred outside the meeting hall. At Ryswyck most of the work was done between the English and French representatives in private meetings. When delegates did meet formally, problems of protocol, and therefore the implied status of their states, could cause difficulties, unless solutions were found. At the Congress of Carlowitz (1699)

A considerable area round the ruined castle of Carlowitz on the Danube was neutralized for the purpose of the meeting, and a temporary conference village was specifically constructed, with a carefully designed negotiating hall, with four sets of doors, so that the delegations could all enter simultaneously.[16]

The congress though was increasingly found to be a cumbrous mechanism. Such meetings were useful in terminating wars, but the more general settlement of international concerns was increasingly dealt with bilaterally through the ever more sophisticated mechanisms of institutional diplomacy.

SUMMITRY AND THE CONCERT OF EUROPE

As the Napoleonic Wars drew to a close Count Metternich, the Austrian chancellor, saw new diplomatic precedents to be established. The inevitable congress at the end of this conflict, because of the nature of the enemies' defeat, would be different. He wrote that

It does not require any great insight to see that this Congress could not model itself on any predecessor. Previous meetings which have been called Congresses have confined themselves to making treaties of peace between parties which either were at war or ready to go to war. This time the treaty of peace is already made, and the parties are meeting as friends, not necessarily having the same interests, who wish to work together to complete and affirm the existing treaty. The matters to be negotiated are a multifarious list of questions, in some cases partly settled by previous discussions, in other cases, as yet untouched.[17]

Metternich was presaging the advent of summitry as a diplomatic tool. Vienna would not only confirm the peace but deal with wider issues concerning the European system, including the ongoing maintenance of discussion through regular summits. By the Treaty of Chaumont (1814), which was subsequently renewed after the war, it was agreed to hold regular summits

to consolidate the connections which at the present moment so closely unite the Four Sovereigns for the happiness of the world, the High Contracting Powers have agreed to renew their Meetings at fixed periods, either under the immediate auspices of the Sovereigns themselves, or by their respective Ministers, for the purpose of consulting upon their common interests, and for the consideration of the measures which at each of those periods shall be considered most salutary for the repose and prosperity of the Nations, and for the maintenance of the Peace of Europe.[18]

This resulted in the holding of four peacetime congresses, at Aix-la-Chapelle (1818), Troppau (1820), Laibach (1821), and Verona (1822). Now, far from feeling a need to meet in desolate neutral locations, the rulers of Europe convened at the best resort towns. These hospitable meetings came to an end when Britain refused to participate further. The Concert of Europe henceforth relied on *ad hoc* conferences held to deal with matters of international concern, consisting of the resident ambassadors of the Great Powers, presided over by the foreign minister of the host Great Power. The congress was, however, used three times in the nineteenth century to settle particularly complex problems at the periphery of European concerns: the Congress of Paris (1856) which ended the Crimean War and admitted the Ottoman Empire to the Concert of Europe; the Congress of Berlin (1878) to settle the most recent version of the Eastern Question; and a further Congress of Berlin (1885) to partition Africa. Modern congresses gave rise to innovative negotiating tactics. Disraeli at the 1878 Berlin Congress at one point theatrically ordered his train to be made ready for departure, to indicate he was not prepared to make further concessions, an action that would be much imitated in the years ahead.

The nineteenth century also saw a marked increase in bilateral summitry, presumably due to increased mobility and decreased insecurity. Napoleon III was particularly attracted to summitry. In 1858 he met secretly with the Sardinian Premier, Cavour, at Plombières and in the course of a drive through the Vosges they concocted a plot to provoke a war with Austria. The incident also illustrates one of the difficulties of secret summits, the impossibility of two such well-known personalities meeting in secret. News soon leaked out of their meeting, increasing international tensions. To allay British suspicions as to his intentions Napoleon III held an impromptu summit soon after, using the visit of Queen Victoria for the opening of the Cherbourg docks to invite Palmerston and Clarendon to Compiégne, ostensibly to hunt.[19]

The Three Emperors' League (1872) was negotiated through personal meetings of the German, Austrian, and Russian rulers. In an age still dominated by ruling dynasties, family gatherings provided a venue for informal summits. Weddings played the role in nineteenth-century diplomacy that state funerals would come to play in the twentieth.[20] Edward VII, during his brief reign, made a great number of state and foreign visits, meeting with a large number of senior political figures. These meetings were useful to British foreign policy.

His experience was immense; his knowledge great; his tact unsurpassed. In his own person he was a most potent Ambassador and his state visits to foreign capitals, as well as conversations which he held with foreign statesmen in continental watering-places, had without question an important, and on the whole a useful, effect upon negotiation.[21]

His successor, George V, loathed state visits and in the latter part of his reign refused to undertake them.[22] Such visits can provide a psychological turning-point in the popular mood between states, such as Edward VII's state visit to Paris in 1902, which instigated the process which resulted in the *entente cordiale* of 1904. On the other hand the goodwill of state visits can temporarily mask real problems. The German Kaiser, Wilhelm II, paid a highly successful state visit to Britain in 1907, in the midst of extreme tension over Anglo-German naval rivalry. Lord Morley noted in his diary of the event:

> The visit of the German emperor has been a great event, and will much improve the chances of a little decent calm over Europe. Even those who were most sceptical about any good coming of it now admit the results have been in every way advantageous.[23]

The two states were in fact well on their way to the apocalypse of 1914. The last important royal summit with diplomatic implications was the sea-borne meeting at Björkö between Tsar Nicholas and Kaiser Wilhelm. The Kaiser, in a meeting aboard his yacht the *Hohenzollern*, convinced his cousin to sign a personal treaty of alliance between Germany and Russia. Subsequently their respective governments refused to accept the agreement as it conflicted with existing commitments. The fall of the dynasties at the end of the First World War ended the era of Great Power dynastic diplomacy, but the state visit remains an aspect of diplomatic contact between the great powers.[24]

SUMMITRY AND THE NEW DIPLOMACY

The aftermath of the First World War saw not only the creation of the League of Nations, but the revival of a particular affection for Great

Power conferences to settle particularly difficult issues. In discussing post-war international relations Sir Maurice Hankey, the secretary to the British Cabinet, expressed the thought that 'there is no panacea, but the best hope appears to lie in the judicious development of diplomacy by conference'.[25] The American President, Woodrow Wilson, was espousing a New Diplomacy, whose processes were seen to be transparent. What better way to accomplish this than by having the democratically elected leaders of states meet and settle matters between themselves? In this he was in accord with the views of the British prime minister, David Lloyd George, who in 1920 observed,

> There is nothing like a heart-to-heart talk.... I wish the French and ourselves never wrote letters to each other. Letters are the very devil. They ought to be abolished altogether ... if you want to settle a thing, you see your opponent and talk it over with him.[26]

Hankey, later the author of a book entitled *Diplomacy by Conference*, told the Institute of International Affairs in 1920, 'It can hardly be doubted that diplomacy by conference has come to stay.'[27] Gordon Craig has observed,

> The cry of the times, then, seemed to be for new diplomatic methods and new diplomatic personnel, and the political leaders of the Western states were quick to respond to what they considered to be the popular desire. Conclaves of ambassadors at the Quai d'Orsay, the Wilhelmstrasse, and the Ballplatz – names now of sinister connotation – gave way to 'frank and friendly conversations' in such charmingly unconventional places as the golf course at Cannes, the bosom of Lake Maggiore, the mountain tavern at Thoiry, and a certain mossy log on the banks of the Potomac. The correctly dressed and distressingly uniform diplomats, who had until now held the center of the stage, ceded their places to a succession of politician–diplomats with such striking and memorable characteristics as plus-fours, Scots brogues, shaggy coiffures, white linen neckties, underslung pipes and various kinds of umbrellas.[28]

This new fashion in diplomacy was inaugurated at the 1919 Paris Peace Conference, summoned to agree a settlement to the First World War. It was, undoubtedly, the single greatest act of mass summitry in history, with 1141 delegates.[29] The key decisions, however, were taken at closed meetings between the leaders of the United States, Great Britain, France and Italy. For the first time an American president travelled abroad during his presidency and participated directly in negotiations with the leaders of

other Great Powers. The United States had retained a suspicion of summitry throughout its history, and as late as 1913 Congress had enacted a
law which forbade the president to attend an international conference
without the explicit authority of law.[30] The subsequent rejection by the
Senate of Wilson's achievements made his successors wary for some years
of emulating his precedent.

Wilson believed in the value of personal attendance. He was the first
president since John Adams to speak before Congress, and he was the first
president to attend an international conference. He informed the chief
Allied powers that he would attend the negotiations provided their pre-
miers did so, in effect summoning a summit conference. Protocol once
again intruded into summitry, as in the days of the early international congresses. Wilson hoped to play the leading role in the negotiations and
therefore wanted to chair the conference. As the only head of state present
he would have precedence, and he cabled Edward House, his representative in Europe, 'I assume also that I shall be selected to preside.'[31] The
French Premier Georges Clemenceau, who wished to exclude his political
rival, the French President Raymond Poincaré, from the negotiations,
argued that it would be impossible to admit one head of state without
admitting all.[32] Eventually a compromise was reached by which Poincaré,
as the head of state of the host country, officially opened the conference,
and Clemenceau chaired the working sessions. Wilson agreed not to press
his claims for precedence, a solution which confirmed the drift to greater
informality at these gatherings.[33] Wilson observed that 'no point of dignity
must prevent our obtaining the results we have set our hearts upon and
must have'.[34] Similar problems would later arise in meetings between
American and Soviet leaders, as until late in Leonid Brezhnev's rule no
Soviet leader held the post of head of state.

The Paris Peace Conference thus served as the introduction of the
United States to summitry, though the experience was not a happy one.
Wilson's decision to attend the conference was controversial, both to his
contemporaries and to historians. Wilson's Secretary of State, Robert
Lansing, was 'convinced that he [Wilson] is making one of the greatest
mistakes of his career and imperiling his reputation'.[35] The American his-
torian Arthur Walworth has observed, 'It is doubtful that without the full
weight of his presence the Americans would have exerted an influence
upon the peacemaking commensurate with the power the nation held'.[36]
Arthur Balfour, the British Foreign Secretary agreed that Wilson's
presence was necessary, otherwise the conference 'would not have run at
all had the president been compelled to contribute his most important
share of the common work from the White House 3000 miles away'.[37]

Venue once again played a role. Wilson at first proposed to hold the conference in Switzerland, but the French persuasively argued the case for Paris. Wilson cabled House:

On second thought it occurs to me that Versailles may be the best place for the peace conference where friendly influences and authorities are in control rather than Switzerland which is saturated with every poisonous element and open to every hostile influence in Europe.[38]

Paris, in fact, was the only city with the hotel capacity to host such a conference.

The conference did finally resolve the question of language at international gatherings. The common language of diplomatic discourse had originally been Latin, shifting to French by the time of Louis XIV. At the Congress of Berlin, Disraeli caused consternation by addressing the participants in English, instead of French. The emergence of two English-speaking Great Powers though brought about a linguistic revision, and at Paris it was agreed for the first time that English would be an official language of the conference, together with French.[39] English and French became the two official languages of the League of Nations, a status they retain under the United Nations.

Having in 1919 enticed the United States onto the conference circuit the Europeans were loath to allow it to slip away again. It was clear though that the reaction to Wilson's European adventure would not encourage his successors to repeat the experience quickly. The solution therefore was to convince the United States to hold the next such jamboree on its own territory, which Britain succeeded in doing in 1921–2 with the Washington Conference, which dealt with questions of naval arms limitation and east Asian stability. President Harding opened the conference, though he proved to be a mere cypher in foreign policy, leaving this to his able Secretary of State, Charles Evans Hughes. The French Premier, Aristide Briand, attended, and his poor performance helped bring about the downfall of his government. The British delegation was led by former prime minister Arthur Balfour, as at the last moment the Prime Minister, Lloyd George, decided not to attend believing the conference was unlikely to succeed and fearing association with a failure.[40]

American presidents remained reluctant to travel abroad in the interwar period, so that leaders wishing direct negotiation with them were forced to travel to the United States. Ramsay MacDonald in particular travelled to meet President Hoover in 1929, two weeks before the Stock Market crash, to discuss arms reduction. Hoover and MacDonald met at

Hoover's fishing retreat at Rapidan, Virginia, where they could be seen sitting on a log informally settling the problems of the world. One result of this meeting was the calling of the five-power London Disarmament Conference in 1930.

In December 1936 President Roosevelt, a disciple of Wilson's, made tentative steps towards renewing overseas presidential travel and participation in summits by attending the Pan-American Conference at Buenos Aires. The question of travel to Europe though was still a sensitive one, and Roosevelt's first meeting with Winston Churchill was a sea-borne summit off the coast of Newfoundland, a meeting fraught with security concerns about German submarines. This meeting produced the Atlantic Charter, which, despite its name, in fact formed part of the press release at the end of this meeting, beginning the practice of embodying the important conclusions of such summits in the final communiqué. Having tentatively broken the stay-at-home mentality, Roosevelt embarked on two major wartime summits with his allies, the Tehran (1943) and Yalta (1945) conferences. The meetings at Tehran also marked the first time an American and Russian leader met one another. Roosevelt's successor, Harry Truman, would continue the practice of summitry at Potsdam (1945), the first time since Wilson's sojourn to Paris that an American president had attended a conference in Europe. The custom of American and Soviet leaders meeting face to face to consider issues of major concern was not a product of the cold war, but rather of their wartime alliance.

British experience of summitry at the political level has not necessarily been any happier than the American. Lloyd George was an enthusiastic participant at summits, with a preference for acting without consultation with the Foreign Office. At the Spa Conference he gave Poland guarantees of protection, an action which had not been authorized by the Cabinet, and which the Foreign Office and the legation at Warsaw only learnt of through the press.[41] He attended the Genoa Conference (1922) without any Foreign Office assistance. The Foreign Secretary, Lord Curzon, was concerned by this, observing, 'when I recall the whole trend of his policy for the past three years – I can feel no certainty that we may not find ourselves committed to something pregnant with political disaster here'.[42] His successors were no better at avoiding interference in the technical details of foreign relations as opposed to the politician's role of setting policy. During the 1923 Ruhr crisis Stanley Baldwin, after a brief meeting with the French government at Paris, allowed a communiqué to be issued which suggested a different policy from that being conducted by the Foreign Office. This led the British ambassador in Berlin to suggest that 'it might be wise to apply to British Prime Ministers the rule governing the peregrinations of a Lord Chancellor and forbid their leaving England'.[43] Ramsay MacDonald, who in his first government had combined the prime minister's and foreign secretary's portfolios, often caused difficulties for the conduct of foreign policy by neglecting to inform the Foreign Office of the substance of his discussions.

The most infamous summit meeting of the interwar period is unquestionably the Munich Conference (1938). It provides a classic case where a political leader, in this instance Neville Chamberlain, felt that the regular mechanisms of diplomacy should be bypassed, and that personal negotiation, leader to leader, would resolve the crisis. As the crisis over the Sudetenland mounted Chamberlain decided to meet Hitler face to face. The brevity of the turnaround time for such a meeting was made possible by the use of air travel, Chamberlain becoming the first Great Power leader to fly to a summit. It was also the first time he had ever travelled in an aeroplane. It is worth considering what would have been the result if technology had made such a meeting harder to arrange, thereby forcing the crisis to be dealt with through diplomatic channels. Hitler and Chamberlain met three times during September and October 1938, and the tempo of the meetings, with Chamberlain flying continually to Germany, gave the crisis a certain momentum and prevented any efforts at what would later come to be termed 'crisis management'. In addition the poor impression Hitler formed of Chamberlain encouraged his aggressive actions. The climactic meeting at Munich, summoned on a day's notice, 'was one of the most disorganised conferences in diplomatic history, a "hugger-mugger" affair' with no traces of Germanic efficiency, and for most of the last five hours 'chaos ruled'.[44] Chamberlain had insisted that for this meeting he would not be accompanied by any official from the Foreign Office. The results are well known, and the experience of Munich called into question the value of summitry. It was against the backdrop of Munich that Harold Nicolson wrote his classic work, *Diplomacy*, which warns of the dangers of diplomacy by conference.

Having created the League of Nations, why did the Great Powers continue to use conferences outside the League to settle outstanding issues? One reason was undoubtedly the American decision not to join the League, making non-League meetings necessary if the United States was to be included. Likewise at Munich neither Germany nor Italy were any longer members of the League. Nevertheless there can also be detected a preference by the Great Powers for dealing with critical matters amongst themselves, avoiding the potential complications of admitting smaller states into the negotiations. As such the experience of summitry during the Concert of Europe and the inter-war years resembles closely the practice of summitry by the nuclear-age superpowers.

CONCLUSION

Summit diplomacy has reflected the evolution of the diplomatic system, adapting at every stage to the latest requirements. The last two centuries have seen three great wars, and after each one, while the international system has tried to evolve better institutionalized mechanisms for dealing with crises (the Concert of Europe, the League of Nations, and the United Nations), each inter-war period has also seen the usage of summitry. A number of factors have contributed to the consistent rise of summitry. Developments in technology and transport have made meetings easier and safer to arrange. The increasing informality of international relations, compounded by frequent meetings as well as developments in telecommunications, has likewise made summitry an easier event to organize than in previous centuries when difficulties of protocol impeded such meetings. The increase of popular involvement in government has also extended to foreign affairs, and politicians in need of a boost in popularity or some assistance in legitimation of their rule have found in the drama and publicity surrounding a summit a useful political tool. The requirements of the professional politician and the diplomatic practitioner vary, and the time-frame they work to can be quite different. Ernst von Weizsäcker, the German State Secretary for Foreign Affairs (1938–44), observed that politicians tended to 'pluck the fruit before it was ripe'.[45] It is this tension which lies at the centre of the debate about the efficacy of summit diplomacy. The historical origins of summitry are diverse, but they tend to suggest that detailed personal negotiations between leaders, as opposed to confidence-building and informative meetings, should be resorted to only sparingly.

NOTES AND REFERENCES

Thanks are due to Thomas Otte and Stuart Croft for their observations.

1. There is no strict difference between the terms 'congress' and 'conference'. Historically the term 'congress' was used for meetings of plenipotentiaries assembled to conclude a peace. Since the late nineteenth century the term 'conference' has increasingly come to be used for all international gatherings. See Lord Gore-Booth (ed.), *Satow's Guide to Diplomatic Practice* (London, Longman, 1979), p. 229.
2. The kings who travelled to Rome and died there were Caedwalla of Wessex in 688, Cenred of Mercia in 709 and Ine of Wessex in 726. Offa of Essex survived his trip of 709, while Sigeric of Mercia abdicated before making the journey. See W. J. Moore, *The Saxon Pilgrims to Rome and the Schola Saxonum* (Fribourg, Society of St Paul, 1937), pp. 126–7

3. Dorothy Whitelock (ed.), *English Historical Documents c. 500–1042*, vol. 1, 2nd edn (London, Eyre Methuen, 1979). Also cited in G. P. Cuttino, *English Medieval Diplomacy* (Bloomington, Indiana University Press, 1985), p. 27.

4. Jonathan Shepard, 'Information, Disinformation and Delay in Byzantine Diplomacy', *Byzantinische Forschungen*, no. 10 (1985), p. 285.

5. Andrew R. Scoble (ed.), *The Memoirs of Philippe de Commynes* (2 vols., London, Bohm, 1855, 1856), pp. 268–80.

6. Ibid., pp. 272–3.

7. Jocelyne Russell, *Field of the Cloth of Gold: Men and Manners in 1520* (London, Routledge, 1969).

8. See Jocelyne Russell, *Peacemaking in the Renaissance* (London, Duckworth, 1986), p. 77.

9. Commynes, vol. 1, p. 121.

10. The best account of language and diplomacy in the Renaissance is the essay, 'Language: A Barrier or a Gateway' by J. G. Russell in her book *Diplomats at Work* (Stroud, Alan Sutton, 1992), pp. 1–50.

11. J. S. Brewer (ed.), *Letters and Papers, Foreign and Domestic, of the Reign of Henry VIII* (London, 1870), vol. 4, Part I, Document 2095, p. 940.

12. Russell, *Diplomats at Work*, p. 39.

13. M. S. Anderson, *The Rise of Modern Diplomacy* (London, Longman, 1993), p. 119.

14. Cuttino, *English Medieval Diplomacy*, p. 40.

15. Russell, *Peacemaking*, p. 79.

16. Richard Langhorne, 'The Decline of Diplomatic Protocol', Paper delivered at the inaugural meeting of the British International History Group, Bristol, September 1988.

17. Quoted in Keith Hamilton and Richard Langhorne, *The Practice of Diplomacy: Its Evolution, Theory and Administration* (London, Routledge, 1995), pp. 83–4.

18. Michael Hurst, *Key Treaties for the Great Powers, 1814–1914*, vol. 1, *1814–1870* (Newton Abbot, David and Charles, 1972), p. 123.

19. Another famous summit was the 1865 Biarritz series of meetings between Napoleon III and Bismarck, a prelude to the Seven Weeks War.

20. G. R. Berridge, 'Diplomacy after Death: The Rise of the Working Funeral', *Diplomacy and Statecraft*, vol. 4, no. 2 (July 1993), pp. 217–34.

21. Harold Nicolson, *Diplomacy* (Washington DC, Institute for the Study of Diplomacy, 1988), p. 33.

22. A. Chamberlain to H. Rumbold, 23 April 1926. Rumbold Papers 26, Bodleian Library, Oxford.

23. Quoted in Jonathan Steinberg, 'The Kaiser and the British: The State Visit to Windsor, November 1907' in J. C. G. Röhl and Nicolaus Sombart, *Kaiser Wilhelm II: New Interpretations* (Cambridge, Cambridge University Press, 1982), p. 138.

24. By convention only one state visit is paid by a head of state to any particular country during his reign or term of office, other visits being merely 'official visits' and attracting a lower level of ceremony.

25. Sir Maurice Hankey, 'Diplomacy by Conference', *The Round Table*, 11 (1920–1), p. 310.

26. Lord Riddell, *Lord Riddell's Intimate Diary of the Peace Conference and After, 1918–1923* (London, Gollancz, 1933), p. 206.

27. Hankey, 'Diplomacy by Conference', p. 309. The institute later became the Royal Institute of International Affairs, commonly known as Chatham House.

28. Gordon Craig, 'The Professional Diplomat and his Problems, 1919–1939', *World Politics*, vol. 4, no. 2 (1952), pp. 147–8.

29. H. W. V. Temperley, *A History of the Peace Conference of Paris* (Oxford, Oxford University Press, 1920), vol. 1, p. 243.

30. Enacted as an amendment to the 1913 Appropriations Bill.

31. Wilson to House, 13 November 1918, in Arthur S. Link (ed.), *The Papers of Woodrow Wilson*, vol. 53, *November 9, 1918 – January 11, 1919* (Princeton, Princeton University Press, 1986), p. 66.

32. Ibid., pp. 71–2, House to Wilson, 14 November 1918; and pp. 84–5, House to Wilson, 15 November 1918.

33. Ibid., pp. 108–9, Wilson to House, 18 November 1918.

34. Ibid., Wilson to House, 16 November 1918.

35. Ibid., pp. 127–8, memorandum by Lansing, 18 November 1918.

36. Arthur Walworth, *America's Moment: 1918* (New York, Norton & Company, 1977), p. 120.

37. Balfour to Close, 13 September 1919, Wilson Papers 4/f324c, Library of Congress, Washington DC.

38. Cited in Walworth, *America's Moment*, p. 84.

39. Keith Hamilton, 'A Question of Status: British Diplomats and the Uses and Abuses of French', *Historical Research*, 60 (1987), pp. 125–9.

40. Erik Goldstein and John Maurer (eds), *The Washington Conference, 1921–22: Naval Rivalry, East Asian Stability and the Road to Pearl Harbor* (London, Frank Cass, 1994).

41. A. L. Kennedy, *Old Diplomacy* (London, John Murray, 1922), p. 337.

42. Harold Nicolson, *Curzon: The Last Phase* (London, Constable, 1937), p. 245.

43. Lord d'Abernon, *An Ambassador of Peace* (London, Hodder and Stoughton, 1929), vol. 2, p. 285, diary entry for 25 December 1925.

44. John Charmley, *Chamberlain and the Lost Peace* (London Macmillan, 1989), p. 139.

45. Ernst von Weizsäcker, *Memoirs of Ernst von Weizsäcker* (London, Gollancz, 1951), p. 69.

Part II
Institutionalized Summits

3 The Group of Seven Summits

J. D. Armstrong

The Group of Seven (G-7) summits emerged against the background of the collapse of the Bretton Woods international financial system during the early 1970s. The central feature of Bretton Woods had been the assumption by the United States of the primary responsibility for upholding international economic stability through its agreement to exchange dollars for gold at a fixed rate. Other states agreed to cooperate to maintain a more general regime of fixed exchange rates, the system as a whole being designed to prevent a recurrence of the competitive and self-defeating currency devaluations of the 1930s, which had contributed to the Depression and the rise of political extremism.

The Bretton Woods regime worked well enough while the United States enjoyed unchallenged economic dominance. However, the combined effects of the rise of German and Japanese economic power and the Vietnam War placed the system under increasing strain during the 1960s. The new economic superpowers came to see the pre-eminence of the dollar as encouraging the United States to avoid the financial discipline that they believed to be incumbent upon the world's economic hegemon, while in the United States itself Bretton Woods was increasingly seen as imposing unwelcome constraints upon domestic policy options. This was the background against which President Nixon took his decision in 1971 to sever the link between gold and the dollar. Two years after this 'Nixon Shock', the international economic system took another body-blow when the Organization of Petroleum Exporting Countries (OPEC) quadrupled the price of oil, thus exacerbating the inflationary pressures that had built up during the 1960s. What had been a managed and relatively stable international financial regime gave way to one governed by the uncertainties of the market. The situation looked in some respects grimly reminiscent of the early 1930s, and it was this consideration, above all others, that led to the emergence of the principal political response to the crisis on the part of the leading economic powers: the Group of Seven summits.

41

The actual origin of the G-7 is to be found in the so-called 'Library Group' meetings of the finance ministers of the USA, Britain, France and Germany, later joined by Japan, which commenced in 1973 with a meeting in the White House Library.[1] Two of the finance ministers present, Valéry Giscard d'Estaing and Helmut Schmidt were shortly to become president of France and chancellor of Germany, and it was their experience of working together in the Library Group that convinced them of the value of regular meetings at leadership level to discuss economic issues. Giscard's original idea was to hold irregular, highly informal meetings of the five leaders of the Library Group countries, without their advisers present and with the world's press also kept at a distance. Such gatherings of what Schmidt termed 'those who really matter in the world'[2] would, Giscard believed, give the heads of government an opportunity to reflect upon the major economic issues of the day without the constraining presence of bureaucrats. A free exchange of ideas amongst individuals whose governmental role was, after all, to stand above the narrow departmental interests of their ministers, would enable a focus to be maintained upon the big picture, and also enable imaginative and far-sighted proposals to emerge from men who had the power to implement them in their respective countries.[3]

There were several problems with this conception of the economic summits from the outset. First, any selection of leaders based upon the criterion of importance would inevitably offend those left out. Italy, which immediately pressed for inclusion, secured admission partly because the original five were apprehensive about the effects of exclusion upon the unstable Italian political situation. Canada was admitted on the insistence of the United States, which wanted a North American ally in what would otherwise have been a European-dominated gathering. The president of the European Community's Commission was reluctantly allowed observer status because of the increasing degree to which it was impossible to consider the economic policies of EC members separately from the broader EC context. Russia became, in effect, the eighth member after the collapse of communism. But several other countries, such as Australia and the Netherlands, believed they had the right to be admitted on the grounds of their economic significance. Their admission would open the door to other claimants, such as China, Brazil or South Korea, and would largely negate the original conception of an intimate elite gathering. However, some believe that states left out of such summits are more liable to indulge in uncooperative or irresponsible international behaviour.[4] The difficulty, as with all summit meetings, is always where to draw the line.

A second major problem stemmed from the fact that although the seven leaders all represented liberal democracies with market economies, their political systems embodied some profound differences which made Giscard's always somewhat romantic notion of the freedom and capacity of the modern leader completely unrealistic. Giscard himself was the beneficiary of a constitution which gave the president seven years of considerable power between elections and election campaigns. Other heads of government were not so fortunately placed. The American president, for instance, enjoyed a much shorter period between elections and was further constrained by a constitution that emphasized the separation of powers. Britain, Germany and Canada all had political systems incorporating more checks and balances than that of France. Italy was in a state of general political disarray, while in Japan the prime minister was merely the representative of a faction in a system that placed the greatest emphasis on consensus formation and found the idea of the political leader as a figure able to take important decisions without prior agreement unacceptable.

A further set of difficulties arose from the different political cultures of the European countries and the United States. Whereas the European (and to some extent Japanese) leaders tended to have held previous government office, frequently as finance minister, American presidents normally emerged from a background of state politics. This meant that they were inevitably less experienced in both foreign and financial policy and therefore less willing to engage in high-level discussions without their advisers present.[5] The Americans were also highly reluctant to exclude the mass media from gatherings that might provide useful photo opportunities for their president. This inevitably made the meetings more of a public event, which had further consequences for the summits themselves. Where Giscard's conception had been for the summits to function essentially as educational events for the leaders, media expectations were for the meetings to produce 'results' in the form of decisions. Moreover, leaders facing elections in the same year as a summit naturally had one eye on the impact of the summit upon their electoral prospects.[6]

A fourth set of problems revolved around the central issues that gave rise to the summits. If the meetings were to be at all meaningful, they would have to be thoroughly prepared by technical experts capable of grasping the complexities. Even Giscard, who in theory favoured a more unplanned and open-ended approach to the summits, showed in the first summit at Rambouillet that he was less willing to leave matters to chance than this public posture implied, since he ensured that the summit was preceded by a series of Franco-American meetings to iron out some of the possible areas of disagreement.[7] As the summits became fixtures in international diplomacy, so the degree of advance preparation increased, particularly after the arrival of the Carter administration in 1977. Carter's approach to the summits was sharply at variance with the Giscard–Schmidt conception, since his administration favoured a much more institutionalized summit, with thorough advance preparation by teams of technical experts. Paradoxically, it was not until the advent of the next Democrat president after Carter that the emphasis in the summits began to shift back to the earlier Giscard notion. President Clinton's influence secured the insertion of the following statement into the 1993 declaration:

> We value summits for the opportunity they provide to exchange views, build consensus and deepen understanding among us. But we believe summits should be less ceremonial, with fewer people, documents and declarations and with more time devoted to informal discussion among us so that together we may better respond to major issues of common concern.[8]

Another problem was that it was difficult for both political and practical reasons to confine the subject matter of the summits to international economics. The political need for the summits to be able to project an image of purposeful action was liable to come up against the awkward fact that resolute action might not always be appropriate to the economic needs of the moment, so it was useful for the summits to have a broader agenda which might yield more opportunities for the leaders to parade their decisive influence upon events before their respective publics. Moreover, in practice it was difficult to disentangle economic issues from other problems. The American Secretary of State, Henry Kissinger, insisted that the summits would need to discuss security as well as economics, and many other issues soon found their way on to the summit agenda, ranging from the environment to terrorism and the war in Bosnia.[9] The 15 brief paragraphs of the 1975 Rambouillet Declaration contained little more than bland assertions of the commitment of all the leaders to such uncontentious goals as 'closer international cooperation and constructive dialogue among all countries', together with slightly stronger assertions of the need for substantial tariff cuts.[10] By contrast the 1988, 1989 and 1990 Declarations had 11, 17 and 20 pages respectively.[11]

A final set of problems stemmed from the complexities of international macroeconomic management. When the summits began, the prevailing economic orthodoxy was still one of Keynesian demand management, although this was already beginning to fall into disfavour in some quarters.

But attempting to implement a Keynesian approach at the global level carried all sorts of potential hazards. First, different national economies were likely to be at different stages of the economic cycle at any point in time, so that a properly coordinated global strategy would require a wide range of responses from the seven economies. Moreover some economies – notably the German and Japanese – with strong currencies and balance of payments surpluses were always likely to be better placed to take reflationary action on behalf of the global economy than the weaker states. This inevitably implied that the burdens of global Keynesianism would not be equally shared. The most successful of the earlier summits is generally judged to have been the Bonn summit of 1978, when West Germany and Japan agreed to reflate their economies in return for American commitments to tighten fiscal policy to reduce inflation and take action to reduce oil imports.[12] However the Germans later came to believe that they had been pushed into policies that exacerbated their own inflation without having any long-term impact on resolving world economic problems. The summit also illustrated the dangers of macroeconomic policy in an uncertain world, since it was followed a year later by the Iranian revolution and a further sharp increase in oil prices which helped to spark the inflation and subsequent recession of the 1980s.

By the 1980s it was, then, already clear that, although the summits might have helped to prevent a 1930s-style rush to competitive and self-defeating protectionism and devaluations, they could not take the place of the Bretton Woods regime as an instrument of global economic management. This was not merely a matter of their inability to take account of unpredictable events like the Iranian revolution, but was also due to more far-reaching structural changes in the world economy. They may have been meetings at the highest level but this did not ensure the economic results they desired. Two of these changes were particularly important. First, international financial movements were becoming increasingly beyond the control of one government, or even of several governments acting in concert. By the mid-1980s the global total of financial exchanges, at around $60 trillion, was many times greater than the total of exchanges of goods and services, at around $4 trillion.[13] As the 1992 crisis in the European Community's exchange rate mechanism demonstrated, attempts to maintain exchange rates at fixed levels merely provided relatively risk-free opportunities to speculate against the weaker currencies until the huge volume of capital involved in the speculation brought about the collapse of the would-be protected currencies. Hence, although the German and French governments continued to believe that currency stabilization policies imposed an important anti-inflationary discipline on governments, they were increasingly flying in the face of market realities. A second structural change was the emergence of a number of Newly Industrialized Countries (NICs) who were posing an increasingly significant challenge to the major Western economies in the production of various goods and services and also in their ability to attract foreign investment. Both of these structural changes contributed to the emergence of a new economic orthodoxy, associated with Ronald Reagan and Margaret Thatcher in the 1980s, which stressed the need for economic and financial discipline to reduce inflation and increase competitiveness, and which also criticized Keynesian and other policies that involved what was derided as government interference with market forces.

The new economic ideology had inevitable consequences for the G-7 summits. Global economic management came to be seen as the chimera it probably always was, and consideration of policy coordination to maintain some exchange rate stability was handed over to regular meetings of the G-7's finance ministers. West Germany and Japan continued to come under pressure from the United States to reflate their economies, but the overwhelming emphasis in G-7 summits was on the need for all to pursue conservative, anti-inflationary policies. For example, shortly before the 1985 summit, the American Secretary of State had publicly called for reflationary measures by Japan and Germany, but the Declaration said that West Germany would 'continue to reduce the claims of the public sector on the economy, the budget deficit and the burden of taxation' and that Japan 'considers it essential to persevere with its policy of budgetary discipline'.[14] Similarly, the 1990 Declaration sternly admonished 'countries with sizeable current account deficits' to reduce fiscal deficits and undertake 'structural reform'.[15] This did not mean that economic issues as such disappeared from the summit agendas. The problem of Third World debt was a regular item, as was unemployment, on which issue a special summit was called in 1994. One significant economic issue that frequently appeared at the summits was the need for further trade liberalization, and the Tokyo summit of 1993 is given credit for achieving a breakthrough that enabled the long-running Uruguay Round of the GATT to move towards its conclusion a year later. However, this should be set against the fact that several summits not only failed to reach agreement on other areas of trade liberalization, such as agriculture, but highlighted the extent of disagreement among the participants. The Houston summit of 1990 marked a particularly low point in this regard.[16]

Notwithstanding these examples of economic issues at the summits, during the 1980s they came increasingly to concern themselves with other matters. President Reagan saw the G-7 summits as an important forum for Western leaders to present a united front against the Soviet Union, including agreeing economic and other sanctions against Moscow for various misdemeanours. Sometimes this led to serious and well-publicized disagreements within the G-7, especially when Reagan was proposing actions that might have adverse economic consequences for his allies. For example, at the 1982 Versailles summit Reagan wanted to pressurize the Soviets by withholding agreement over the proposed trans-Siberian pipeline that was to be built with Western aid. Such sanctions would have jeopardized many European jobs and the eventual supply of gas from the Soviet Union, and a lengthy argument on the issue failed to reach agreement. Some analysts believed that the summit had actually exacerbated the disagreement on this issue rather than illuminated it. This was certainly a case where more careful advance preparation might have prevented a public falling-out over the issue by revealing the extent of European opposition to Reagan's proposals.[17] The next summit, at Williamsburg, managed to avoid a débâcle like Versailles over an issue where there was real potential for a major clash. This was the question of the British and French nuclear deterrents, which the Soviets were arguing should be thrown into the overall equation in arms control negotiations going on between themselves and the United States. The issue was further complicated by the Soviet insistence that their agreement to remove SS-20 missiles from their European territory did not imply that they could not simply shift their location to the Soviet Far East. This naturally alarmed the Japanese, as it was doubtless intended to do given the strong Japanese support for the United States that had been forthcoming from the recently elected Prime Minister Nakasone. In the event the summit provided an opportunity both to reassure Japan and to draw it closer into the broader Western alliance system. These purposes were achieved by a joint statement on security that included a crucial passage to the effect that 'the security of our countries is indivisible and must be approached on a global basis'. More generally it could be argued that one unquestionable benefit of the G-7 summits has been to provide a means of seating Japan and Germany at the international top table.

Many other non-economic issues have made their appearance at the summits. The environment took up no less than a quarter of the communiqué in 1990. General security questions and the overall Western strategy *vis-à-vis* the Soviet Union were frequent items, as were various regional issues, especially relating to the Middle East. Human rights, drugs and terrorism also appeared several times on the summit agenda. But from 1985 the dominating summit issue was how to deal with Mikhail Gorbachev's revolutionary new approach to East–West affairs and from 1989 how to respond to the rapidly changing European scene as the cold war ended and the Soviet empire collapsed.

By 1990 Gorbachev had been transformed from the apparent prime mover of events to a supplicant for Western aid. From Gorbachev's perspective, having to work through the G-7 process turned out to be nothing short of disastrous. His request for an aid package in 1990 brought him several semi-public lectures on how to get his economic house in order and what amounted to an agreement to disagree about the best response to his request from the G-7 leaders. West Germany and France decided to go ahead with their own bilateral aid programmes – giving the Soviet Union aid it would have received through normal, less public diplomacy – but the US called for further concessions on security issues, Japan for aid to be linked to the return of the contested Kurile islands and Britain for a more thoroughgoing restructuring programme than Gorbachev envisaged.[18] Similarly in 1991, when Gorbachev sent a lengthy letter to the G-7 leaders calling for a substantial aid and investment package prior to meeting them at the London summit, he received somewhat patronizing advice about his lack of understanding of the workings of market economies together with cynicism about the continuing high levels of Soviet military spending, but much less aid than he had anticipated. His failure at the summit was undoubtedly one factor in his downfall and the collapse of the Soviet Union over the next year. While these were not necessarily unwelcome events in the West, they had not been deliberately planned outcomes of the summit and they brought a less desirable element of additional instability to European affairs. Whether more traditional diplomacy would in the long run have prevented what might have been an inevitable sequence of events in the Soviet Union is perhaps debatable but there can be little question that the summit was not the most appropriate forum for such highly sensitive issues to be determined.

The Soviet question overshadowed other issues that appeared before the 1991 meeting to such an extent that one potentially very significant part of the summit declaration received relatively little attention.[19] This was a statement to the effect that the G-7 states intended to make much greater use of the UN for such purposes as conflict resolution, preventive diplomacy and cooperation in various political, economic, ecological and humanitarian areas. Since the G-7 had itself appeared at times to be assuming some of the UN Security Council's roles and prerogatives in global policy-making, the statement amounted to a declaration that the end of the cold war was providing new opportunities to shift such responsibilities to a global, as opposed to a Western forum. There was much rhetoric at this time from President Bush and others, in the aftermath of the Gulf War, about building a new world order with a greatly enhanced role for the UN, and the summit declaration was essentially a reflection of this.

The new world order proved harder to construct than to talk about and the G-7 soon found itself confronting the numerous European crises that flowed from the collapse of communism there. By this point the G-7 summit was beginning to find itself somewhat trapped by its earlier image as the world's most important international policy-making forum, an image that had been deliberately fostered by the seven leaders largely for domestic political reasons. Full membership became a cherished Russian policy goal, pressed strongly at the 1994 Naples summit by the host premier, Silvio Berlusconi.[20] Mr Yeltsin's failure to gain membership added significantly to his credibility problems with an increasingly restless opposition in Russia and contributed to the adoption of a more negative and confrontational posture by Moscow over the ensuing months. Had he succeeded, however, he would perhaps have won an important symbolic victory and an opportunity to be seen acting in an important diplomatic theatre, but very little more. Similarly, several Soviet successor states, including Russia itself, tended to look to the G-7 for solutions to some of their political and economic problems, and in particular for economic aid. Although more aid was forthcoming than the unfortunate Mr Gorbachev had received, this was inevitably less than had been requested. Many Third World countries had already formed a view of the G-7 as an exclusive rich man's club and a similar impression was clearly emerging in the former Soviet Union.

In recent years, the summits have encountered far more criticism than praise. They have been widely derided as pointless exercises, especially since the end of the cold war removed what many saw as the one remaining source of cohesion within the group. Particular criticism has focused upon the fact that their 'conclusions' are normally prepared in detail beforehand, and that the summit communiqués have increasingly come to resemble little more than resounding declarations on the value of motherhood, which are forgotten until the next year.[21] Similarly, many believe that other institutions are better suited to deal with most of the specific issues that confront the summits: the UN in the case of security questions, the IMF and World Bank for economic matters.[22] Moreover, the summits, by encouraging the largely misleading impression that leaders actually have the power to control events in the economic and political spheres over which they have less and less real influence, tend to raise hopes and expectations which are inevitably liable to be dashed. In this sense they are seen as having contributed to a general disillusionment with governments that is apparent in all of the G-7 states. Indeed, they may even be counterproductive. Where summits have been followed by coordinated interventions to influence exchange rates or growth (decreasingly the case in the last five years), their attempts to intervene in markets that nowadays largely follow their own logic have frequently been counterproductive.[23] Likewise, at the political level, the summits are unpopular with states which feel they are entitled to membership, they are a source of humiliation for importunate states that have to go through an annual ritual of begging for crumbs from the rich men's table, and the fact that they have frequently been unable to agree decisive action in some of the world's trouble spots, such as former Yugoslavia, adds to an impression of irresolution that may actually encourage warring parties.[24]

Much of this is true but much of it also stems from a highly unrealistic conception of what is and what is not possible in international relations. If the summits are at times little more than a form of theatre, so is much of domestic politics, and for similar reasons. If the modern state is increasingly perceived as ungovernable because of the complexity and intractability of some of the problems it faces, this must be even more true of the international arena, where the sovereignty of states still poses an insuperable obstacle in relation to one set of problems, while the size and autonomy of the international financial market constrains choices in another domain. In such circumstances, the role of political leaders becomes increasingly one of enacting certain symbolic rituals, overseeing the vast bureaucracies that carry on the day to day tasks of governance and, very rarely, taking meaningful decisions. But the theatrical and symbolic roles of leaders are not entirely without meaning. Their function inside states is to provide reassurance that democratic government has not become an oxymoron: not an insignificant task given the precarious status of democracy in much of the world, including the former Soviet Union. On the international stage, the role of diplomatic theatre is similarly to provide some degree of reassurance but, in this case, reassurance that there is some degree of governance as such in the international system: some sense that leaders are in control of events which, in reality, frequently control them. Such an essentially psychological role should not be underestimated, especially during an era, such as the present, of momentous transitions: from American hegemony, from the cold war, and from an age of relatively secure economic expectations in areas like employment and currency stability towards an uncertain future in all cases.

This bleak assessment of the summits is not, of course, the whole picture. During the 1970s they may have been one factor working against a global slide towards protectionism, through a collective stiffening of the summiteers' backbones. Individual leaders are said to have found them valuable. Mr Nakasone was able to enjoy a relatively long period of office for a Japanese premier, partly because he played the role of international statesman effectively; other leaders have used the summits to help in overcoming domestic opposition to unwelcome economic policies. More generally the summits played a crucial role in bringing West Germany and Japan to the centre of the international stage. This was to prove of great significance when their financial support was needed to fund the Gulf War.

Even if the most cynical views of commentators – that the summits consist of little more than verbiage – are justified, this contention in itself needs further consideration. Events are not simply determined by such structural attributes of the international system as the global distribution of power or wealth. Relationships between individuals and systems, including those between individual states and the international system, involve a constant two-way flow of ideas, ideas that are mediated primarily through words. Over time such interactions have profound consequences for the identities of both 'agents' and 'structures', as each feeds back into the other.[25] The fashionable terms 'discourse' and 'discursive practices' are useful here. We are defined not so much by unchangeable material structures as by 'ideational' structures, or by sets of ideas, and practices embodying these ideas, that are constantly evolving and reforming. In this sense, the G-7 meetings should be seen as an aspect of, and a contributory factor in 'international discourse': the ongoing exchange of ideas, symbols and words which interprets and gives meaning to 'reality'. To move from the highly abstract to the particular, a very clear change took place in the ideological underpinnings of economic policy between the 1970s and the 1980s. Leaders like François Mitterrand in the early 1980s who tried to resist this trend found in the end that they had to go along with it. This emerging 'discourse' and the practices associated with it (monetarism, use of interest rates to control inflation and so forth) were absolutely crucial in shaping events during the 1980s, including the end of the cold war. In the most simple terms, a discourse is a conversation and the G-7 summits embodied this conversation in its most literal form as the seven leaders helped to persuade each other of the validity of their new interpretation of economic and political reality.

NOTES AND REFERENCES

1. W. R. Smyser, 'Goodbye, G-7', *The Washington Quarterly*, vol. 16, no. 1 (Winter 1993), pp. 15–28.
2. Robert D. Putnam, 'Summit Sense', *Foreign Policy*, vol. 54 (1984–5), pp. 73–91.
3. Robert D. Putnam and Nicholas Bayne, *Hanging Together: Cooperation and Conflict in the Seven-Power Summits* (Cambridge, Mass., Harvard University Press, 1987), pp. 27–34.
4. J. Robert Schaetzel and H. B. Malmgren, 'Talking Heads', *Foreign Policy*, vols 38–41 (1980–1), pp. 131–42.
5. Robert D. Putnam and Nicholas Bayne, *Hanging Together*, p. 34.
6. Ibid., p. 277.
7. Robert D. Putnam, 'Summit Sense', p. 76.
8. *Financial Times*, 11 July 1993.
9. Ibid., p. 35.
10. *The Times*, 17 November 1975.
11. Nicholas Bayne, 'The Course of Summitry', *World Today*, vol. 48, no. 2, (February 1992).
12. *Financial Times*, 17 July 1978.
13. Philip G. Cerny, 'The Infrastructure of the Infrastructure? Toward "Embedded Financial Orthodoxy" in the International Political Economy', in Ronan P. Palan and Barry Gills (eds), *Transcending the State–Global Divide: A Neostructuralist Agenda in International Relations* (Boulder and London, Lynne Rienner Publishers, 1994).
14. *Economic and Political Weekly*, 18 May 1985.
15. *The Times*, 12 July 1990.
16. *Financial Times*, 13 July 1990.
17. Robert D. Putnam, 'Summit Sense'.
18. *Economic and Political Weekly,* 21 July 1990.
19. Although not, interestingly, in the Soviet Union itself, where commentators saw it as a direct result of earlier Soviet policy initiatives. Sergei Lavrov, 'Seven-Plus-One Plus UN', *International Affairs*, Moscow, October 1991.
20. *The Independent*, 8 July 1994.
21. 'To Naples for a Game of Charades', *The Independent*, 8 July 1994, for example.
22. W. R. Smyser, 'Goodbye G-7', p. 24.
23. See, for example, Norman Macrae, 'Wasted Work of the World's Seven Dwarves', *The Sunday Times*, 10 July 1974.
24. W. R. Smyser, 'Goodbye G-7'.
25. For a discussion of such 'structurationist' ideas in international relations, see Alexander Wendt, 'The Agent–Structure Problem in International Relations Theory', *International Organization*, vol. 41 (Summer 1987), pp. 335–70.

4 From 'European Community Summit' to 'European Council': The Development and Role of Summitry in the European Union
John Redmond

I

Summitry has a somewhat controversial history in the European Union (EU) because it is a clear manifestation of intergovernmental cooperation which was anathema to the (federalist) founding fathers of the EU. Its early history is particularly 'tainted' in this way. Summitry was the favoured method of cooperation of de Gaulle and, indeed, he was the instigator of the first two EU summits, in Paris in February 1961, and then in Bonn in July 1961. However, these summits were principally geared towards preparing the ground for the 'Fouchet Plan',[1] a French initiative named after the French ambassador to Denmark who chaired the committee which produced it in late 1961. It is perhaps not entirely unfair to characterize this as a Gaullist attempt to hijack the fledgling European Union and reinvent it on a firmly intergovernmental basis. The Fouchet Plan sought to institutionalize EU summits and create a permanent secretariat and intergovernmental committees in key areas. It was not well received outside France and was not taken up in the EU. However, de Gaulle's antagonism to supranationality continued and was to culminate in the 1965 crisis and the paralysis of the (then) European Community.

Consequently when the European Council did emerge as a permanent EU 'institution' it was variously described as 'the epitome of intergovernmentalism'[2] and 'an extra-treaty manifestation of institutionalized intergovernmentalism'[3] (which indeed it was). Thus EU summits have particular undertones, represent an aspect of probably the most fundamental underlying debate in the EU (intergovernmentalism versus federalism and supranationalism) and are therefore, unlike other summits, set in a very specific context. None of this means that EU summitry cannot be analysed using the methodology employed in the rest of this book to examine other summits; rather, it adds an interesting extra dimension to the subject.

In addition to this very specific context, EU summits are characterized by an ambiguity surrounding their role and position which is amply illustrated by the history of their development. In fact, there was no reference to either the European Council or summits in the Treaty of Rome and their development has therefore been informal and *ad hoc*. There were three early EU summits. Two of these – in 1961 (Paris and Bonn) – were atypical and, as already indicated, concerned primarily with de Gaulle's intergovernmental agenda. The third, in 1967 in Rome, was simply a ceremonial celebration of the tenth anniversary of the signing of the Treaty of Rome. The history of the European Council effectively began with the Hague summit in December 1969. This was called in response to the perception that the steam had gone out of European integration and a new impetus was needed. This was certainly provided by the Hague summit which agreed (amongst other things):

- the EMU 1980 project;
- negotiations for the first enlargement of the EU;
- European political cooperation;
- development of the 'own resources' financial system; and
- the completion of financing arrangements for the common agricultural policy.

The success of the Hague summit was potentially a good omen for the future of EU summitry.

However, there was controversy. Some did see this first 'real' summit as simply an expedient to get integration back on track but others saw it as a sinister development in the shape of a reassertion of the importance of intergovernmental cooperation and the nation state. Perhaps not surprisingly, the main support for the summit framework came from leading government figures who saw an obvious way of reinforcing the relevance and centrality of the EU – that is, their own direct involvement. Moreover, the optimism surrounding the Hague summit was short-lived. The Paris 1972 and Copenhagen 1973 summits were somewhat less successful, getting bogged down over economic and monetary union (EMU) and the development of an EU regional policy. Nevertheless, at the Paris 1974 summit it was agreed to institutionalize and regularize EU summits and hold them three times per year. In fact this was generally a successful summit with consensus reached on regional policy and eventual direct elections to the European Parliament; a commitment to pursue convergent economic policies; and agreement over the UK renegotiations and in other areas. EU summits then continued on an *ad hoc* basis for more than ten years and were not given a constitutional and legal status until they were formally recognized in the Single European Act (SEA) in 1987. This states (Article 2):

> The European Council shall bring together the Heads of State or of Government of the Member States and the President of the Commission of the European Communities. They shall be assisted by the Ministers for Foreign Affairs and by a Member of the Commission.
> The European Council shall meet at least twice a year.

However, the SEA merely lays down membership and frequency of meetings and does not define the role and tasks of the European Council. These continued to evolve informally in the actual European Council meetings themselves. The Maastricht Treaty was a little more forthcoming but, at the same time, rather vague. It restated the composition of the membership and frequency of meetings but went further: 'The European Council shall provide the Union with the necessary impetus for its development and shall define the general political guidelines thereof.'[4] This would seem to add to the fears of those who do not favour intergovernmentalism because it cuts across the (supranational) Commission's role of initiator of EU policy.

In practice the original arrangement of meeting three times per year was discontinued in 1985 and since then the European Council usually only meets twice, at the end of each six-monthly EU presidency (in June and December), unless there is a special summit (as, for example, at Birmingham in October 1992). EU summits usually last 24 hours (lunch to lunch) and the preparatory work is done by the Committee of Permanent Representatives (COREPER) and the Political Committee which serves the European Political Cooperation (EPC) framework, now superseded by the Common Foreign and Security Policy (CFSP). EU summits are chaired by the leader of the country which holds the presidency of the Council of Ministers.

Thus the format for the meetings is clear but the precise nature of the European Council remains ambiguous. If it is not a summit then is the European Council an EU institution? Superficially, this seems quite plausible, and the European Council has frequently been characterized as a 'super-Council (of Ministers)'. It is serviced partly by the Council's bureaucracy (COREPER) and, after all, the Maastricht Treaty does formally define the Council of Ministers as consisting of 'a representative of each Member State at ministerial level, authorized to commit the government of that Member State'.[5] Clearly the European Council is this, but to consider it as merely a 'super-Council' is simplistic in the extreme. The real situation is much more complex and ambiguous: the European Council is both rather less and rather more than the Council of Ministers. It is less in the sense that it has little specific formal power and takes no actual decisions; it is a kind of 'talking shop' that merely issues a statement outlining its conclusions at the end of each meeting. It is much more in that it sets the agenda of the European Union and effectively directs the Council of Ministers to take the necessary formal decisions to implement its will. In fact, it is rather easier to define what the European Council is not than what it actually is.

Nevertheless, despite this ambiguity, there is no doubt that the European Council has evolved into the most authoritative body in the EU. Since its creation it has launched all the major initiatives – the European Monetary System (EMS) and the (Maastricht) Treaty of European Union, for example – and taken most of the major decisions. Indeed, its role as one institution amongst several in the European Union is something which differentiates it from other summits. Most summits stand apart or alone and have a particular function (or perhaps no clear function at all) but the European Council has, in some ways, not had to create but rather usurp a role (at the expense of the European Commission and, to some extent, the European Parliament). However, there have also been failures and the European Council has on occasion become enmeshed in internal disputes. This is perhaps sometimes inevitable given the magnitude and nature of such disputes. The British budgetary dispute is an obvious case of internal wrangling; but the European Council has also tied itself in embarrassing political knots over other issues – like the choice of the Commission president for the incoming 1995 Commission – which ought to be straightforward.

II

There are a number of similarities between EU summits and the others examined in this volume. For example, it is patently true that all 'summit meetings are to a greater or lesser degree public relations exercises'.[6] For this reason the version of what happened at any particular summit will differ amongst participants (sometimes markedly so) as each strives to present an interpretation of the event which shows them in the best light to their electorate. More fundamentally, different leaders have differing degrees of power in their own countries. In the EU context, the French president traditionally has substantial power whereas, by late 1994, Chancellor Kohl's support had been reduced to only a small majority in Germany, the Italian leadership was in disarray and John Major had been compelled to link EU measures to a vote of confidence to get them through the British Parliament. Of course, circumstances change over time – for example, Kohl previously enjoyed much greater support, and, in her heyday, Mrs Thatcher could be certain of getting anything she agreed at a summit approved with ease.

An underlying factor is of course the nature of the government a leader leads – that is a single-party government, a two-party coalition or a multi-party coalition. A leader may also be constrained by the degree of scrutiny back home. This may take a variety of forms:

- formal parliamentary scrutiny through a parliamentary committee system as in Denmark (which has been imitated by the new Nordic members of the EU);
- informal parliamentary scrutiny by MPs which can create difficulties for a government with a small majority which may have to appease its internal critics – this was effectively the situation in the UK in 1995 as the government's majority dwindled to single figures (as a result of by-elections) and the Eurosceptics on the Conservative backbenches became increasingly vociferous; or
- formal scrutiny by the general public – in some cases EU summit decisions have to be ratified after referenda in some member states; this notably concerns treaty changes such as the Single European Act and the (Maastricht) Treaty of European Union.

The personality of the leader is also important in determining performance at the summit. The two key factors here are strength and experience. Political strength can be significant, and EU summits provide many examples of 'strong' and 'weak' leaders, but experience can also be important; for example, economic experience (usually derived from a previous post as finance minister) can be useful. Personality can also be critical in determining the capacity of a head of state to form coalitions with other EU leaders to push policies through: the personalities involved in the Franco-German axis obviously come to mind, with the frequent isolation of Mrs Thatcher, who represented the other extreme.

These three factors – power, scrutiny and personality – significantly affect the performance of participants at summits. Most obviously, they determine the ability of leaders to get their own way and have an impact on the summit. Similarly, they influence the capability of leaders to push what was agreed at the summit through their own systems and actually deliver what they have promised; this, clearly, has implications for future credibility. A less obvious result is to make reaching agreement at EU summits at least more complicated and possibly more difficult because of the differing degrees of domestic authority and strength of personality that the various leaders possess, and the differing kinds of domestic scrutiny that they face.

However, the EU summits differ from other summits in certain key respects. Most of the others are either limited-issue summits (NATO, G-7, and, frequently in practice, the superpower summits) or one-off/infrequent summits (the 'Earth' summits, funeral summits). The European Council is a 'serial' rather than an *ad hoc* summit (to use Berridge's terminology). The EU leaders meet much more frequently and with a much broader agenda. Furthermore, EU summits are embodied within a broader institutional framework – indeed they are not called summits but the European Council. These differences have a number of implications for the role and the activities of EU summits which make them unique in some respects:

- They have a much clearer function than many other summits – that is (in effect) they determine overall policy direction and settle disputes.
- EU summits are thus much more proactive than most other summits – NATO, the G-7 and the 'Earth' summits, for example, are (or were) much more reactive. EU summits potentially have a much more positive ethos; in principle, each member state has some sense of the ultimate purpose of European union.
- This positive ethos is made stronger by the fact that the EU is perceived as a distinct entity. Consequently, the European Council is much more than a defence club (NATO) or an economic talking-shop (the G-7). EU summits are one of several fora within the organization and there is a much stronger sense of partnership underlying these meetings than is the case with other summits. There is also a much greater pressure to cooperate than in other summits.
- For the same reason (because it is only part of the whole) the EU summit is potentially much more significant; its decisions have a much greater force, are more binding and are more likely to lead to concrete results than the decisions taken by other summits.

- EU summits are nearly always tied to EU Council presidencies and usually occur at the end of a presidency. This has two implications: first, it raises issues of national prestige – every member state wants to make a good job of the presidency and wants to finish with a good summit that achieves something (all of which adds to the pressure to make progress); second, the presidency tries to shape the summit by attempting to set the agenda during its period of office, which can either accelerate or slow down policies. Hence the conclusions of the Corfu summit (Greece) in June 1994 included a reference to Cyprus (and Malta) being in the next round of EU accessions; whilst those of the Edinburgh summit (Britain) in December 1992 made very little reference to EU social policy (which the British have traditionally opposed).
- There is much more scope for a second chance within EU summitry. Indeed many issues are deliberately discussed and developed over several summits, such as the creation of the EMS and the Treaty of European Union; and the outcome of the 1996 Intergovernmental Conference will also be developed over several summits. Thus the European Council is not only unique in terms of its nature and identity but also in its practices and functions. The purpose of the next section is to provide a more detailed analysis of these functions.

III[7]

Since the European Council was not part of the EU's original institutional framework, there is no single clear statement of what it is supposed to do. However, the functions or objectives of the European Council can be determined by examining various summit communiqués. There would appear to be eight, as listed below:

1 Facilitating Informal Exchanges of View

This was emphasized at the 1977 summit in London and was particularly favoured by Schmidt and Giscard d'Estaing. These are the 'fireside chats' of which no records are kept, thereby encouraging frankness but making it very difficult for researchers to determine to what extent the purpose of the interview has been achieved. There is some evidence that informal exchanges played an important role in the establishment of the EMS which has been described as 'a triumph of politicians ... over the scepticism of central bankers, government officials and other participants in the "normal" policy making hierarchy'.[8] But generally it is difficult to show that informal consultations have achieved a great deal and they went out of fashion somewhat during the rather confrontational summits of the early 1980s. However, it is difficult to disagree with the presumption that they at least facilitate contact between EU leaders and encourage a kind of 'coordination reflex'.

Moreover, informal contacts at EU summits have to be set within the broader context of personal interaction between EU leaders which takes place in a variety of other ways. At the simplest level this involves telephone calls which may assist progress in the European Council and, in turn, may be facilitated by meetings at European Councils. Of course, EU leaders also meet at other summits; sometimes these may involve all EU leaders (or their representatives), sometimes only some of them. The net result of this contact, primarily through summits, is that EU leaders have very frequent discussions and know each other well. Although animosity is perhaps not uncommon, this is usually overcome by the recognition of a need to get on, and the cumulative outcome of frequent contact is arguably more likely to be positive. Alliances will be forged and this will facilitate progress. Indeed, personal relationships, particularly between French and German leaders, have been a driving force in the process of European integration. Thus the role of summits in providing an opportunity for informal exchanges of view is perhaps more important than it may first have appeared.

2   Defining the Guidelines for Integration

This role involves defining a strategy for consolidating EU integration and developing it further. The European Council clearly has insufficient time to do this itself so it tends to commission small committees of experts to prepare reports – for example, the Tindemans Report on European Union (1976), and more recently and productively the Dooge Report (1984), which led to the Single European Act, and the Delors Report (1990) on Economic and Monetary Union.

3   Policy Orientation

This relates to particular policies rather than the general orientation of EU policy. (This overlaps in practice with dispute settlement – discussed below – where orientation takes the form of guidelines as to how to solve a particular problem, for example the UK budget rebate.) Policy orientation not connected with dispute settlement has mainly related to aspects of economic

policy, where it is difficult to judge the impact of EU summit recommendations and energy policy, which is ill-defined at EU level. Policy orientation
has therefore proved to be a difficult function to carry out in practice.

4 Scope Enlargement

This involves the initiation of policy in new areas. On the face of it the
European Council has been very successful in initiating new policy in
many areas, including:

- European Political Cooperation (The Hague, 1969)
- European Monetary Cooperation Fund (Paris, 1972)
- European Regional Development Fund (Paris, 1972)
- Environmental policy (Paris, 1972; Luxembourg, 1985)
- Energy policy (Copenhagen, 1973)
- European passport (Paris, 1974)
- Cooperation against terrorism (Rome, 1975; Brussels, 1976)
- EMS (Copenhagen, Bremen and Brussels, 1978; Strasbourg, 1979)
- Cultural cooperation (Stuttgart, 1983)
- Security policy discussions in EPC (Stuttgart, 1983)
- 'People's Europe' (Fontainebleau, 1984)
- Technology (Luxembourg, 1985)
- Home affairs etc. (Maastricht, 1991).

However, what is important is the follow-up, since having initiated these
policies it is not the European Council but the other EU institutions which
have to bring them to fruition. In some cases the policies have not progressed much beyond the European Council's drawing-board, but a
significant number of the above policies have indeed been realized. In short,
there has been a fair measure of success, although several notable failures.

5 Policy Coordination

This is a fairly obvious function for the European Council but one which it
has not carried out particularly well. It has been difficult to agree on priorities and reach consensus amongst member states on strategies.

6 Issuing Declarations on Foreign Relations

The European Council has responsibility for expressing a 'common position in questions of foreign relations' according to the 1983 Stuttgart

summit communiqué. This it has done regularly in response to international crises, by and large without significant disagreements. Developments in the Middle East and in East–West relations have been the focus of many of these declarations but the scope has been very broad and declarations are frequently concerned with internal political developments in some non-EU country. Whether these declarations have had much effect is another question.

7 Dispute Settlement: Problem-Solving as a 'Court of Appeal'

This involves settling issues unresolved from discussions at lower levels; essentially, the European Council intervenes to take decisions that cannot be agreed in the Council of Ministers because they are too difficult (usually involving high political stakes). Heads of government have not been too keen on promoting this function for fear that all difficult decisions will be passed upwards. Nevertheless, this has become one of the main functions of the European Council. It has had to settle many important disputes – involving the budget, the common agricultural policy, the common fisheries policy, and many more trivial cases (such as the siting of the JET Euratom research centre).

8 Policy Monitoring

The European Council obviously reviews its previous policy decisions. Since it is not responsible for implementing them it has to make sure that others do (mainly the Council of Ministers). In practice, however, it is actually quite lax in this regard – as indeed is the EU generally.

To summarize, the European Council has, in general terms, two purposes which, though not unimportant, are nevertheless perhaps less important than others and difficult to assess in terms of effectiveness. These purposes are:

(i)   informal exchanges (function 1, above)
(ii)   declarations on foreign policy (function 6)

However, the two main activities at EU summits would appear to involve:

(I)   determining policy at various levels (functions 2,3,4,5,8)
(II)   dispute settlement (function 7)

The European Council much prefers to be involved with (I) and, indeed, largely was in its first phase in the 1970s. It then became increasingly preoccupied by dispute settlement (II) – effectively hijacked by the British budgetary dispute and related issues in the early 1980s. However, since the mid-1980s it has successfully reverted to its preferred role of policy determination (I), particularly at the grand design level (function 2) which it is uniquely equipped to undertake.

Finally, some reference must be made to a function of the European Council which may sometimes have little to do with the actual summit itself. EU summits provide opportunities for what might be called 'sub-summits' – that is separate meetings between two or more individual leaders. These may directly relate to the summit and could, for example, involve bartering to assist agreement on some policy proposal, or the leader of the country currently holding the Council presidency trying to broker a deal between two member states in disagreement. However, the 'sub-summit' may relate to an issue which has nothing to do with the business of the European Council: two EU leaders may simply be using the opportunity of being in the same place at the same time to discuss a matter of mutual interest, away from the glare of publicity to some extent. A good example would be the meetings between British and Irish prime ministers to discuss the situation in Northern Ireland. This has little to do directly with the functions of the European Council, except insofar as it is an example of an informal exchange of views, but is potentially extremely useful.

It is clear that, after a shaky start, the European Council has carved out a role for itself and by and large fulfils its primary functions reasonably well, and in that sense it is successful. In fact, if the European Council had not existed in the early 1980s then it would probably have had to be invented to deal with the budgetary disputes, since these were only ever going to be resolved by agreement between heads of government. Equally, it is difficult to believe that anything on the scale of the Maastricht Treaty of European Union could have been agreed through the Commission's normal decision-making channels, except at the level of heads of government. Thus the Callaghan remark in 1977 – that the European Council was 'strong on discussion, not so strong on decisions'[9] – seems to have been rendered inaccurate by subsequent events. Essentially the European Council has filled a gap and has made a major contribution to consensus-building and consequently decision-making because it has a political authority which the general Council of Ministers lacks.

IV

Whilst much of this chapter has focused on the uniqueness of EU summits it is also necessary to address a number of comparative questions which can usefully be asked about all summits:

1. **Are EU summits mainly symbolic?** The appropriate answer is strongly negative. The outcome is variable but European Councils are rarely simply a photo-call (although one or two have amounted to little more than this). Both the discussion and the outcome are potentially, and often actually, substantial. Moreover, even when they are not, an 'unsuccessful' summit is still part of an evolutionary process and may help pave the way to subsequent success.

2. **Are summit negotiations 'pre-cooked'?** To some extent they are in the sense that the European Council sometimes prepares the ground by commissioning expert committees to provide reports on particular issues or policy proposals. However, this only really 'pre-cooks' the agenda in part and not the outcome (although this may be given a push in a very specific direction); moreover, the real purpose of these committees is simply to undertake detailed preparatory work. In general, European Councils are not 'pre-cooked' but are fairly 'free-ranging', and the performance of individual participants can be important; for example, the final Maastricht compromise was largely shaped by the Germans, the Dutch and the British.

3. **Are EU summits best suited to high or low politics?** The answer would seem to be that they are flexible enough to deal with both and, indeed, their range of functions does cover both.

4. **To what extent do summits serve domestic as well as foreign policy goals?** The nature of EU summits is rather different from many others and part of this difference is that they are very largely concerned with what might be defined as domestic matters. This is still true, albeit somewhat less so, if domestic is defined as 'national' rather than 'European'.

5. **To what extent are EU summits now institutionalized as part of a fixed regime?** Clearly, the European Council has a place in the EU framework and a degree of permanence. Moreover, whilst it is still evolving to some extent, its functions have become fairly well specified and are unlikely to change much.

How precisely the European Council has been institutionalized is not quite so clear and raises the specific (to EU summits) question as to how the European Council fits in to the EU framework. This has already been addressed and the answer would seem to be ambiguous. At one level the European Council is an intergovernmental riposte to the supranational Commission. However the Commission, of course, actually attends summits so still has an input, and arguably the original model of the Commission as exclusive policy initiator had already failed by the 1970s and the system needed to evolve. The Commission has always had to take account of different constituencies, including heads of government. With regard to potentially usurping the role of the Council of Ministers it should be remembered that there have been some issues the Council actually wanted to pass up to the European Council. The relationship which is perhaps potentially the most fraught is that with the European Parliament.

V

EU summitry – the European Council – was an inevitable development. From the early 1970s, events in the international political and economic arena demanded immediate and authoritative reaction which could not be provided by the EU institutions. Moreover, the fact that many international developments impacted more or less equally on all member states blurred the line between domestic and foreign policy and required a coordinated response. Only the heads of state or government had the authority and position to act and respond in the appropriate manner. Given the already prevalent fashion for summits, then the establishment of EU summits was the obvious next step.

Whether the European Union has a federal or intergovernmental agenda, the European Council will remain an important *de facto* part of the EU's institutional machinery. It has arguably been one of the most effective examples of summitry of all. On numerous occasions it has 'kick-started' the EU when it has become moribund and bogged down in internal dissension. It has acted as the initiator of nearly all major EU policy developments since summits began in earnest in 1969 and has settled seemingly intractable disputes, notably involving British budget rebates and the reform of the common agricultural policy. It has promoted policy coordination of EU member states, economically and politically, and has been flexible and inventive in its response to problems. It has been the channel through which the European Political Cooperation Procedure (EPC) has been developed and will take the lead in the development of the common foreign and security policy (CFSP).[10]

However, it is noticeable that the effectiveness of the European Council has been significantly reduced in areas for which the EU has lesser provision in its treaties. Thus the European Council has been able to engineer significant progress in the economic sphere – for example, the European Monetary System and the Single European Market – which is well covered by EU treaties but it has achieved much less with EPC and (as yet) the CFSP which are covered much more vaguely by the treaties. Perhaps European Union summits are not that different from other summits in some ways and the main lesson they provide for summitry is that 'stand alone' summits are of very limited usefulness; the effectiveness of summits is very closely related to the degree of back-up and follow-up, and the extent to which a summit is the apex of a much larger organization. Perhaps this is most starkly illustrated by comparing EU summits with the 1992 'Earth Summit' in Rio de Janeiro.

NOTES AND REFERENCES

1. The Fouchet Plan was a French proposal for a form of European political union along intergovernmental lines. It is described and set in context in J. D. Armstrong, L. Lloyd and J. Redmond, *From Versailles to Maastricht: International Organisation in the Twentieth Century* (London, Macmillan, 1996), chapter 6.
2. J. Weiler, 'The Genscher–Colombo Draft European Act: The Politics of Indecision', *Journal of European Integration*, vol. 4, nos 2 and 3 (1983), p. 140.
3. D. Cameron, 'The 1992 Initiative: Causes and Consequences' in A. Sbragia (ed.), *Euro-Politics: Institutions and Policymaking in the 'New' European Community* (Washington, Brookings Institute, 1992), p. 62.
4. Treaty of European Union (1992), Title I, Article D.
5. Treaty of European Union (1992), Title I, Article 146.
6. A. Morgan, *From Summit to Council: Evolution in the EEC* (London, Chatham House, 1976), p. 56.
7. This section bases its framework and draws heavily on S. Bulmer and W. Wessels, *The European Council* (London, Macmillan, 1987), chapter 5, pp. 75–102.
8. Bulmer and Wessels, *The European Council*, p. 84.
9. Comment by James Callaghan at the closing press conference of the June 1977 London summit, quoted in Bulmer and Wessels, *The European Council*, p. 100, and Agence Europe, *Daily Bulletin*, 1 July 1977.
10. Treaty of European Union (1992), Title V, Article J8.

5 Superpower Summitry
Michael Andersen and Theo Farrell

Superpower summitry is history. Since the collapse of the Soviet Union in December 1991 only one superpower remains and, like the tango, it takes two superpowers to have a superpower summit. The term superpower grew out of the cold war and the special conditions of that period. Post-war bipolarity was based on US and Soviet military dominance, especially in terms of nuclear weapons. There was a series of summit meetings between the four victorious powers after the Second World War but, by 1949, it was clear that the world had split into two blocs led by the United States and Soviet Union respectively. From then on, with the exception of a meeting in 1955, real summits were bilateral affairs.[1] This chapter will look at the development of superpower summitry from the first such meeting in 1959 (although the 1955 summit between all the

Table 5.1 Superpower Summits

Location	Date	Participants
Camp David (US)	15–27 September 1959	Khrushchev and Eisenhower
Vienna	3–4 June 1961	Khrushchev and Kennedy
Moscow	22–26 May 1972	Brezhnev and Nixon
Washington, DC	16–24 June 1973	Brezhnev and Nixon
Moscow	27 June–3 July 1974	Brezhnev and Nixon
Vladivostok (USSR)	23–24 November 1974	Brezhnev and Ford
Vienna	15–18 June 1979	Brezhnev and Carter
Geneva	19-20 November 1985	Gorbachev and Reagan
Reykjavik	11–12 October 1986	Gorbachev and Reagan
Washington DC	7–10 December 1987	Gorbachev and Reagan
Moscow	29 May–2 June 1988	Gorbachev and Reagan
New York	December 1988	Gorbachev and Reagan/Bush
Malta	2–3 December 1989	Gorbachev and Bush
Washington DC	30 May–4 June 1990	Gorbachev and Bush
Helsinki	9 September 1990	Gorbachev and Bush
Moscow	30 July–1 August 1991	Gorbachev and Bush

allied powers will be discussed) to the last one in 1991. Summitry, like foreign policy in general, exists at the juncture of international and domestic politics: it simultaneously affects, and is affected by, developments in both these political spheres. This chapter is structured accordingly.

INTERNATIONAL POLITICS OF SUPERPOWER SUMMITRY

During the cold war, summitry proved to be a very useful device for regulating the superpower relationship. It did this in three ways: firstly, by providing opportunities for US and Soviet leaders to meet and get a feel for each other; secondly, by providing a non-violent means for the superpowers to assert their standing, with both allies and enemies, in the international system; and thirdly, by providing an impetus to arms control and disarmament. Each of these will be discussed in turn from the US and Soviet perspectives.

Getting Personal

Every US president and most Soviet general secretaries (the exceptions being Andropov and Chernenko), had a summit with their counterpart on at least one occasion.[2] Part of the appeal of a superpower summit was the opportunity it provided for the leaders and their advisers to check out the opposition and to present their views in person (although the only superpower leader who used the summit occasion to get first-hand experience of *life* in the adversaries' country was Nikita Khrushchev who toured the United States for two weeks in 1959). The views of John Kennedy's advisers are typical on this score:

> It would be useful, all agreed, for the President to size up Khrushchev, to find out his views on [a range of] issues, to gain a firsthand impression against which he could then judge Khrushchev's words and deeds, and to make more clear and precise than his letters could ... the vital interests for which this nation would fight.[3]

Similar views are expressed in Eisenhower's and Jimmy Carter's autobiographies, and in Ronald Reagan's biography.[4] In Reagan's case, summitry enabled him to develop a warm personal relationship with Gorbachev which greatly aided the winding-down of the cold war.

Claiming Parity and Asserting Primacy

The cold war can be seen as a dispute between the superpowers over their relative position in the world. From this perspective, the Soviets were constantly trying to achieve parity with the United States and the United States was continuously asserting its primacy.[5] Thanks to the innovative styles of Khrushchev and Gorbachev, the Soviets managed to seize the initiative in this struggle during two seven-year periods: 1956–63 and 1985–92. The rest of the time the ball lay in the Americans' court. Both sides used military force to advance their claim, be it to parity or primacy, often producing tense crises in the process. Summits provided an alternative, safer, way for superpowers to assert their position in the world.

In the late 1950s and early 1960s, the United States faced a series of challenges to its primacy from the Soviets which became the focus of superpower summitry in that era. At the twentieth party congress in 1956, Khrushchev, establishing himself as the *primus inter pares* in the Kremlin, not only denounced Stalin but also proposed fundamental revisions in Soviet ideology and thinking on international relations. Dismissing the long-standing doctrines on the inevitability of war between the two antagonistic camps in the world, Khrushchev announced the doctrine of 'peaceful coexistence' based on the assumptions that Soviet military strength would deter a capitalist attack and that the correlation of forces in general now favored the Soviet Union.[6] This new optimism served domestic purposes which will be discussed in the next section. The international purpose of Khrushchev's reassessment was straightforward, namely, to persuade Western policy-makers that Soviet power had risen to a level equal with that of the United States. Khrushchev's drastic revision of the international image and status of the Soviet Union was based on a combination of boasting and bluffing. Thus he declared before the 1956 Party Conference that 'capitalism has lost its former superiority'. And indeed, most observers agreed, the momentum in world affairs between 1957 and 1960 seemed to be with Moscow; as Western empires were rapidly crumbling the Soviet Union was gaining influence in Africa, Asia and in the Middle East.[7] Khrushchev's ultimate challenge to the Americans was the launching of Sputnik in 1957, followed by the first test of an intercontinental ballistic missile (ICBM). In reality, the Soviet Union had neither the economic nor the military capacity to back up the General Secretary's hefty rhetoric; yet a strange synthesis of the West's battering experience of Sputnik, the overwhelming perspective of a nuclear holocaust and Khrushchev's flamboyant catchphrases ('we will bury you!') allowed him to bluff his way through for a period.[8]

In late 1958 Khrushchev decided to apply the same strategy in the heart of Europe: Berlin. The fact that allied forces still were in West Berlin was 'a bone in Moscow's throat'; it was literally crippling the East German economy with tens of thousands of the best educated citizens fleeing for better lives in the West. The allied presence in the heart of East Germany also placed a question mark over Soviet control of Eastern Europe. By threatening Berlin, Khrushchev also hoped to exact a German peace treaty banning West German possession of nuclear weapons, a development Moscow feared might come about as a result of West German membership of NATO.[9] Consequently, on 27 November 1958 Khrushchev issued an ultimatum to the West, stating that the Soviet Union, unilaterally, would conclude a peace treaty with the East German government within six months thereby effectively cancelling the allies' rights of occupation in Berlin.[10] This precipitated a crisis which became the main theme of the 1959 summit. For Eisenhower, the primary purpose of his meeting with Khrushchev was to communicate 'our firmness on Berlin and our rights elsewhere in the world'. It is hardly surprising that this summit did not produce any kind of substantive agreements. But for Khrushchev it was a big success as he attached great symbolic importance to the fact that the world had witnessed him and the American president discuss world affairs as equals, on America's initiative and on American soil.[11]

The Vienna summit, 3–4 June 1961, was doomed from the beginning; if Berlin in 1958 had been an irritating bone in Khrushchev's throat, he was now desperately choking on it. Kennedy sought, as Eisenhower had done two years earlier, to use the summit to communicate US resolve on the Berlin issue.[12] Khrushchev went to his meeting with Kennedy in Vienna 'on probation', so to speak. With the emergence of a Sino-Soviet split over Mao's objection to Khrushchev's conciliatory line to the West, and the revelation that the missile gap favoured the United States, the Soviet premier's political survival now depended on progress on Berlin. The flow of refugees from East to West Berlin had increased to more than 20 000 people a month creating not only bad publicity for the Soviet way of life but also a threat to the very existence of the East German state. Once again the summit ended in stalemate; the two men spent most of two days snapping at each other. Khrushchev eventually solved his Berlin problem, at least in part, by erecting a wall around the Western enclave in August 1961.

In the early 1970s, summitry assumed an even greater role under Richard Nixon, and his National Security Adviser Henry Kissinger. Nixon and Kissinger sought to de-emphasize the function of military power in the superpower competition. They believed that the Soviets were catching up with the United States in nuclear forces and so they sought to shift the basis of superpower status to economic and ideological power where the US would remain superior. Summitry, combined with arms control, was to provide the concrete manifestation of this new policy of détente. For this reason Nixon had follow-up summits with Brezhnev in 1973 and 1974 even though nothing substantial was expected to come of them; it was the symbolism that really mattered.

Continuing an ideological line remarkably similar to Khrushchev's a decade earlier, Leonid Brezhnev, in the late sixties and first half of the seventies, judged the correlation of forces as favouring the Soviet Union. Firstly, during the late sixties, Brandt's Ostpolitik had created a *de facto* peace settlement in Europe. Secondly, seen from Moscow, developments in the capitalist world looked promising; the Americans were in trouble in Vietnam, and had lost their former economic superiority over their allies. Most importantly (as discussed later), the Nixon administration recognized in 1970 that the Soviets had reached nuclear parity with the United States. However, contrary to Khrushchev's aggressive brinkmanship which triggered off all sorts of crises, Brezhnev's approach was a combination of newfound Soviet self-confidence and diplomatic caution[13] – an approach that paid off, not least in the direct dealings with Nixon at the summit in 1972. The summit itself and the multitude of agreements were a clear demonstration of the newly recognized parity between the United States and the Soviet Union. Obviously, this was the case with the agreement on the Strategic Arms Limitation Treaty (SALT). However, SALT for the Soviets had much broader political significance and purpose. Besides achieving the substantive goal of establishing a ceiling on future nuclear missile developments, which in itself was an important goal for the Soviet leadership, Brezhnev more than anything else wanted SALT to symbolize the American acknowledgement of political parity between the two superpowers.[14] The difference in approaches is striking if we consider the other main agreement at the 1972 summit: the agreement on the basic principles of relations between the two sides. Ironically, it is not quite clear whether Nixon ever bothered to read this mere 1000 words; Brezhnev, however, estimated the agreement to be more important than SALT itself. Indeed, he later said that this document was the most important thing ever agreed at a US–Soviet summit.[15] The key words in the agreement were 'peaceful coexistence' and 'normal relations based on the principles of equality and non-interference in internal affairs', leading to 'recognition of security interests on the basis of equality'. Thus, the Americans, in print and in public, recognized that there now existed an equal relationship between the two. Moreover, crucially for the future superpower relationship, the summit thus saw the American recognition of the concept of 'peaceful coexistence'. While excluding military confrontation between the superpowers, this concept nevertheless remained a central part of the international class struggle, which assumed a continuation of the economic competition and ideological conflict, including continued support for national liberation movements in the Third World.[16] The failure of the Nixon administration to identify differences in the understanding of this concept is nothing less than extraordinary, and was interpreted by the Soviets as giving them a free hand in the Third World. Thus, after an initial period of caution, Soviet attempts to seek or assert influence in the Middle East, North Vietnam, Portugal, Mozambique and Angola gained momentum with disastrous consequences for the longer-term détente.[17] In general terms, the following two summits between Nixon and Brezhnev saw a Soviet policy along the same lines, following up on the basic objectives set out by Brezhnev's evaluation of the correlation of forces and consequent détente initiatives; stressing the continuation of the process, trying to sustain the momentum, even when the process had been reduced to nothing more than a hollow shell.[18]

After three Nixon–Brezhnev tête-à-têtes in two years, the rest of the decade saw only two far less significant summits: the 'getting-to-know-you' Ford and Brezhnev meeting in Vladivostok in November 1974 at which agreement was reached on the principles for the SALT II accord, and the bland 1979 summit between Carter and Brezhnev which staged the eventual signing of that agreement, a treaty which was never ratified. In his first term, Ronald Reagan rejected all suggestions about meeting the leaders from the country he described as 'the evil empire'; Reagan never met his counterparts Brezhnev, Andropov or Chernenko before they died.

The later part of the 1980s was without doubt the golden age of superpower summitry, with a string of increasingly successful summits, featuring the 'Great Communicator', Reagan (and, from 1989, his successor George Bush), and the master of summitry, Gorbachev. During those years, Gorbachev and Shevardnadze repeatedly stunned the West with a 'da' on all the occasions the world had come to expect a 'njet'; whether it was democratization, openness (*'glasnost'*), human rights or disarmament. There is no doubt that Gorbachev, backed by a set of hand-picked civilian advisers with a de-ideologized world view, saw summits as the ultimate opportunity to communicate his 'New Political Thinking' to friends and erstwhile foes alike. A vivid illustration of this strategy was his announcement, before the UN General Assembly and televised to the rest of the world, on the eve of the Washington summit in December 1988, that the Soviet Union would unilaterally eliminate its conventional superiority in

Europe. According to Gorbachev's advisers, this announcement had a double aim: firstly, to kick-start the negotiations on the reductions of the conventional forces in Europe; and secondly, to create an irreversible breakthrough in relations with the West; not least by enabling the European NATO members, already smitten with 'Gorbamania' (or 'Gorbasm' as the French called it), to put pressure on the still sceptical US administration.[19] The US Congress, which was more impressed than the Bush administration with Gorbachev's UN speech, successfully applied pressure on the administration to speed up its review of policy towards the Soviet Union. Less than a year later both the Berlin Wall and the division of Europe were history.

Naturally, superpower disputes over specific policy and geographical areas came up in summits and these can be seen as part and parcel of the overall dispute between the United States and Soviet Union about their relative positions in the international system. An example of this is the Soviet uneasiness about the American–Chinese rapprochement. During the 1973 and 1974 summits Brezhnev tried to make the Americans realize that the relationship between Washington and Moscow was much more important than closer US ties with China, culminating with his proposal at the 1974 summit for the establishment of 'a superpower condominium', which was rejected outright by Nixon.[20] For the United States, superpower summits afforded good opportunities to discourage Soviet 'adventurism' in the Third World and to embarrass the Soviets publicly over their human rights record. This was particularly useful for Nixon and Kissinger. For them, détente was not about developing a cooperative relationship with the Soviets on an equal basis but rather about persuading the Soviets to accept their appropriate position in the world, in other words below that of the United States. So the Soviets were expected to abide by international 'rules of conduct' which US policy-makers did not apply to themselves. In this case, US intervention in the Third World was deemed acceptable whereas Soviet intervention was not.[21] Nixon's concern in the lead up to the 1972 Moscow summit was with Soviet support for North Vietnam in the war against the United States and South Vietnam. He hoped to persuade the Soviets to assist the United States in withdrawing from Vietnam without losing face. Indeed, as Kissinger was leaving for preparatory talks with Brezhnev, Nixon instructed his National Security Adviser to 'just pack up and come home' if the Soviet leader was not willing to play ball over Vietnam.[22] Fifteen years later, the tables had turned and Shevardnadze approached Shultz in pre-summit talks to ask for US assistance in a Soviet withdrawal from Afghanistan.[23] Carter, likewise, used the 1979 summit to attack the Soviets for their 'adventurism' in the Third

World. In one of his statements he claimed, 'In the Horn of Africa, in Southern Africa, in the Middle East, and in Southeast Asia I have tried to achieve peace, but the Soviet leaders have done just the opposite.'[24] Carter was being hypocritical, particularly with regard to the Horn of Africa and south-east Asia. Up to this time he had overseen the supply of arms to Somalia (as he put it to 'aggressively challenge' the Soviets in their own sphere) for its war against Ethiopia, to North Yemen for its war against South Yemen, and to Indonesia for its truly genocidal invasion of East Timor.[25] Reagan also attacked Soviet 'adventurism', especially in Afghanistan, in the 1985, 1986 and 1987 summits. Although, as already noted, by 1987 the Soviets had already privately indicated to the Americans their intention to withdraw from Afghanistan and, by the 1988 summit, both sides were negotiating the synchronization of this withdrawal with the termination of US arms supplies to the Afghan rebels. At the same time, US adventurism in the Third World had increased. Under the Reagan Doctrine, the United States had increased its military support for anti–left-wing rebels and governments in the Third World.

Reagan was most forceful in his condemnation of the Soviets' human rights record. This issue did not really concern Nixon whereas Carter claimed it to be central to his foreign policy. However, when it came down it, Carter rather lamely raised the issue of human rights at the 1979 summit and then promptly accepted Brezhnev's reiteration of the standard Soviet position that it was not an appropriate topic for discussion at the summit.[26] There was little discussion about human rights in the 1985 summit but the fact that there was any formal discussion at all was a significant concession by the Soviets. The discussion in 1987 amounted to no more than an angry exchange, with Reagan criticizing the Soviet Union for refusing to let more Soviet Jews emigrate and Gorbachev criticizing the United States for using armed patrols to prevent Mexicans from illegally immigrating. By 1988, however, with no expectation for progress towards a Strategic Arms Reduction Treaty (START) agreement, Reagan decided that human rights should be top of the US agenda for the Moscow summit. Consequently he spent the summit giving private and public speeches on this theme. Again the Soviets attempted to counter US criticisms in the pre-summit talks but with little success. In one meeting Shevardnadze asserted that 'the United States systematically denies women and blacks the opportunity to advance, to undertake important tasks' while he was facing an American delegation which included a woman assistant secretary of state and a black chairman of the Joint Chiefs of Staff (JCS).[27] Once again, Carter and Reagan were being hypocritical: under their presidency the United States sponsored serious human rights abuses (for instance in Iran under the Shah; Iraq; East Timor; and the Contras in Nicaragua) and supported oppressive regimes around the world (such as those of most Central American states). Of course, the Soviets were unable to attack the United States on these counts as the Soviet Union acted in a similar manner.

Advancing Arms Control

In the public eye arms control, and especially the official signing of agreements, were by far the most significant feature of superpower summits. The main superpower agreements on arms control and disarmament were SALT I, SALT II, the Intermediate-range Nuclear Forces (INF) Treaty, and START. These were signed respectively at the 1972, 1979, 1987, and 1991 summits.[28] However, for the most part, these agreements were not negotiated by the leaders at summits but rather were constructed through lengthy (often painstaking) negotiations by specialists. Still summitry could be used to help this process in three ways. First, on occasion, the prospect of a summit was held out by one side as a carrot to induce the other side to be more forthcoming in ongoing arms control negotiations. Eisenhower instructed the State Department to issue a conditional invitation to Khrushchev to visit the United States for a summit in 1959, the condition being that progress was made in the arms control talks at Geneva.[29] In contrast, Reagan's Secretary of State, George Shultz, reports in his memoirs that Gorbachev tried 'to exact a price in exchange for his agreement to come to Washington' for a summit in 1987, the price being progress in the START talks.[30] These particular attempts failed: the State Department neglected to issue Eisenhower's proviso along with the invitation to Khrushchev and, since the Soviets were as keen as the Americans on a summit in 1987, Shultz was able to ignore pressure from Gorbachev. In a more general sense, the prospect of a summit may be held hostage by both sides in order to make progress in arms control negotiations as was the case in 1971.

This leads to the second way in which summits can provide impetus to arms control negotiations, that is by creating a deadline for negotiators to work towards. The objective would be, if not to close a deal, then at least to present a nearly completed one which could be finished off at a summit. For instance, the announcement by both sides in October 1971 that they would hold a meeting seven months later served to apply more pressure on the negotiators in Helsinki to pull together a SALT agreement in time for the Moscow summit. The desire on both sides to conclude a SALT II Treaty which could be signed at a summit in mid-June 1979 led to four months of talks in early 1979 of renewed intensity during which time an agreement was successfully reached. The INF talks were also given a big push in the months leading up to the 1987 summit in Washington. In each of these cases, progress in the negotiations was aided by numerous meetings between Kissinger and the Soviet Ambassador to Washington, Anatoly Dobrynin, between Secretary of State Cyrus Vance and Dobrynin in 1979, and between Shultz and Soviet Foreign Minister Eduard Shevardnadze in 1987.

Thirdly, summits may also give impetus to arms control negotiations by providing opportunities for direct intervention by leaders in order to overcome the final hurdles to an agreement. In so doing, leaders may rely on their immediate advisers or, alternatively, a larger group of advisers to help them wrap up the negotiations. In the 1972 summit, Nixon and Brezhnev, along with Kissinger and Gromyko, took over the final stages of the negotiations. In order to ensure that he got all the credit for SALT, Nixon wanted to keep the action as close to the White House as possible. This suited Kissinger's negotiation preference for high-level direct talks and served his own egotistical desire to grab the limelight.[31] In typical style, Kissinger overcame stumbling blocks to a SALT agreement by personally engaging in secret high-level negotiations in Moscow without Nixon's approval or the support of the US military or any governmental agencies.[32] In stark contrast, Reagan and Gorbachev took far larger negotiation teams with them to their summits, including representatives from all concerned agencies.[33] This difference reflects the divergent approaches taken by Nixon and Reagan to summitry. Reagan wanted to allow for the possibility of substantive negotiations during the summits, at least the ones in 1985, 1986 and 1987. In general, his summits tended to be less stage-managed affairs than Nixon's. For instance, the joint communiqué for the 1972 summit was agreed upon beforehand by Kissinger and Dobrynin, whereas Reagan wanted the summit discussions to determine the joint communiqués and not vice versa.[34] Likewise, Gorbachev's announcement on the eve of the Washington summit in December 1988 of significant unilateral Soviet withdrawals from eastern Europe injected new life and purpose into the long frozen negotiations on conventional forces in Europe.

Every cold war superpower leader professed to be keen to reach arms control agreements. In reality, however, a serious arms control agreement was simply not on the cards until the late sixties: Eisenhower and Kennedy were not prepared for reductions, and the Soviets, trying to reach nuclear parity, consequently couldn't be.

Each of Eisenhower's arms control proposals was designed to favour the United States. In his first arms control initiative, announced in 1953 and called 'Atoms for Peace', the President proposed that the superpowers divert nuclear materials from their weapon programmes to civilian projects under UN supervision. This plan favoured the United States because, as Eisenhower noted in his diary, the United States could contribute far more materials from its atomic stockpile than the Soviets 'and still improve our *relative* position in the cold war and even in the event of the outbreak of war'.[35] In the 1959 summit, Eisenhower proposed negotiating a ban on nuclear testing for military purposes which he then intended to circumvent by using nuclear explosives in large civilian projects from which the military could gather test information.[36] It is also clear that many people in the Eisenhower administration were firmly against substantive arms control. The military services and defence officials argued that it was not technically possible to provide adequate verification for arms control agreements and so the Soviets were bound to cheat. Thus it was noted in a National Security Council (NSC) paper in 1955 that US arms control proposals were designed for public relations purposes and not for the purpose of reaching any actual agreements.[37] Fundamentally, Eisenhower's 'New Look' defence policy ruled out substantive nuclear arms control as it called for the United States to depend on nuclear weapons rather than conventional forces to deter Soviet aggression. This policy was driven by an Air Force campaign which persuaded the public and policy-makers that Soviet conventional forces were far larger than they were in reality and that nuclear weapons provided the most cost-effective way of meeting this threat.[38] In light of this, Eisenhower could ill afford to agree any substantial cuts in nuclear armaments, or even cap them. Indeed, in 1957 the United States rejected a Soviet proposal at the Geneva talks for the exchange of inspection teams and in March that year, in a complete reversal of policy, the President's special assistant on disarmament renounced the US objective of nuclear disarmament.[39]

Kennedy was not about to cut any major arms control deals with Khrushchev either. In his 1960 presidential campaign he had attacked Eisenhower for not being hard enough on the Soviets. Echoing most Democrats and some Republicans, Kennedy argued that the United States needed to be more assertive in its dealings with the Soviet Union and in order to do this, the United States had to build up its military forces. Indeed, Kennedy claimed that the Soviets were acquiring more ICBMs than the United States and that Eisenhower was doing little about this. A 'missile gap' did exist but it favoured the United States and not, as Khrushchev and US alarmists claimed, the Soviet Union. Kennedy, who had full knowledge of this, went ahead anyway with a massive armament programme; within two years defence expenditure rose from $40 billion to $56 billion.[40] Not surprisingly, no arms control agreement was reached at the 1961 summit in Vienna. Like his predecessor, Kennedy was interested in building up arms, not trading them away.

Despite Khrushchev's public utterances to the contrary, the Soviet nuclear capability was still inferior to the American. This basic fact of life combined with the Soviet military assumption that a major conflict would inevitably escalate into a full-scale nuclear war, led from 1959 onwards to a Soviet surge for nuclear parity. And, consequently, until that goal had been achieved in 1970, the Soviets could not allow themselves to sign up for any agreement that would constrain this nuclear race on their side.[41]

In contrast, the major arms control agreements of the 1970s, SALT I and II, were brokered because arms control suited the rearranged policy preferences of Nixon and Carter on one hand, and Brezhnev on the other. Arms control was hailed as the fruit of détente – that is, Nixon's and Kissinger's policy to de-emphasize the function of military power in the superpower competition. For this reason Nixon actually downplayed US nuclear superiority and, in 1970, declared that the two superpowers had reached parity in terms of nuclear forces. This was true in that both sides were able to destroy each others' cities but false in that the US still had a larger nuclear arsenal. Nixon allowed the meaning of parity to remain unclear, so that he could negotiate SALT with the Soviets on the basis of parity while at the same time tell Congress that the treaty did not undermine US nuclear superiority.[42] For the Soviets, their achievement of nuclear parity and NATO's shift to a 'flexible response' strategy (which the Kremlin as well as the French saw as American reluctance to extend the nuclear guarantee to Europe), opened up the strategic prospect that a superpower conflict could be contained at the conventional level and the Soviet Union would be spared nuclear devastation even in the event of conflict. If a Soviet conventional 'blitzkrieg' could neutralize NATO's nuclear forces in Europe, they would be able to deny the United States a bridgehead on the continent from which it could stage an offensive against the Soviet Union, and some kind of peace agreement might be possible before the war escalated into an all-out nuclear one. Thus, from the beginning of the seventies, the Soviets focused on maintaining their conventional superiority, with the role of nuclear weapons being to deter and not to attack the United States, and to maintain nuclear parity at as low a level as possible.[43]

Carter was even more keen on arms control. He had made no secret of his deep dislike of nuclear weapons and once in office he was impatient to reach an arms control agreement with the Soviet Union. For this reason Carter initially suggested a 'rapid' SALT II agreement on the basis of the Vladivostok principles followed by a more comprehensive SALT III agreement. He subsequently changed his mind and made far more bold arms control proposals for SALT II than the Soviets had expected or were ready to accept. Ironically, Carter's eagerness for arms control was self-defeating in that it raised Soviet suspicions and put the arms control talks off track thereby delaying the conclusion of the SALT II agreement for about two years.[44] In addition, as will be discussed later, Carter felt compelled to approve the nuclear armament programmes of the military services in order to gain their support for the SALT II agreement.

In contrast to most of his predecessors, Reagan came up with a simple formula which synchronized his administration's disarmament proposals and defence policy. It was called 'negotiation from strength'. Reagan declared that the United States would only engage in substantive arms reduction talks after it had built up its nuclear forces. Thus, for most of the first Reagan administration, US negotiators only went through the motions at the INF and START talks for public relations purposes. By his second term in office, Reagan followed the changing tide of opinion which favoured real progress in arms reduction talks. He sought to use the US position of strength to force the Soviets to make all the concessions. This they did, and more, by making far-reaching arms reduction proposals which were closer to US rhetoric from the early 1980s (for example, the 'zero-option') than US policy in the mid-1980s.[45]

THE DOMESTIC POLITICS OF SUMMITRY

The political environment of every president and general secretary consisted of two interdependent parts: the international and domestic spheres. Thus, while superpower summitry was obviously about international affairs, it was also very much about domestic politics.

The United States

To talk of the United States having a 'position' or a 'policy' in specific superpower summits disguises the fact that, while the president was the most important actor in formulating policy, he still had to contend with, and rely on, plenty of other policy and political actors. The key aspect of superpower summitry which attracted most domestic political attention in the United States was arms control. Three domestic political arenas will be discussed in this section: election politics, bureaucratic politics within the administration, and institutional politics between the administration and Congress.[46]

Superpower summits, especially ones involving arms control treaties, provided presidents with opportunities to appear to be peacemakers. Both Nixon and Carter used summits in this way to improve their re-election fortunes. Clearly, with an election looming, Nixon used the 1972 summit and the SALT Treaty to boost his image as a peacemaker. This was particularly important for Nixon as he had been elected in 1968 on a promise to end the Vietnam War and with no end in sight to that war he hoped the summit in Moscow would placate public opinion. Equally, Carter sought to capitalize on the 1979 summit and SALT II Treaty in his bid for re-election. It is reasonable for presidents to seek to use summits in this way provided that US interests are not undermined in the process. In Nixon's case, they were. Nixon sought to ensure that he got all the credit for SALT. In order to take all the glory, he prevented the US arms control team from closing a deal in the Geneva talks in March 1972 and then he prevented the team from joining him in Moscow for the summit. Thus, closing negotiations were left up to Kissinger and his immediate aides who lacked the technical expertise for the task and who favoured a bad deal over no deal.

There is intensive bureaucratic warfare surrounding the formulating and implementation of US national security policy. Many agencies have interests at stake and these lead them to advocate conflicting policies. This is particularly evident in arms control. In this case the pattern of bureaucratic conflict has been fairly constant and predictable. The State Department has largely favoured arms control agreements, because it involves diplomacy, whereas the military services (represented by the JCS) have largely opposed any agreements which hinder their weapon acquisition programmes. However, the JCS have supported arms control agreements which only affect obsolete weapons and which provide them with arguments for acquiring new weapons in their place. JCS support in the mid-1980s for abiding by the unratified SALT II treaty is a good example of this. The other main agencies involved are the NSC staff, the Arms Control and Disarmament Agency (ACDA), and the civilian offices of the Department of Defense. Where they stand on arms control depends on the current incumbent of the White House. Under Carter, Paul Warnke, an arms control advocate, was appointed to head ACDA, whereas under Reagan the first two chiefs of ACDA, Eugene Rostow and Kenneth Adleman, were fundamentally opposed to arms control. Equally, Carter's Secretary of Defense, Harold Brown, had formerly been a member of the SALT I delegation and so was far more willing to contemplate arms control than Reagan's hardline Defense Secretary, Casper Weinberger. Under both Carter and Reagan, the NSC staff tended to be very hardline on arms control, although the NSC staff under Carter were broadly supportive of some arms control in order to contain Soviet power. This array of battling agencies has led different presidents and their advisers to pursue different strategies to advance arms control at summits. As noted previously, Kissinger simply excluded everybody from the process whereas Shultz included everybody. Shultz's approach made more sense as it gave the president access to the full spectrum of advice and ensured that every agency had a stake in any agreements reached at the summit.

Congress is also involved in the whole process from negotiating treaties to ratifying them. It doesn't take much for Congress to block a treaty, just 34 senators or one-third of the Senate. Moreover, if senators wish to avoid the stigma of attacking a popular treaty, there are a variety of other ways, such as 'killer' amendments or compensatory action, by which they can render a treaty meaningless. A president has good reason, therefore, to woo doubters in the Senate. In this way, the Senate was able to influence the formulation of a US negotiation position in the run-up to a superpower summit. For instance, Carter decided to replace the Vladivostok principles with a bolder proposal for a SALT II Treaty in order to win the support of a prominent hardline senator, Henry Jackson. Carter's new proposal satisfied Jackson but was rejected by the Soviets and served to throw the SALT II talks off track for a few years. Informal discussions with congressional advisers on SALT II also preceded the 1979 summit. This form of consultation increased under Reagan. In 1984, when a resumption of superpower arms control talks was expected, a bipartisan Arms Control Observer Group was formed in the Senate, and between 1985 and 1989 this group had informal discussions with both US and Soviet delegations to the arms control talks in Geneva. In the 1980s power shifted within Congress, from the Senate Foreign Relations Committee, which is responsible for reporting to the floor on treaties, to the four committees responsible for controlling defence expenditure (Armed Services Committees and Defense Appropriations Subcommittees of the Senate and House). This, in turn, served to increase congressional influence over the formulation of policy on arms control since Congress's greatest power resides in its control of the purse-strings. However, members of these committees tended to be more pro-defence than the rest of their respective chambers. So when Congress stalled funding for the new MX ICBM in mid-1982, in retaliation for Reagan's apparent refusal to make any genuine effort to pursue arms control talks with the Soviets, it was members of these committees who managed to rescue the programme. They pulled together a deal whereby Congress agreed to fund the MX in exchange for a promise from Reagan to get serious about arms control.

After the president, the JCS generally had the most influence in arms control negotiations during the cold war as their views were listened to in Congress; if they voiced opposition to a treaty then the Senate would never ratify it. As a result, Nixon and Carter had to promise more funds for nuclear weapon programmes to buy military support for the SALT I and II treaties respectively. Things changed with the end of the cold war. Congress gained greater influence in arms control and since legislators found the budget deficit more worrying than the Soviet Union they didn't care so much what the military thought of the START agreement.

The Soviet Union

The Soviet approach to, and behaviour at, summits clearly illustrates the interdependent relationship between foreign policy and domestic politics. In accordance with the central tenet of Marxist–Leninist ideology, and foreseeing the inevitable clash with capitalism, military security had to be the Soviets' ultimate priority: any Soviet general secretary would first and foremost be expected to initiate the necessary programmes to cover all eventualities.[47] Domestic priorities came second. This primary consideration, combined with general economic and political misdevelopment, created a pattern for every Soviet leader after Stalin: the new man in office would realise the need to curb military spending and develop more relaxed relations with the West. He would then initiate an ideologically correct reassessment of developments in the world, stating that the correlation of forces benefited the Soviet Union and that this fact opened up the opportunity for international détente. In most cases, the General Secretary was met by internal opposition which he was initially able to keep at arm's length. His next step would be to seek a summit with the adversary, looking for a breakthrough to secure his programme and his position back in the Kremlin. Consequently, the successful outcome of the summit would be a vital component in this strategy.

Khrushchev's boasting and bluffing offensive was aimed at increasing the international standing of the Soviet Union in order to curb the military's claim on economic resources.[48] Unfortunately for Khrushchev, his brinkmanship never paid off and the summits he had counted on did more than anything else to expose his failures. The U2 humiliation in Paris in 1960, the lack of progress over Berlin (a factor in all Khrushchev's meetings with Western leaders) and the break with China rapidly eroded his position *vis-à-vis* the military, and he was eventually ousted in 1964.

Brezhnev's détente was partly a result of growing Soviet self-confidence, not least on the basis of the American recognition of nuclear parity. However, anxieties generated by chronic economic difficulties were also part of Brezhnev's equation. The Soviet leadership was well aware that the economic gap between East and West was growing and that it faced great difficulty in meeting the twin necessities of maintaining Soviet military strength on the one hand, and satisfying the internal demand for consumer goods on the other – the well-known 'guns-or-butter' question. The previous winter, riots over food prices had forced the Polish leader Gomulka to leave office. As John Lewis Gaddis says about the situation: 'It began to look as though the Soviet Union would not be able to compete with the West without help from the West, in the form of trade, investment, and most important, technology transfers.'[49] Brezhnev invested a lot of personal interest and prestige in his summits with Nixon and in the détente process in general. Brezhnev was still in the process of consolidating his own position and had to face opposition to his policies, in the Kremlin as well as in China and the Soviet satellites, who criticized him for selling out politically for selfish interests. Nevertheless, Brezhnev pushed hard to improve relations with the Americans. As Raymond Garthoff has pointed out: 'Brezhnev and by then most of his colleagues were prepared to accept the risks and costs of such reactions ... rather than to jeopardize the long-sought recognition of parity, the general launching of détente and the unveiling of a virtual flood of co-operation and Soviet–American endeavours.'[50]

Gorbachev knew better than any of his predecessors that the Soviet Union could only be revitalized with the help of the West. He also realized that summits were an important tool, a short cut, to implement this strategy. He started out, like Khrushchev and Brezhnev, by internally communicating his re-evaluation of the international situation; except that Gorbachev's analysis pointed towards the chance of disarmament and cooperation based on the radically new assumption that it would be possible to avoid a conflict with the West.[51] Gorbachev told the Politbureau that the Soviet Union now would have to indicate that they did not want a conflict either. Shervardnadze brought home the point about the direct connection between domestic and international realms more clearly than ever before when, in a speech to the Soviet foreign ministry, he stated that the goal of diplomacy was to create an external environment favourable to the internal development of the state. He added that Soviet diplomacy had failed to fulfil this role, and that the Soviet Union had declined economically as a consequence of shortcomings in the conduct of foreign policy.[52] Summitry was an integral part and successful component of Gorbachev's and Shevardnadze's strategy. For a time they were able to keep internal opposition against reforms at bay, then slowly start to confirm their own positions, not least by actively seeking and achieving results at summits. In the end, however, the population at large ran out of patience with Gorbachev's reforms. He underestimated the problems and the forces he had so courageously let loose and, in the end, he received little more than supportive words from the West. The popularity and prestige he enjoyed in the West never impressed the average Soviet citizens; in this respect summitry did him no good.

CONCLUSION

Three questions remain to be addressed in this concluding section. First, was superpower summitry an institution? Second, did summitry really matter to the superpower relationship? Last, how does US–Russian summitry differ from superpower summitry? Each of these questions will be addressed in turn.

Superpower summitry was an institution in that it encompassed norms of superpower behaviour and through this regulated the superpower relationship. Summits became forums for asserting primacy or parity, including the raising of specific issues of concern in particular geographical and policy areas. Summits also provided the leaders of both superpowers with opportunities to regulate the 'arms race' between them. But for an institution, superpower summitry was a rather *ad hoc* affair. In this way, rather predictably summits followed the overall ups and downs of the superpower relationship: summits were more likely to be held and to be successful when relations were good. In the early cold war and new cold war years of the early 1950s and early 1980s, the superpowers held no summits. In contrast, in the optimism of the early détente period and the twilight years of the cold war, the superpower summits were more frequent and far more productive.

Summitry only really mattered to the superpower relationship if it could improve poor superpower relations or wreck good relations. So far it has been suggested that summitry was dependent on superpower relations. Indeed, détente deteriorated from 1972 onwards despite four summits in the rest of the decade. But, in fact, summitry could affect superpower relations. Hence the summits in the latter half of the 1980s, coming after six-and-a-half years of no face to face contact, clearly played an important role in improving superpower relations and eventually ending the cold war. The warm personal relationship that developed between Gorbachev and Reagan facilitated frequent summits. This, in turn, gave Gorbachev time to sell his New Political Thinking to the Americans, to realize the issues on which Reagan was not going to budge (in particular, space weapons), and to chart a series of agreements that were to end the cold war.

The international and domestic politics of US–Russia summits are completely different. The cold war bipolarity has been replaced by US unipolarity. Consequently, US goals have shifted from regulating their relationship with a rival power to regulating the affairs of a far weaker power; summits are used by the United States to promote political and economic reform in Russia, a restrained Russian foreign policy, and nuclear disarmament in the former Soviet Union and nuclear non-proliferation from that region. The US president faces greater competition from domestic political rivals than his cold war predecessors. In particular, Congress is more willing and able to promote alternative visions of US policy towards Russia. Money matters far more than missiles to Russia. The Russian president, Boris Yeltsin, goes to summits not to compete with the United States but to ask for funds to bail out Russia's failing economy and support its embryonic democracy. During the cold war, the concessions made by Soviet leaders to the United States could get them into trouble with political elites back home, especially if the concessions did not pay off. Similarly, Yeltsin's failure to secure US financial assistance at summits, in spite of the restraint he has shown in his foreign policy, has got him in trouble with rival political elites. Perhaps not surprisingly, the Yeltsin administration is moving towards a more assertive foreign policy which promotes Russian interests in conflict with US ones.

NOTES AND REFERENCES

1. There was a summit between the United States, Soviet Union and France in Paris in 1960 but it was a wash-out as Khrushchev stormed out over the U2 affair.
2. Lyndon Johnson may be the exception in that he only met the official Soviet Premier, Alexi Kosygin, when the *de facto* leader was Leonid Brezhnev.
3. Theodore C. Sorensen, *Kennedy* (NY, Harper and Row, 1965), p. 542.
4. Dwight D. Eisenhower, *Waging Peace* (NY, Doubleday, 1965), p. 432; Jimmy Carter, *Keeping Faith* (London, Collins, 1982), pp. 241, 246; Lou Cannon, *President Reagan: Role of a Lifetime* (NY, Simon and Schuster, 1991), p. 263.
5. William Curti Wolhforth, *The Elusive Balance* (Ithaca, NJ, Cornell University Press, 1993).
6. *20 s'ezd Kommunitisticheskoi Partii Sovetskogo Soiuza: Stenograficheskii octhet* (Moscow, Isdatal'stvo Politicheskoi Literatury, 1956).

7.   Wohlforth, *The Elusive Balance*, p. 141.
8.   Martin Walker, *The Cold War* (London, Vintage, 1994), pp. 133, 156.
9.   Adam Ulam, *Coexistence: The History of Soviet Foreign Policy* (Oxford, Oxford University Press), pp. 294–5.
10. Ulam, *Coexistence*, p. 294.
11. Nikita Khrushchev, *Khrushchev Remembers: The Last Testament*, tr. Strobe Talbott (Boston, Little, Brown and Company, 1974), pp. 368–416.
12. Sorenson, *Kennedy*, pp. 584–6.
13. Wohlforth, *The Elusive Balance*, pp. 184–6; Peter J. Mooney, *The Soviet Superpower; the Soviet Union 1945–80* (London, Heinemann, 1982), p. 120.
14. Gordon R. Weihmiller and Dusko Doder, *US–Soviet Summits: An Account of East–West Diplomacy at the Top, 1955–1985* (Lanham, University Press of America, 1986), p. 32.
15. Raymond L. Garthoff, *Détente and Confrontation* (Washington DC, Brookings Institution, 1985), pp. 294–5.
16. Michael MccGwire, *Perestroika and Soviet National Security Policy* (Washington DC, Brookings Instituton, 1991), p. 82.
17. John Lewis Gaddis, *The Long Peace: Inquiries into the History of the Cold War* (Oxford, Oxford University Press, 1987), p. 271.
18. Garthoff, *Détente and Confrontation*, p. 320.
19. Michael Andersen, interview with Gorbachev adviser and director of IMEMO, Moscow, April 1992; Andersen interview with Andrei Kortunov, USA–Canada Institute, Moscow, April 1990.
20. Weihmiller and Doder, *US–Soviet Summits*, p. 68.
21. Garthoff, *Détente and Confrontation*, pp. 33–4.
22. W. Isaacson, *Kissinger* (London, Faber and Faber, 1992), p. 433.
23. George Shultz, *Turmoil and Triumph* (NY, Scribner's, 1993), p. 987.
24. Carter, *Keeping Faith*, p. 254.
25. Garthoff, *Détente and Confrontation*, pp. 630–60; Carmel Budiardjo, 'Indonesia: Mass Extermination and the Consolidation of Authoritarian Power' in Alexander George (ed.), *Western State Terrorism* (Oxford, Polity Press, 1991), pp. 180–211.
26. Carter, *Keeping Faith*, pp. 259–60.
27. Shultz, *Triumph and Turmoil*, pp. 1094–6, 1101–4.
28. In addition, there was the Conventional Forces in Europe (CFE) Treaty which was signed at a meeting of the Conference on Security and Co-operation in Europe (CSCE) in Paris in 1990.
29. Eisenhower, *Waging Peace*, p. 407.
30. Shultz, *Turmoil and Triumph*, p. 1000.
31. Isaacson, *Kissinger*, pp. 429, 433; Kissinger, *White House Years* (Boston, Little, Brown and Company, 1979), p. 1217.
32. Garthoff, *Détente and Confrontation*, pp. 448–9.
33. Shultz, *Turmoil and Triumph*, p. 752.
34. Weihmiller and Doder, *US–Soviet Summits*, p. 66; Shultz, *Turmoil and Triumph*, pp. 597, 751.
35. Robert Ferrell (ed.), *The Eisenhower Diaries* (NY and London, W. W. Norton and Co., 1981), p. 262 [italic added].
36. Stephen E. Ambrose, *Eisenhower the President: Volume Two, 1952–1969* (London, George Allen and Unwin, 1984), p. 565.

37. Matthew Evangelista, *Innovation and the Arms Race* (Ithaca, NY, Cornell University Press, 1988), p. 263.
38. Matthew Evangelista, 'Stalin's Postwar Army Reappraised', *International Security*, vol. 7, no. 3 (1982–3), pp. 110–38.
39. David Goldfischer, *The Best Defense: Policy Alternatives for US Nuclear Security from the 1950s to the 1980s* (Ithaca, NY, Cornell University Press, 1993), p. 109.
40. Stephen E. Ambrose, *Rise to Globalism* (NY and London, Penguin Books, 1985) pp. 171–2, 175.
41. MccGwire, *Perestroika and Soviet National Security Policy*, pp. 21–3.
42. Richard K. Betts, *Nuclear Blackmail and Nuclear Balance* (Washington DC, Brookings Institution, 1987), pp. 182–8.
43. MccGwire, *Perestroika and Soviet National Security Policy*, pp. 24–30.
44. Garthoff, *Détente and Confrontation*, pp. 802–3.
45. Raymond L. Garthoff, *The Great Transition* (Washington DC, Brookings Institution, 1994), pp. 765–6.
46. The best sources to consult on the domestic politics of national security policy, and on which much of the discussion in this section is based, are: Steven E. Miller, 'Politics Over Promise: Domestic Impediments to Arms Control', *International Security*, vol. 8, no. 4 (1984), pp. 79–90; (on bureaucratic politics) Hedrick Smith, *The Power Game* (NY, Random House, 1988), chapters 15 and 16; Strobe Talbott, *Endgame: The Inside Story of SALT II* (NY, Harper and Row, 1980); Talbott, *Deadly Gambits* (London, Picador, 1984); (on Congress) Barry M. Blechman, *The Politics of National Security: Congress and US Defence Policy* (NY and Oxford, Oxford University Press, 1990); Paul N. Stockton, 'The New Game on the Hill: The Politics of Arms Control and Strategic Force Modernization', *International Security*, vol. 16, no. 2 (1991), pp. 146–71.
47. For a brilliant summary of the Soviet preoccupation with military security and its implications, refer to MccGwire, *Perestroika and Soviet National Security Policy*, pp. 1–44.
48. Wohlforth, *The Elusive Balance*, pp. 140–1.
49. Gaddis, *The Long Peace: Inquiries into the History of the Cold War*, p. 260.
50. Garthoff, *Détente and Confrontation*, p. 297.
51. MccGwire, *Perestroika and Soviet National Security Policy*, pp. 1–13.
52. *Vestnik, MID SSSR 2*, 26 August 1987, p. 31.

6 NATO Summits
Bill Park

INTRODUCTION

In the conduct of diplomatic relations between states, the concept of a 'summit' is normally taken to refer to meetings between heads of state and government. Beyond that basic observation, 'summits' as diplomatic and political phenomena can take a variety of forms. There may be few participating states, or many. Summits might be held between adversaries or between allies. They might be held relatively regularly, or on an *ad hoc* or even one-off basis. Summit agendas might leave heads of state and government with a creative role, free to explore the scope for and content of political agreement, or they might be so pre-prepared as to leave heads of state and government with little more than symbolic roles to play. With these differing possibilities in mind, there are a number of introductory observations we can make about summits of the North Atlantic Treaty Organization. Participants are relatively numerous – sixteen – but vary enormously in size and significance, from the United States to Luxembourg or Iceland. Furthermore, NATO summits take place at the apex of a permanent bureaucracy composed of national and international civil servants provided by allied states keen to display unity. Excessive disarray could appear to undermine the very nature and purpose of the alliance. It might also be added that, although issues of defence and security can have extremely high salience, NATO summit agendas have relatively rarely engaged the passions of the wider public except during those periods when the alliance's nuclear debate has been at its most intense. As a rule, then, NATO summits produce little drama and few surprises.

By and large this chapter shows why this is so. It begins by locating NATO summits within the framework of the alliance's standing bureaucracy. It then goes on to discuss the way in which the frequency with which NATO summits have been held has varied with changes in the overall political and security context of the alliance's affairs. The chapter considers what role the heads of state and government actually play during a NATO summit, and the manner in which the very fact of an impending summit both feeds into and drives the alliance policy process – this last, indeed, is identified as perhaps the primary utility of NATO summits. The broad conclusion presented here is that NATO's business is conducted intensively and continuously, formally and informally, bilaterally and multilaterally, and at many levels. NATO summits can best be understood both as offering occasional symbolic expression to at least some of that more hidden, less glamorous, but vital diplomatic and political activity, and as a device by which it might sometimes be given additional shape, purpose and impetus.

INSTITUTIONAL EVOLUTION

With the signing of the North Atlantic Treaty in April 1949, the North Atlantic Council was established as the highest guiding body of the new alliance. All members of the alliance were to be represented on the Council, which was tasked to consider all matters concerning the implementation of the treaty and to work towards the fulfilment of the treaty's basic objectives. The Council was expected to meet at short notice should the need arise, and was empowered to establish 'such subsidiary bodies as may be necessary'. Initially, the Council met at the foreign minister level, and at their first meeting in September 1949 the foreign ministers decided to meet annually in normal circumstances. They quickly set about the task of establishing subordinate committees, such as the Defence Committee composed of the defence ministers of the member countries, and a Military Committee consisting of chiefs of staff. As the organization of the alliance and the issues it was grappling with grew more complex, so Council deputies were appointed and a small international staff built up to enable the alliance to conduct its business in permanent session. Then, at the ninth Council meeting in February 1952 in Lisbon, it was decided that NATO should become a permanent organization, which it did on 28 April 1952. Each member state was to appoint a Permanent Representative (PermRep) to the headquarters of the alliance, to be supported by a national delegation of advisers and experts. The international staff of the alliance also continued to expand, and it was further decided at Lisbon that this staff should be headed by a secretary-general who was also to be an international civil servant rather than a member of one of the national delegations.

Thus, although NATO quickly developed an international infrastructure to reflect the depth, functions and goals of the alliance, its supreme political body, the North Atlantic Council, was and remains an intergovernmental forum. The decision to appoint PermReps was necessitated by the

intensity and the significance of intergovernmental consultation and cooperation in the alliance, so that NATO headquarters contains a curious
mixture of national delegations and international bureaucrats drawn from
the same member states. PermReps' meetings, which normally occur at
least once each week, function as the North Atlantic Council 'in permanent session'. However, the Council also meets at foreign minister level.
Such 'ministerial meetings' of the Council, at which foreign ministers
might be joined by defence or finance ministers as appropriate, usually
take place biannually, once in Brussels and once in the national capital of
a member state. Less frequently, and on an *ad hoc* basis, Council meetings
might bring together the heads of state and government of the alliance.
Council meetings at this level are more popularly referred to as NATO
'summits', and there have been thirteen such summits to date. According
to the official NATO handbook, Council meetings enjoy 'the same authority and powers of decision-making, and its decisions have the same status
and validity, at whatever level it meets' – PermRep, foreign minister, or
head of government and state. In this sense, NATO summits can be seen
as routine meetings given special form. Yet the handbook also states that
'Summit Meetings ... are held whenever particularly important issues confronting the whole Alliance have to be addressed.'[1]

From this account, it can be seen that because NATO summits take
place astride a standing bureaucratic alliance structure, and because they
are in a sense a more elevated variant of regularized and lower-level
Council meetings, they represent a rather unique manifestation of the
general summit phenomenon. They display less of the drama that can
characterize equally high-level but more *ad hoc* summits such as those
held between the superpowers. And the emphasis on the active contributions made by heads of state and government is less than we might expect
from, say, G-7 summits, where there is less scope for 'pre-cooking' the
summit outcome.

THE CHANGING FREQUENCY OF NATO SUMMITS

Notwithstanding the scope for differences of view regarding what exactly
constitutes a 'particularly important issue', even a superficial glance at the
historical record, at least for the first two decades of the alliance's existence, suggests that a NATO summit meeting need not be a prerequisite for
the consideration of issues important to the alliance as a whole. NATO's
first ever summit, or Council Meeting at the level of heads of state and
government, was not held until December 1957, in Paris, more than eight

years after the signing of the North Atlantic Treaty. This intervening period, between the establishment of the alliance and the holding of its first summit meeting, was full of significant developments both within the alliance itself and in the broader political and strategic context in which it operated and from which it drew its *raison d'être*. It saw the formation of a permanent civilian and military alliance infrastructure which is broadly intact to this day, including the creation of the posts of Supreme Allied Commander, Europe (SACEUR) and the Secretary-General; it witnessed the accession of new members in Greece, Turkey and – above all – the Federal Republic of Germany; it incorporated profound developments in the alliance's military strategy; and it experienced the internal dissension among its leading members which resulted from the Suez crisis in 1956. Developments external to the alliance were hardly less dramatic. The Korean War, the death of Stalin and the emergence of Krushchev, the formation of the Warsaw Pact, and the 1956 Soviet intervention in Hungary all came and went without a NATO summit being called. NATO's second summit did not take place until June 1974 in Brussels. The erection of the Berlin Wall, the Cuban missile crisis, the withdrawal of France from the integrated military structure of the alliance, the tortuous debate over and the eventual adoption of the alliance strategy of 'flexible response', the adoption of the so-called 'Harmel Report' – 'The Future Tasks of the Alliance' – in 1967, and the Warsaw Pact invasion of Czechoslovakia in 1968 all failed to generate enough pressure for the holding of a NATO summit.

On the other hand, after this rather slow start, subsequent years saw a more frequent resort to 'summitry' on the part of NATO. North Atlantic Council meetings at the level of heads of state and government were held in 1975, 1977, 1978, 1982, 1985, 1988, twice in 1989, 1990, 1991 and 1994. Periodic summits have in more recent years become almost a part of the routine way in which NATO goes about its business. Why this should be so, given the capacity of lower-level North Atlantic Council meetings to make decisions on serious issues, is one of the mysteries of NATO summitry. Yet, given the regular occurrence of NATO summits in recent years, it is similarly curious that summits were held so infrequently during the earlier phases of NATO's history. This is particularly so in the light of the fact that the first summit in 1957 was held in the immediate aftermath of the adoption by NATO's foreign ministers of the Report of the Committee of Three on Non-Military Cooperation in NATO at their ministerial meeting in December 1956. The leitmotif of this report of the 'Three Wise Men' – namely, Gaetano Martino of Italy, Halvard Lange of Norway and Lester B. Pearson of Canada – was that political consultation between the member states of the alliance should be intensified.[2] Prepared against the backdrop of the intra-alliance wrangling over the Suez crisis, the report reflected the aspiration that NATO should become something deeper and more substantial than just a military alliance. Member states were called upon to inform the Council of any development significantly affecting the alliance; they were requested not to adopt policies or make pronouncements in areas of interest to the alliance without first consulting their alliance partners; and they were asked to reflect any alliance-wide consensus in the formation of national policies.

The commitment to political consultation encouraged by the 'Three Wise Men' in 1956 has since been reaffirmed on countless occasions. It could almost be described as NATO's mantra. In the words of a former UK PermRep to the North Atlantic Council, 'Political consultation is the lifeblood of the alliance.'[3] The centrality of political consultation to the proper functioning of the alliance was a feature of the Harmel Report adopted in 1967 outlining the need for NATO to pursue détente whilst maintaining credible defence forces;[4] and of the 'Declaration on Atlantic Relations', agreed by the foreign ministers in Ottawa in June 1974 and signed by the government heads at the NATO summit – only the second in the history of the alliance – in Brussels just a few days later.[5] As one former NATO official put it, 'The nerve centre of the consultative process is the North Atlantic Council.'[6]

Why, though, were there no NATO summits between 1957 and 1974? One can only speculate, but two possible explanations spring to mind. The first is that developments in East–West relations during much of this period essentially underlined the rationale for forming the alliance in the first place, and strengthened rather than weakened the commitment to it. Notwithstanding Khrushchev's 'thaw', these were the cold war years during which the Soviet threat appeared to be at its least ambiguous and when such a large proportion both of NATO's external responses to the Soviet threat and of its internal deliberations were towards the military rather than the political end of the spectrum. Such matters could be more easily left to the 'experts' and did not self-evidently lend themselves to the high-profile interventions of presidents and prime ministers. Secondly, the European partners generally showed greater deference to American leadership during this period. Goodwill towards the United States earned as a result of the exertions of the Second World War had not yet evaporated in the face of the Vietnam War. The economic gap between North America and Western Europe had not yet been sufficiently closed, which left the Europeans with a sense of weakness and inferiority reinforced by the still too recent memories of the Second World War. And the United States' strategic lead over the Soviet Union meant that, for all the intra-alliance squabbling that characterized this as well as subsequent phases in NATO's history, there was a more profound faith in the American protective umbrella – or at least a more resigned recognition that Europe had little alternative but to accept it in the form it was offered. One might also add that, following the withdrawal of France from the Integrated Military Structure in 1966, summits offered a useful device for more fully involving the French in the political management of the alliance. For all these reasons, although high levels of political consultation may nevertheless have been the norm during this early period, there seems to have been less need to call summit meetings to give symbolic reinforcement to this diplomatic practice.

By the early 1970s, arguments over burden-sharing, differences over the meaning and implications of détente, and strains resulting from Soviet strategic parity with the United States, were all coming to a head. The Declaration on Atlantic Relations issued by the 1974 summit sought to address itself to all of those issues. It is perhaps not surprising that the Declaration reportedly took a year to prepare.[7] All this suggests that the role of summits in NATO affairs has evolved with changes both in the broader political and strategic context within which the alliance operates, and with shifts in the relationships between its members. NATO's affairs had become increasingly difficult to handle, and a perceived need for suitable political rhetoric grew. It might be added in support of this general contention that the Secretary-General did not begin to hold Defence Planning Committee press conferences until well into the 1980s. The particular frequency of NATO summits in the wake of the cold war – there have been six in the period 1988–94 – reinforces at least the first of these suppositions. It is additionally interesting to note that the increased frequency of NATO summits enables each summit to build upon the work of the previous one and to lay down guidelines for subsequent meetings at this level. One should also recognize that the increased frequency of NATO summits may simply reflect the increased frequency of summits of all kinds, as interdependency, cooperative diplomacy, the role of the media and ease of travel have improved and increased.

Certainly the adaption of NATO to the changed security environment in recent years can be seen as a continuous process of adjustment and transformation in which summits have played a central role. Thus the London Summit of July 1990 ordered a fundamental review of alliance strategy. The Rome Summit 16 months later heralded the new Strategic Concept for the alliance which resulted from this directive.[8] The Combined Joint Task Force initiative of the 1994 Brussels Summit has been described by the then Secretary-General Manfred Wörner as 'the next logical step in this adaption of our force structure'.[9] Similarly, the invitation to the then Warsaw Pact states to establish diplomatic missions at NATO headquarters issued at the London Summit in July 1990 evolved into the creation of the North Atlantic Cooperation Council at the Rome Summit in November 1991, and then the Partnership for Peace initiative of the January 1994 Brussels summit. From an earlier period, Sir Clive Rose reminds us how 'the London Summit of 1977 established a programme of work for the Alliance, the results of which were reviewed at the Washington Summit in 1978'.[10] There might also be something in the related but more mundane assertion that summits – or NATO summits at any rate – are habit-forming; that once a number of summits have been held in quick succession, an expectation builds up that such frequency should be maintained, and that it is appropriate for heads of government to be more visibly involved in the conduct of NATO business. In this context, it will be interesting to see how frequently NATO resorts to summitry during the forthcoming decade, particularly if the broader security environment settles down and stabilizes.

HEADS OF STATE AND GOVERNMENT AND NATO SUMMITS

In any case, NATO summits have come to occur on a relatively frequent if still *ad hoc* basis. But what do these summits achieve? If the difference between NATO summits and other North Atlantic Council meetings is the presence of the alliance's heads of state and government, one could infer that these events loom large in the political lives of the latter. Yet if the available memoirs are to serve as a guide, this does not appear to be the case. President Nixon recalls having attended 'ceremonies marking the twenty-fifth anniversary of NATO' – which indeed they were – rather than the June 1974 NATO summit. His memoirs then consist of half a dozen lines on his formal presentation at the summit, which was rather standard fare for addresses at these summits: a brief discussion of his personal ailments, followed by a far more excited account of the rest of his European tour.[11] On the 1975 summit, President Gerald Ford writes that, 'From the perspective of our European allies, I'm sure that the NATO meeting loomed as a very significant opportunity [*sic*]. They would have a chance to talk with the new American President, whom many of them had not met before.'[12] He then recites how he met the prime ministers of Greece and Turkey, had lunch with Chancellor Schmidt, visited some Danish officials, sat down with Portugal's new prime minister, and made a speech. Carter's memoirs reveal nothing at all of the events of the 1977 and 1978 summits although those of his National Security Adviser, Zbigniew Brzezinski, recall that 'although differences on the nuclear issue were only papered over, Carter established a personal rapport with the allies' and that his speech to the other NATO leaders 'set the tone and pace for the entire meeting and demonstrated vital American leadership'.[13] Harold Wilson says very little about the 1974 summit, and only recalls that the 1975 NATO summit was one of the increasing number of high-level meetings to which government heads were subjected.[14] Of the remarkable total of six NATO summits which took place during her premiership, Margaret Thatcher's memoirs devote less than a couple of pages to the March 1988 summit, and less or nothing at all to the others.[15]

The same set of political leaders cannot be said to have been so seemingly unmoved by all the summits they attended. Superpower and G-7 summits, for example, generally receive far more attention in the memoirs of heads of state and government. There appears to be something about NATO summits in particular rather than summits in general which induces these bouts of amnesia on the part of government heads. Perhaps a clue is offered by the Canadian prime minister, Pierre Trudeau, whose recollection of NATO summits is of 'the tedious business of reading speeches drafted by others with the principle objective of not rocking the boat ... any attempt to start a discussion or question the meaning of the communiqué – also drafted by others long before the meeting began – is met by stony embarrassment or strong opposition'.[16] NATO summits are by and large pre-drafted, pre-cooked, choreographed, and formalized. Even where heads of government might have been heavily involved in the issues before a summit takes place, at the summit itself they might be reduced to little more than 'talking heads', at least in the formal sessions. Again, to quote Sir Clive Rose, 'No one expects the participants to discuss in detail the documents they approve. There is never enough time for this.'[17] Indeed, the 1982 Bonn summit lasted just a few hours.[18] The former Dutch Foreign Minister, Ernst Hans van der Beugal, whilst complaining that 'there is sometimes too much hoo-la and too little time' at NATO summits, nevertheless has gone on to assert that the role of heads of state and government at NATO summits should indeed be to 'generally only put finishing touches to previously negotiated agreements or, even better, confine themselves to sealing them ceremoniously'.[19] It is difficult to avoid the conclusion that, at least at the formal sessions of a NATO summit, heads of state and government are barely active participants at all. Important informal discussions might well take place at summit gatherings, but between this particular group of countries consultation is a fairly routine and continuous activity and occurs in all sorts of fora.

What purpose, then, does the presence of heads of state and government at North Atlantic Council meetings serve? Sir Clive Rose has argued that 'a Summit provides a useful catalyst for demonstrating the cohesion of the Alliance, for reaffirming its objectives and for setting a course for future action'.[20] The need to demonstrate cohesion should not be underestimated in the case of a politico-military alliance such as NATO. Although conflict and dissent might be the stuff of politics, it is anathema to the concept of collective defence and to the need to show political and military will. Given the high salience of security issues, especially during the last two decades or so with the persistent differences of view concerning the role of nuclear weapons and the more recent need to respond to the enormous changes in the alliance's security environment, intra-alliance arguments have indeed been fierce at times. Summits have been seen as useful and necessary devices to counter the impression of endless dispute and potential fragmentation. It helps too that, for all their importance, the issues which make up NATO's politico-military agenda can generally be dealt with by carefully worded communiqués, or by the making of commitments which do not require domestic legislation or even the unambiguous commitment of scarce resources. NATO summits generally produce agreements which even the most reluctant government heads can live with domestically.

In this light, the presence of government heads has two purposes. Firstly, prime ministers and presidents function as political symbols in a way that PermReps or even foreign ministers never could. The media circus that generally accompanies NATO summits, and the associated photo opportunities, banquets and the like, are all encouraged by the presence of the top political leaders. This has something to do with the social psychology of political systems, but agreed communiqués purporting to demonstrate unity and consensus issued in the name of smiling and hand-shaking government leaders have a totemic quality. It all seems to be important, even if it all equally defies rational analysis by flying in the face of the evidence of dissent and disagreement.

SUMMITS AND THE POLICY PROCESS

Secondly, however, because 'a meeting of all the Alliance heads of state and government is in itself an important event, it has to be a success'.[21]

Politicians abhor public failure, and the calling of a summit thus raises the stakes. The fact of, and fear of, a looming deadline serves to force the pace and creates pressure to decide rather than defer. An impending summit casts a shadow in front of itself. It concentrates the minds of the officials and politicians whose careers and reputations might hinge on it to some degree. In this way, it is less the summit itself than the way in which a forthcoming summit impinges on the policy process that precedes it which is important.[22] This is a more substantive and more readily analysable point, and it has two parts. Firstly, it means that the background preparations for a summit are crucial. The process can be intense and lengthy. In this sense a NATO summit itself can be seen as just the tip of an iceberg. The 'real' summit work, which supports the actual – in the sense of visible – summit and without which it could not take place, is largely hidden from view.

However, although much of the preparatory activity might appear to be directed towards the drafting of agreed communiqués, or even the organ-ization of banquets and the like, the more substantive preparations might in themselves make a significant contribution to the policy process. This is the second part of the argument about the importance of the preparation of summits. Communiqués might be worded in order to express consensus – or the appearance of it – but the activities which lead to their drafting, or to the establishment of a summit agenda, might help to create that unity. To quote Sir Clive Rose again: 'It is hardly an exaggeration to say that the preparatory work is equal in value to the Summit meeting itself, since it is here that genuine efforts are made by all the Allies to reconcile differences of view and approach, with the aim of reaching agreement on the texts to be submitted to the heads of Government.'[23] A more recent NATO official has referred to the significance of summit communiqués 'as tools for forging unity among Allied Governments and in shaping perceptions among decision-makers'.[24] The word used here is 'forging', not merely 'expressing'.

In the light of these arguments, it is not entirely digressive to draw attention to the role NATO plays as an institution and as an alliance in helping to create consensus amongst its member governments. As with the European Union, NATO proceeds on the sometimes tacit or even uncon-scious assumption that, in the modern international system, the preserva-tion of sovereignty might paradoxically require some surrendering of it. For a functioning and bureaucratized alliance such as NATO, this observa-tion is not of a purely abstract quality, but permeates activities, institu-tions, perceptions and even career profiles within the member states as well as within the alliance itself. A recent and as yet unpublished paper on the evolution of NATO from 'alliance' to 'organization' to 'institution' has identified 'the development of a transnational community of opinion formers, sympathetic to the interests of an institution even though they may owe formal loyalty to their own government's national interests'. Officials sent to represent their own government's interests may nevertheless 'become socialised into taking a progressively more internationalist perspective'. Furthermore, 'this may remain within them once they return to national government departments'. In this way, officials and representatives can become the means by which any consensus worked out between them at NATO is injected into national policy formulation. National governments may not only become so sensitized to collective alliance positions that they become disinclined to rock the boat, but they may also come to regard their own national positions as to some degree synonymous with whatever it is that permits alliance-wide agreement to emerge.[25] Thus the German 'NATO community' may have been highly instrumental in shifting German policy away from the development of the Conference on Security and Cooperation in Europe (CSCE) as the dominant institutional vehicle for forging security links with the East, towards the 'NATO' preference for the creation of the North Atlantic Cooperation Council (NACC) at the 1991 NATO summit.[26] Because NATO summits in effect exclude the option of failure, they serve to reinforce those impulses which encourage the search for common alliance-wide policy positions and the adoption of 'alliance perspectives' by nominally national officials.

The consultative process which precedes a NATO summit and which is tasked with arriving at a consensus position suitable for presentation to the heads of state and government can be very lengthy. We have already noted how the Atlantic Declaration issued by the 1974 summit was a year in preparation. The documents emanating from the June 1982 Bonn summit, which lasted just a few hours, nevertheless 'were, as usual, the outcome of many weeks of hard discussion'.[27] A leading British participant recalls how the Strategy Review Group (SRG), established in July 1990 within a month of the London summit's call for a new alliance strategy, had a full draft of the strategy document ready by October 1990, more than a year ahead of the Rome summit at which the New Strategic Concept would be unveiled. Nevertheless, work was still progressing in February 1991 when France decided to participate in the process, and was not completed even in May 1991 when NATO defence ministers made important decisions on conventional force restructuring in advance of the approval of the concept as a whole – in itself a revealing insight. All in all, it took 16 months for the SRG to develop the new concept in time for the November 1991 Rome summit.[28]

The Partnership for Peace idea, eventually unveiled at the January 1994 summit, was discussed at a NATO defence ministers' meeting at Travemunde in October 1993.[29] However, it was NATO's foreign ministers at their meeting in June 1993 who had agreed that there would be a winter summit, and who had determined that security links with eastern Europe would be on the agenda.[30] On the other hand, it appears to have been President Bill Clinton's idea to call the summit.[31] Although serious work on the summit agenda does not appear to have begun at NATO HQ until early in September,[32] during the summer an interagency work group was established in Washington under the supervision of Jennone Walker, the US National Security Council's senior director for European affairs, to grapple with the Clinton administration's agenda for Europe and NATO.[33] On the other hand, most of the flesh seems to have been put on PFP's bones by NATO staffs rather than US specialists between the October defence ministers' meeting at Travemunde and the summit itself in January. During this period, a major difficulty appears to have been the differences of view between the Defence and the Foreign Ministries in Bonn, with the Foreign Ministry lobbying for a more explicit offer of alliance membership to the East Europeans until just a few weeks before the summit took place.[34]

Two additional observations can be gleaned from a perusal of the preparatory work which precedes NATO summits. First, there are no fixed channels through which pre-summit consultations are handled. Although we might expect that the Council in the form of the PermReps would handle a great deal of the work, particularly in the later stages or where the political issues are especially delicate, in fact much depends on the issue and on other bureaucratic factors. NATO has at any one point in time literally hundreds of committees.[35] They take a variety of forms – standing committees, steering committees, *ad hoc* groups, and so on. In preparing for summits, NATO is free to use any fora it considers appropriate. As a former Belgian PermRep to NATO put it, 'There is no rigid codification nor are there any procedures carved in stone .... NATO is an organisation that evolved on the basis of the demands made on it. Neither its architecture, nor its operation was designed on the basis of any overall plan or on a pre-established blueprint. Over the years, annexes and extensions have been added .... The result is great flexibility of operation.'[36] These comments should be borne in mind when considering how NATO goes about the task of preparing for summits. It is similarly necessary to take into account the intense bilateral, multilateral and intranational consultations which go on, both formally and informally and within and outside the alliance bureaucratic infrastructure. It is no secret that the more influential

members of the alliance – the US, the UK, Germany and France – sometimes meet, at a variety of levels, to thrash out differences on the eve of or
during a summit, so as to develop a consensus view which the smaller
members would find difficult to resist. This appears to have happened at
the Rome summit, for example.

Second, it is evident that the role of the United States remains central to
NATO summitry in a number of respects. Summits often result from
American initiatives, as with the 1994 summit. They offer US presidents
the opportunity to present themselves as world leaders, to both domestic
and international publics. This might be especially important to a president
new to the office, as with Clinton in 1994 or Bush in 1989. In contrast, for
some of the smaller NATO members it is doubtful that NATO summits
have much domestic political significance at all. Washington usually
determines much of the agenda, particularly where nuclear weapons
issues, relations with the East, or transatlantic relations are concerned –
and most NATO summit agendas are dominated by one or more of these
areas. An interesting variant on the summit theme took place in November
1985, the main purpose of which was to afford an opportunity for
President Reagan to brief most of the other government heads on his
Geneva summit meeting with the new Soviet leader, Mikhail Gorbachev.
Only the US can truly offer leadership, or galvanize the other alliance
members. This stems not simply from the power of the US relative to the
other members, but also from the very foundation of the alliance as a US
security guarantee to Europe. Little can emerge from a NATO summit
unless it meets with Washington's approval. On the other hand, this is true
of NATO affairs more generally. Furthermore, the bilateral links which
Washington enjoys with each of the members, and particularly the more
important ones, are not only very strong but are intensively exploited in
the conduct of NATO business generally and in the preparation of
summits specifically.[37]

CAN NATO SUMMITS FAIL?

What happens though if NATO officials are unable to reach agreement in
time for a summit meeting, or if member states are intent on raising issues
and points of view which do not form part of the official agenda? What
role do NATO summits have when such instances occur? Certainly the
stakes can be high. As Ernst Hans van der Beugal put it, 'at the Summit
the decision of last resort has been abolished. If Heads of State and
Government disagree, there is nobody left to limit the damage.'[38] If

political agreement has not been possible during the preparation for a summit, then the pressure to resolve issues at the summit itself can become truly overwhelming. The most dramatic example of this was the May 1989 summit in Brussels, which saw the members deeply divided over the issue of the modernization of short-range nuclear weapons. The PermReps had been tasked to come up with an agreed position but, according to a former Belgian PermRep, 'At the beginning of their work, the gap between national positions was such that for almost a year it was impossible to agree on a single line of text. It was only after two years that a document, containing square brackets around the several points still in dispute, was submitted to the Brussels Summit on 30 May 1989. The last hurdles were overcome during a memorable night session at which Foreign Ministers themselves sat as a drafting committee.' He goes on to note that, 'the solution was found, as usual, by accommodating the various conflicting positions'.[39]

There are two important points to note from this account. Firstly, even at a summit it was the foreign ministers (apparently assisted by a team of PermReps and special representatives) and not the heads of government who were given the task of finding a suitable compromise. Secondly, the agreed document can be seen less as an expression of a positive agreement and more as a clever form of words which left the core differences between the member states intact. Margaret Thatcher recalls the differences with Bonn on the tactical nuclear weapons modernization issue at the March 1988 summit, and notes that 'it was possible for the Americans and us to take account of German sensitivities in the NATO communiqué'. Her clear implication is that a form of words was substituted for a meeting of minds.[40] Sir Clive Rose has noted that the 1982 Summit Declaration was 'naturally' worded 'in terms which all sixteen Governments were able to accept', even though it was evident that serious differences of view persisted.[41] It does not take a particularly careful reading of NATO summit communiqués to recognize the frequency with which blandness takes the place of substance.

It is evident that the pressure to avoid summit 'failure' can mean that intense negotiations take place right up to a summit's commencement. Thus, American delegations were sent to European capitals during the week before the 1989 Brussels summit to explain President Bush's proposals for cuts in conventional forces, reflecting concerns expressed by Defence Secretary Cheney and Joint Chiefs Chairman Admiral Crowe about the possible allied reaction. Argument was still taking place within the US administration the weekend before the summit.[42] Just before the July 1990 summit in London, US Secretary of State James Baker sent an advance copy of the NATO communiqué to the Soviet foreign minister, Eduard Shevardnadze, saying: 'This is a draft. I think we can get it, I'm going to work hard to get it, but it's a draft and it could change.'[43]

An aggrieved participant, or a crisis which blows up after a summit agenda has been prepared, can on occasion bring a contentious issue to the attention of a summit in an impromptu manner. For example, the French were determined that the January 1994 summit should address the Bosnian crisis, which was intensifying as the summit approached. The Americans were reportedly equally determined to keep the issue off the agenda, partly because if would detract from the agenda centre-piece, the PFP initiative, but also because there were serious differences within the alliance on the issue of NATO air strikes and characteristically it was felt that a NATO summit was not the appropriate place to air serious differences. Nevertheless, the issue was raised and, as might have been expected, a document for all seasons was produced which essentially reasserted the pre-existing NATO position but which left sufficient scope for varying interpretations. Indeed, the 1982 summit took place in the midst of considerable intra-alliance squabbling over relationships with the Soviet Union in the wake of the invasion of Afghanistan and the declaration of martial law in Poland, which was probably the closest a NATO summit has ever been to complete failure. According to Rose, this was 'the result of a breakdown of effective consultation' and of the fact that the summit 'evidently failed to get to grips with the real issues'.[44] Indeed, he chastizes the heads of state and government for leaving the foreign and defence ministers subsequently to tackle the outstanding issues 'in the absence of clear guidance'.[45]

There are occasions when the objections of a member state to the wording of a communiqué are simply overridden, which might lead to that country 'reserving its position' on those passages to which it objects. At NATO's very first summit in 1957, Norway refused to accept those portions of the communiqué which had been drafted without its participation.[46] Greece has been a relatively frequent dissident where NATO communiqués are concerned.[47] In general it is only ever likely to be the smaller countries which are ignored in this way, although the French have chosen to distance themselves from passages on strategic doctrine with which they have been uncomfortable, in keeping with their policy of non-integration with the military side of the alliance. Thus, although France joined the review of NATO's strategy in preparation for the 1991 Rome summit, Paris nevertheless reserved its position on those paragraphs dealing with collective defence planning.[48]

CONCLUSION AND SUMMARY

NATO summits are rather curious affairs in that they represent a routine forum in special form. To some degree this might emphasize their symbolic value because it is quite possible to argue that they are not really necessary. The North Atlantic Council, meeting at lower levels, could just as adequately deal with the substantive issues. Indeed, at summits the heads of state and government generally simply endorse agreements which have already been arrived at lower down the political and bureaucratic hierarchy. Nor is it the case that this particular set of political leaders otherwise have few opportunities to meet each other. Nevertheless, NATO summits are summits of politico-military allies, and shows of unity have a special significance for such a grouping. Even where there are profound differences of view, summits offer an opportunity to redress an image of dissension and decay as well as an opportunity for the government heads and their entourages to address these differences in behind-the-scenes discussions.

Perhaps the real virtue of NATO summits, though, is unintentional. It is that impending summits force participating governments to face and try to resolve issues which they might otherwise defer. Summits demand energetic consultation and highlight the need for consensus and compromise. The downside of this is that summit communiqués can often appear bland. NATO summits should be seen as punctuation points or organizing devices around which this never-ending flow of mutual opinion-shaping takes place. Any agreement arrived at by 16 sovereign states might be regarded as an achievement. The capacity which the alliance has demonstrated in recent years to adapt to profoundly changed circumstances is testimony to the way NATO conducts its internal affairs, and much of this progress has been expressed through summit communiqués. In these changed circumstances, the very occurrence of summits might serve to convey the continuing relevance of an alliance which might otherwise come under greater scrutiny. NATO is characterized by continuous multilateral consultation, and the result has generally been a remarkably high level of consensus, although we must await the passage of time before we can make a full assessment of the impact of the removal of the Soviet threat on NATO's capacity to achieve consensus. The alliance might indeed come to seem less relevant in the years to come, and its summits might become less important and even less frequent. Should the day arrive when NATO's demise has to be announced, it might well take the form of a summit communiqué expressing a universal consensus reached after months of tortuous and fractious consultation.

NOTES AND REFERENCES

1. *NATO Handbook* (Brussels, NATO Office of Information, 1992), pp. 23–4. These early passages are otherwise gleaned from *The North Atlantic Treaty Organization: Facts and Figures* (NATO Information Service, 1989).
2. See ibid., pp. 384–401 for the text of the Report.
3. Sir Clive Rose, 'Political Consultation in the Alliance', *NATO Review*, vol. 31, no. 1 (April, 1993), p. 1.
4. For the text of the Report, formally known as the 'Report of the Council on the Future Tasks of the Alliance', see *The North Atlantic Treaty Organization: Facts and Figures* (1989), pp. 402–4.
5. For the text, see ibid., pp. 405–7.
6. Fredo Dannenberg, 'Consultations: the political lifeblood of the Alliance', *NATO Review*, vol. 33, no. 6 (December, 1985), p. 8.
7. According to Sir Clive Rose, 'The 1982 Summit and After: a personal view', *NATO Review*, vol. 30, no. 4 (September, 1982), pp. 8–9.
8. See Michael Legge, 'The Making of NATO's New Strategy', *NATO Review*, vol. 39, no. 6 (December, 1991) for detail on this.
9. In his 'Shaping the Alliance for the Future', *NATO Review*, vol. 42, no. 1 (February, 1994), p. 4.
10. Rose, 'The 1982 Summit and After', p. 9.
11. See his *Memoirs of Richard Nixon* (London, Sidgwick and Jackson, 1978), pp. 1026–7.
12. *A Time to Heal: The Autobiography of Gerald R. Ford* (London, W. H. Allen, 1979), p. 288.
13. Zbigniew Brzezinski, *Power and Principle: Memoirs of the National Security Adviser 1977–1981* (London, Weidenfeld and Nicolson, 1988), p. 293.
14. Harold Wilson, *Final Term: The Labour Government, 1974–1976* (London, Weidenfeld and Nicolson and Michael Joseph, 1979), pp. 57 and 86.
15. Margaret Thatcher, *The Downing Street Years* (London, Harper Collins, 1993).
16. Quoted in S. McLean, *How Nuclear Weapons Decisions Are Made* (London, Macmillan, 1986), p. 209; and requoted in Dan Smith, *Pressure: How America Runs NATO* (London, Bloomsbury Press, 1989), p. 16.
17. Rose, 'The 1982 Summit and After', p. 8.
18. Ibid., pp. 9–10.
19. Ernst Hans van der Beugal, 'The Atlantic Family: managing its problems', *NATO Review*, vol. 34, no. 1 (February, 1986), p. 17.
20. Rose, 'The 1982 Summit and After', p. 8.
21. Ibid.,
22. These points were strongly made by Sir Michael Alexander in an interview with the present author on 1 February 1994.

23. Rose, 'The 1982 Summit and After', p. 8.
24. Ambassador Henning Wegener, 'The Transformed Alliance', *NATO Review*, vol. 38, no. 4 (August, 1990), p. 1.
25. See Martin Smith and Owen Greene, 'NATO as an International Institution: its strengths and weaknesses in the post-Cold War era', presented to the Annual Conference of the British International Studies Association, University of Warwick, December 1993, pp. 3–4.
26. Ibid., p. 15.
27. Rose, 'The 1982 Summit and After', p. 10.
28. Legge, 'The Making of NATO's New Strategy'.
29. See 'Bosnia Unites NATO Defence Ministers', *Defense News*, 25 October 1993, p. 4.
30. See 'NATO Makes Plans for Crucial Post-Cold War Summit', *Defense News*, 30 August 1993, p. 20.
31. According to his Secretary of State, Warren Christopher. See his 'Towards a NATO Summit', *NATO Review*, vol. 41, no. 4 (August, 1993), p. 1.
32. 'NATO Makes Plans', *Defense News*, 30 August 1993.
33. 'Wörner Seeks to Rally US–NATO Ties' *Defense News*, 11 October 1993, p. 11.
34. Interview conducted with UK Ministry of Defence official, 3 February 1994.
35. A US Ambassador to NATO during the 1980s, David Abshire, apparently counted 435 committees! Smith, *Pressure: How America Runs NATO*, p. 10.
36. Ambassador Prosper Thuysbaert, 'The Changing Face of Political Consultation', *NATO Review*, vol. 41, no. 5 (October, 1993), p. 27.
37. These points were reinforced by interviews conducted with NATO officials in Brussels, 21–24 February 1994; with a UK MoD official, 3 February 1994; and with Sir Michael Alexander, 16 February 1994.
38. van der Beugal, 'The Atlantic Family', p. 17.
39. Thuysbaert, 'The Changing Face of Political Consultation', p. 25. Sir Michael Alexander, himself a British PermRep at the May 1989 summit, confirmed in an interview on 16 February 1994 the intensity of the pressure to come up with a solution to ensure that the summit did not end in disarray.
40. Thatcher, *The Downing Street Years*, pp. 774–5.
41. Rose, 'The 1982 Summit and After', p. 12.
42. See Michael R. Beschloss and Strobe Talbott, *At the Highest Levels: The Inside Story of the End of the Cold War* (Boston and London, Little, Brown and Company, 1993), pp. 74–8.
43. Ibid., p. 237.
44. Rose, 'Political Consultation in the Alliance', p. 4.
45. Rose, 'The 1982 Summit and After', p. 14.
46. Robert S. Jordan, *Political Leadership in NATO: A Study in Multilateral Diplomacy* (Boulder, Colorado, Westview, 1979), p. 69.
47. Smith, *Pressure: How America Runs NATO*, pp. 14–16.
48. Legge, 'The Making of NATO's New Strategy', p. 11.

7 Funeral Summits
G. R. Berridge

Ceremonial occasions of exceptional national importance generally attract guest lists on which foreign dignitaries, including heads of state and government, are prominent. As a result, they are often significant diplomatic events – in the relations between enemies as well as friends. Imperial enthronements, royal coronations, presidential inaugurations, papal investitures, royal weddings, independence day celebrations, and anniversaries of the revolution, are characteristic occasions of this kind. There seems little doubt, however, that the funerals of major political figures – 'working funerals' – are now the most important of these occasions.

Funeral diplomacy goes back at least to the Feast of the Dead celebrated by the Algonkians of the Upper Great Lakes of Canada in the seventeenth century,[1] and probably a great deal further. Indeed, passing reference to at least some stunted version of it is made by Queller in his authoritative account of diplomacy in the Middle Ages,[2] while Cohen notes that the Amarna Letters contain hints of the practice in the Near East as early as the fourteenth century BC.[3] Nevertheless, evidence of practice is one thing; evidence of the institutionalization of a practice within a particular system is quite another.[4] And the fact remains that, as far as the post-Westphalian system of states is concerned, it appears to have been as late as the 1960s before funeral diplomacy became at least a significant institution.[5]

The growth in funeral diplomacy in the 1960s was obviously encouraged by the enormous improvements at this time in air transport. Another reason seems to have been that it was at roughly this juncture that advances in the technology of embalmment and refrigeration were achieved. These made it possible to preserve bodies for longer in hot climates, thus giving time for foreign dignitaries to assemble before burial or cremation of the deceased luminary became unavoidable if the health of his retainers was not to be put at serious risk.[6] The theatrical potential of these funerals also became more attractive to publicity-hungry leaders such as General de Gaulle with the spread of television during this decade. Secularization, too, may have made it seem less outrageous that funerals should be so obviously exploited for the conduct of business. Finally, it was in the 1960s that severing relations became fashionable as a political gesture and the availability of other avenues of discreet diplomatic contact became important. In any event, it was in 1967 that, according to Harold Wilson, the term 'working funeral' was invented.[7] By the early 1980s, with the huge international gatherings at the funerals in fairly rapid succession of three Soviet leaders, the working funeral had clearly come of age.

What are the characteristics of these funerals? What diplomatic risks are associated with them? Why, nevertheless, do they provide such important diplomatic opportunities?

WHAT IS A 'WORKING FUNERAL'?

This is the funeral of a major political leader who dies either in office or in retirement. It is attended by scores of high-level delegations from abroad who use the occasion in order to conduct diplomatic business. Perhaps the most remarkable in recent years was the funeral of the Emperor Hirohito of Japan, which was attended by representatives from almost 160 countries, including 55 heads of state, 11 prime ministers and 14 representatives of royal families.

Working funerals are not necessarily 'state funerals'; nor are state funerals necessarily of greater diplomatic significance than political funerals of lesser grandeur. For instance, at the state funeral of former US President Herbert C. Hoover in 1964 only 15 of the 300 diplomats invited actually turned up; by contrast, a galaxy of foreign dignitaries attended the merely 'official' funeral in 1959 to which former US Secretary of State John Foster Dulles was entitled.[8] Nevertheless, since the most important leaders tend to receive state funerals, working funerals are generally of this kind; they are distinguished by the 'lying-in-state' of the fallen hero in an imposing edifice at the heart of the state's institutions; in the United States, for example, in the Capitol rotunda.

On the day of the burial or cremation eulogies over the body are delivered by leading figures among the politically bereaved, and visiting foreign delegations pay their last respects. Despatch of the corpse is then followed by a state reception for the guests, which is in turn followed hotly by the private conduct of diplomatic business between different visiting delegations as well as between the visitors and their hosts.

The working funeral has now become so institutionalized that no sense of shame is felt at this mingling of business with obeisance to the dead. No attempt is made to conceal the discussions: leaders make press statements within minutes of the conclusion of their discussions with the leadership of the bereaved state, and joint statements are commonly issued following conversations between visiting delegations which have proved fruitful. Even at the funeral of Emperor Hirohito, where controversial Shinto rituals were employed, 'the standard international model' was much in evidence.[9] Provided that there are incentives for diplomacy, the atmosphere in which the funeral is conducted does not necessarily make much difference either. Thus the usual round of meetings was held in the emotional atmosphere of Nasser's funeral in 1970, when there were fears in the government that – despite the presence of three entire divisions of the army – the Cairo crowds would get out of hand and burn the city to the ground.[10] They were also held in the supercharged climate of the funeral of President John F. Kennedy, a young, charismatic leader cut down by an assassin.[11]

THE DRAWBACKS OF FUNERAL DIPLOMACY

Despite their own drawbacks, normal summit meetings between world leaders are now widely regarded as an essential feature of modern diplomacy – at least by politicians. By and large, they signal top-level commitment to diplomacy, engage the attention of heads of state and government on foreign issues, set the clock on negotiations, and, among other things, provide splendid opportunities for solemnizing international agreements.

These advantages flow not least from the fact that normal summits are usually arranged well in advance. By contrast, international funerals, even those of leaders whose age and poor health suggest that they have not long to live, are still usually held at very short notice. This means that these 'impromptu summits'[12] – a special case of the *ad hoc* summit – carry several risks not associated with other summits.

First, top-level attendance can seriously upset existing diplomatic schedules (as well as domestic timetables) and, at the least, risk causing offence. President Reagan did not lead the American delegations to any of the Soviet funerals, and one reason for this – admittedly not the most important – was that it would have meant his absence from Washington at a time when visits by important foreign leaders had been arranged: newly elected Chancellor Kohl of West Germany at the time of Brezhnev's funeral;[13] King Hussein of Jordan and President Mubarak of Egypt on the occasion of that of Andropov. By the same token, personal attendance in Moscow by these leaders would have meant causing offence in Washington. Vice-President George Bush, who led the American delegations to all of these funerals, had to interrupt an African tour to participate in Brezhnev's rites. In a further example, attendance by President Tito of Yugoslavia at Nasser's funeral in September 1970 would have meant cancelling an imminent visit by President Nixon, though, ironically enough, when the news broke the Americans assumed that Tito would cancel (Tito and Nasser had been founder members and subsequently pillars of the Non-Aligned Movement) and frantically worked on alternative plans while Nixon slept on board the US aircraft carrier *Saratoga*. To the relief of Nixon's staff, 'He [Tito] attached more importance to the symbolism of the first Presidential visit to Belgrade', records Kissinger, 'than to the funeral of his fallen friend'.[14]

Secondly, there is now such a widespread assumption that the funeral of a major figure will be attended at a high level that failure to comply with this norm on grounds of pressing business carries the opposite risk: offence to the politically bereaved. Whether or not relations between Belgrade and Cairo suffered as a result of Tito's non-appearance at Nasser's funeral is not clear. However, it was widely held at the time that relations between Turkey and the Atlantic powers had been impaired by the relatively low level of Western attendance at the funeral of the Turkish president, Turgut Ozal, who died suddenly of heart failure (aged only 65) in April 1993. This was not overlooked in Turkey, where there is widespread suspicion that ethnic and religious considerations underly the West's determination to keep the country at arm's length. The Ozal funeral was not a good day for Western diplomacy.[15]

Of course, if all states or, more likely, a group of allied states can agree beforehand on the level of attendance at a funeral the political damage will individually be less if the level is relatively low. This probably happened at the time of the Ozal funeral. However, the short notice for funeral summits also means that there is very limited time available for gathering information on the intentions of other states and making the necessary preparations. On the evidence of a cable sent to the Foreign Office from the British embassy in Tokyo on the occasion of the funeral of President Kennedy, problems of this kind seem to have led the Japanese cabinet to be seized by something little short of panic. 'At first, the plan seems to have been that the former Prime Minister, Mr Yoshida, should attend the funeral as the official Japanese representative. Later it was decided to send Mr Ohira, the Foreign Minister. At the last minute, however, when it became known that Royalty and Prime Ministers would be representing other countries, the Cabinet decided that Mr Ikeda should also attend.'[16] The Japanese ultimately made the right decision but it was a close call. In New Delhi, however, 'no-one thought about the question of sending someone from India to Washington' until it was too late.[17]

Sometimes decisions on attendance at the funeral of an incumbent also have to be made in the absence of certainty about who the successor is likely to be and what manner of reception will be granted to the visiting delegation. This increases a third risk, especially, of course, if relations between the countries concerned are poor – the risk of humiliation. In the event, this did not materialize for US Vice-President George Bush at the funeral of Andropov – despite the fact that Chernenko was not appointed to succeed Andropov as Party Leader until the day before the funeral and the Vice-President had no guarantee that he would be able to meet with Chernenko before deciding whether or not to attend.[18] However, the Soviet funerals in the 1980s produced more mixed fortunes for the Pakistani and Chinese governments.

Even old friends have to take irrevocable decisions in the absence of complete certainty that a top-level delegation to the funeral of an allied leader will be received appropriately. For example, after a brief period of indecision in the hours following the assassination of President Kennedy as to whether to attend the funeral in person,[19] the new British Prime Minister, Sir Alec Douglas-Home, instructed the Foreign Office to cable the Washington Embassy in the middle of the following day that he had 'now definitely decided to come himself'. This cable was despatched at 1.15 p.m. on 23 November 1963 under 'Emergency/Top Secret' classification. It added that the United States government should be informed of the proposal and that it was the aim to make it public 'as soon as it is clear that the Americans have no objection'.[20] Ten minutes later, but later nevertheless, Downing Street cabled the British Ambassador with instructions to try to arrange a meeting between the new president, Lyndon Johnson, and the prime minister. It was understood that, in the circumstances, this could only be 'the shortest of talks', and Sir Alec was prepared to delay his departure slightly if this 'would make all the difference to the chances of seeing the President ... . For your information, however', added Downing Street, 'the Prime Minister does feel that it might look odd if he comes to Washington and did not have any time with the President at all'.[21]

As well as making risky decisions almost inevitable, the short notice for funeral summits also means that they are unlikely to provide opportunities for serious negotiations. This is because it is impossible to undertake the lengthy and detailed preparation of briefs which normally precedes summit meetings. (In any case, little time is available and many delegations have to be contacted.) Arrangements for personal security and media coverage are also much more difficult to make at short notice. The unexpectedness of funeral summits also means that they cannot function as deadlines for the completion of negotiations, which is one of the more important functions of the regular *ad hoc* summit; while this – as well as their formal character – means that they cannot be used to solemnize international agreements either.

Finally, it should be added that the sheer informality and confusion which attends some part of these occasions, particularly when inexperienced leaders are not accompanied by aides, can lead to inadvertent public encounters between 'unfriendly powers'. One such incident, much relished by the leader of the Liberal Party in Britain, David Steel, occurred in a crowded palace ante-room in Belgrade at the funeral of Marshall Tito in 1980. Here, records Steel, who was himself a guest, 'our relatively new Prime Minister, Mrs Thatcher, was glad-handing those present ("I'm Margaret Thatcher, *so* pleased to meet you"). Being without any aides in this distinguished gathering, she gave the distinct and understandable impression of not knowing who everybody was – she had not dealt much with foreign affairs in her political career. Among those she greeted with happy incomprehension was Yasser Arafat.'[22]

Altogether, then, these impromptu summits upset diplomatic schedules, present a higher risk of mistakes and rebuffs, and clearly lack some of the diplomatic attractions of ordinary summit meetings. Nevertheless, they have a great many compensating advantages.

THE DIPLOMATIC POTENTIAL OF FUNERAL SUMMITS

Funerals of incumbent leaders, or of retired ones which happen to coincide roughly with a transfer of power,[23] are usually the most valuable to diplomacy. This is because they provide the visiting dignitaries with probably their first opportunity to meet the new government. If this is the government of a major power, aid donor, or key client, allies or patrons will attend in order to show respect, establish a personal rapport with the new leadership, and seek reassurance that there will be no change in policy to their disadvantage. It is for reasons such as these that the British generally crowd to American presidential funerals;[24] that Warsaw Pact leaders were always the first to be received by the new Moscow bosses at Soviet funerals; and that a large and high-powered Soviet delegation descended on Cairo for the funeral of Nasser in September 1970.[25]

Some of the visiting delegations at international funerals, however, are rivals if not outright enemies of the politically bereaved – for example, the Turks at the funeral of Stalin; de Gaulle at that of Churchill; and Mrs Thatcher at that of Chernenko. Such mourners may be there in order to explore the possibility of a *rapprochement* with their hosts. Indeed, it is of special diplomatic significance that the enemies of the bereaved government as well as its friends can normally attend these funerals without serious fear of attack from supporters at home or friends abroad. Paying respects to the dead (unless extravagantly depraved or the object of religious anathemas) is above reproach in all cultures of which I am aware, including that of the Chicago mob. International funerals, in other words, are usually times of political truce.

Furthermore, while the short notice for these funerals presents the difficulties noted earlier, it has three compensating advantages. First, a head of government or other major figure might *want* to break an existing diplomatic schedule, possibly for an urgent discussion with another foreign leader in circumstances which will not arouse excessive public expectations. The funeral summit provides good cover for this type of meeting. What is really significant about the Tito case is that the Yugoslav leader could have broken his engagement with Nixon if he had wanted to go to Nasser's funeral for business reasons; the Americans expected this. Secondly, the short notice means that a decision to attend is unlikely to prove embarrassing as a result of changed circumstances by the date of the event. An apposite contrast in this connection is provided by the Gorbachev–Deng summit in Peking in May 1989. This was publicly announced in February when all was quiet in Tiananmen Square but ended up being held against the humiliating background of its occupation by pro-democracy students.[26] Thirdly, there is little time for opposition to attendance at a funeral summit to be mobilized.

It also seems reasonable to suggest that the atmosphere at most major funerals is conducive to a diplomacy of reconciliation. In the West at any rate funerals of statesmen – no less than those of private individuals – are customarily occasions for reflecting on the transitoriness of life itself. With the eternal verities thrown into strong relief, the righteous indignation of everyday political strife begins to look petty. Moreover, because the funeral of an incumbent coincides with the creation of a new leadership, because, that is, the political wake is also a political baptism, there may well be a sense of change and opportunity in the air. It is thus not surprising that major funerals are often a time for urging a more energetic search for peaceful solutions to the world's problems.

In light of the foregoing, it is perhaps not surprising that de Gaulle's presence at Kennedy's funeral in 1963 should have 'helped to reconcile Americans to his unaccommodating stance as an ally',[27] or that the long conversation which he had with President Nixon at Eisenhower's funeral in 1969 should have 'laid the groundwork', according to Nixon, 'for

Kissinger's secret trips to Paris, which resulted four years later in the Paris Peace Agreement and the end of American involvement in Vietnam'.[28] At Churchill's funeral in January 1965, a 50-minute conversation at the French Embassy between the indefatigable de Gaulle and the new British Prime Minister, Harold Wilson, broke the ice which had formed over Anglo-French relations following the veto by Paris two years previously of Britain's application to join the Common Market. At Brezhnev's funeral General Zia was encouraged to believe that Moscow was now serious about a diplomatic solution to the Afghan conflict, and at Chernenko's funeral Mrs Thatcher had a private conversation with Mikhail Gorbachev in which she clearly advanced the good relationship with him established during his visit to Britain in the previous December.[29]

Among the most successful attempts in recent years to exploit the potential of funeral summits for bilateral diplomacy between visiting delegations were those made by the leaders of East and West Germany at the Soviet funerals. These began at Brezhnev's obsequies, when Erich Honecker was met privately by President Karl Carstens and the Foreign Minister of the recently elected CDU/CSU-FDP government, Hans-Dietrich Genscher. At the next funeral Chancellor Kohl himself met Honecker for the first time, and they met again at that of Chernenko.[30] It is widely acknowledged that these encounters were of the greatest significance in the improvement of relations between the two halves of divided Germany, and helped pave the way for eventual reunification. Chernenko's funeral was also the scene of a private meeting between Mrs Thatcher and President Samora Machel of 'Marxist' Mozambique, a country which was soon to be virtually the latest recruit to the British Commonwealth. Following discussions between President Suharto of Indonesia and Chinese Foreign Minister, Qian Qichen,[31] at Hirohito's funeral in February 1989, China and Indonesia resumed diplomatic relations after breaking them off over 20 years earlier.

Finally, it should be noted that these funerals, especially those of incumbent leaders, provide first-class opportunities for diplomatic signalling as well as private diplomatic conversations. These opportunities exist for both the bereaved and the mourners, though as hosts the former probably have more scope for subtlety.

For potential guests at the wake, the scope for signalling, as already noted, is normally confined to decisions on attendance. These, however, are not insignificant opportunities. An interesting case of a decision to attend prompted largely by symbolic considerations, and for which there is documentary evidence, is provided by the Turkish decision to accept the

Soviet invitation to Stalin's funeral in 1953. This was a cause of general astonishment, not least in Moscow, because Turkish–Soviet relations were very bad at the time. The Turks had nevertheless decided to accept for three reasons, as M. Aÿikalin, Secretary-General of the Turkish Foreign Ministry and the man who led the special mission, explained to the mystified British ambassador on his return. First, there had been a desire to repay the earlier Soviet gesture, albeit made in very different circumstances, to send a mission to the funeral of Ataturk. Secondly, they wanted to take a look inside Moscow (though Turkey did have a mission in the Soviet capital). And thirdly – and this seemed to be the most important consideration as far as Aÿikalin was concerned – the Soviet invitation was seen as a challenge which, 'from the point of view of the cold war', it was important to take up. In line with this, Molotov had invited Aÿikalin to call on him during the visit but the interview had been confined to formalities: 'It would, he said, have been a sign of weakness if he had started talking politics; and M. Molotov showed no disposition to do so himself.'[32] Behind each of these reasons prompting the decision of the Turks to go to Moscow there was perhaps also, as a British Foreign Office official suspected, 'the feeling that after all they are a limitrophe [bordering] state of Russia'.[33]

As far as manipulating the level of attendance at a funeral for purposes of diplomatic signalling is concerned, obviously a decision to attend at head of government level amounts to a major olive branch to the new leader. This is what Mrs Thatcher, who had come a long way since Belgrade, presented to Chernenko by her personal presence at Andropov's funeral in February 1984 after several years of 'megaphone diplomacy' (she had only sent her Foreign Secretary to the funeral of Brezhnev).[34] It is also what President Mubarak of Egypt, previously ostracized in the Arab world following the peace treaty with Israel, delivered to King Fahd of Saudi Arabia by his own attendance at the funeral of King Khalid in June 1982.[35] Conversely, a decision not to be represented at all – especially if publicly announced in a manner which is gratuitously offensive – is obviously a gesture of deep hostility. An example of the latter was provided by the British government on the death of the Iranian leader, Ayatollah Khomeini. To a written question in the House of Commons as to whether the British government would 'express sympathy to the peoples of Iran on the death of their nation's spiritual leader' and if it 'sought to be represented at the funeral', the Foreign Office spokesman replied 'No, in both cases'.[36] In between these extremes, however, there is a host of nuanced possibilities. At the more flattering end, these include sending the Vice-President (the American strategy), the Foreign or Defence Minister (a common strategy), or the wife of the head of state (a uniquely Filipino strategy). At the less flattering end, they include sending the Minister of Agriculture, an ex-Governor General, or the Ambassador, who happens to be there anyway. As for the bereaved government, this is able to grant or withold a private audience with the new leadership at an appropriate level. However, it is also able to display any change in its attitude to the more hostile among the funeral guests by drawing on a range of other actions, though the rigidity of the funeral format and the multiplicity of guests makes it more difficult for the host government to manipulate ceremony and hospitality to develop a 'political theme' than is the case in other settings for diplomatic theatre. At the Soviet funerals, the new leaders signalled a desire to improve relations with particular states by giving them manifestly warm welcomes in the Kremlin and the earliest and longest, as well as the most high-level, private audiences which protocol would allow. At Brezhnev's funeral this was notably the case with China, Pakistan, and West Germany. At the funeral of Chernenko in March 1985, the new General Secretary, Mikhail Gorbachev, immediately showed his own determination to improve relations with China by having its delegation (along with that of India) 'whisked ahead of the line' at the Kremlin reception. Like Andropov at the Brezhnev funeral, Gorbachev also signalled his goodwill towards Western Europe by devoting more attention to the states of this region in his bilateral conversations than to the Soviet Union's own allies.[37]

The working funeral became an institution of the world diplomatic system in the 1960s, at a time when conventional channels of diplomacy were at a discount in many areas of the East and South – and to some degree in the United States, for that matter. It should not be forgotten, however, that funeral summits are often as important for allies looking for reassurance as they are for enemies seeking to find a way out of an impasse. On the occasion of the funeral of the Showa Emperor, *The Times* summed up the subject well: 'They are public ceremonies,' it wrote, 'which offer more a convenience for the living than a tribute to the dead.'[38] There are risks in this diplomacy for the unwary, it is true, but these are probably fewer now that the funeral summit has been so completely institutionalized. This process is thus cause as well as effect of the rise of the working funeral.

NOTES AND REFERENCES

This is a revised version from my book *Talking to the Enemy* (London, Macmillan, 1994).

1.   H. Hickerson 'The Feast of the Dead among the Seventeenth Century Algonkians of the Upper Great Lakes', *American Anthropologist*, vol. 62, no. 1 (1960).

2.   D. E. Queller, *The Office of the Ambassador in the Middle Ages* (Princeton, NJ, Princeton University Press, 1967) p. 99.

3.   'On the Origins of Diplomacy: The Amarna Letters', paper delivered to the Annual Conference of the British International Studies Association, York, December 1994.

4.   There is a useful discussion of this point in Maurice Keens-Soper, 'The Practice of a States-System', in M. Donelan (ed.), *The Reason of States: A Study in International Political Theory* (London, Allen and Unwin, 1978) p. 44, note 29.

5.   In a major book published in 1926 on the character and functions of funeral customs, containing an entire chapter on 'State and Public Funerals', the author makes no mention of any diplomatic function at all. B. S. Puckle, *Funeral Customs: Their Origin and Development* (London, Werner Laurie, 1926).

6.   A spectacular recent example was provided by the funeral on 7 February 1994 of Ivory Coast leader, Félix Houphouët-Boigny, who died two months earlier. His corpse was kept frozen while the elaborate preparations for the funeral were made. The *Independent Magazine*, 19 February 1994.

7.   H. Wilson, *The Governance of Britain* (London, Weidenfeld and Nicolson, 1976) p. 87.

8.   B. C. Mossman and M. W. Stark, *The Last Salute: Civil and Military Funerals, 1921–1969* (Washington DC, Department of the Army, US Government Printing Office, 1971) p. 264.

9.   T. Crump, *The Death of an Emperor: Japan at the Crossroads* (Oxford, Oxford University Press, 1991) p. 211.

10. M. Heikal, *The Road to Ramadan* (London, Collins, 1975) pp. 110–11; Lord Home, *The Way the Wind Blows* (London, Collins, 1976) p. 199.

11. W. Manchester, *The Death of a President* (London, Pan Books, 1967) pp. 844–52.

12. This phrase was employed in the *Guardian*, 13 February 1984.

13. See *Public Papers of the Presidents, Ronald Reagan, 1982*, vol. II, The President's News Conference, 11 November 1983.

14. H. A. Kissinger, *The White House Years* (London, Weidenfeld and Nicolson, 1979) pp. 926–7.

15. The Americans were represented only by the former Secretary of State, James Baker, and his successor's deputy, Cliff Wharton. Britain was represented by its Minister of Overseas Development, Baroness Chalker. The Germans, it is true, sent President Weizsäcker, but the French despatched merely their Minister of Foreign Trade. *Financial Times*, 28 April 1993.

16. Public Record Office (British Embassy (Tokyo) to Foreign Office, 26 November 1963, FO371/168406.

17. PRO, British High Commission (New Delhi) to Commonwealth Relations Office, 30 November 1963, FO371/168408.

18. *Public Papers of the Presidents, Ronald Reagan, 1984*, vol. I, Radio Address to the Nation on United States–Soviet Relations, 11 February 1984.

19. PRO, Downing Street to British Embassy (Washington), despatched 12.43 a.m., 23 November 1963 and classified 'Emergency/Confidential', FO371/168487. In immediate reply, the ambassador urged him to come to Washington. Ibid.

20. PRO, Foreign Office (FO) to British Embassy (Washington), 23 November 1963, FO371/168487.

21. PRO, Personal for the Ambassador from de Zulueta, despatched 1.25 p.m. (Emergency/Top Secret), 23 November 1963, FO371/168487.

22. D. Steel, *Against Goliath* (London, Pan, 1991) p. 231.

23. For example, Churchill's funeral coincided with the election of the Labour government in Britain in late 1964; Eisenhower's with the inauguration of Nixon in early 1969.

24. Manchester, *The Death of a President*, p. 771. In a brief report to the Cabinet on his meeting with President Johnson at Kennedy's funeral, Sir Alec Douglas-Home stated that 'he had been assured by President Johnson that there would be no change in United States foreign policy and that the United States Government would wish to maintain close relations with the United Kingdom', PRO, CM(63)8, 28 November 1963, CAB128/38.

25. M. Riad, *The Struggle for Peace in the Middle East* (London, Quartet, 1981) p. 168. See also Heikal, *The Road to Ramadan*, pp. 111–13.

26. P. Cradock, *Experiences of China* (London, Murray, 1994) p. 221.

27. *The Times*, 24 February 1989.

28. R. M. Nixon, *Leaders* (London, Sidgwick and Jackson, 1982) p. 76.

29. *Guardian*, 14 March 1985; and G. Howe, *Conflict of Loyalty* (London, Macmillan, 1994) pp. 429–30.

30. *The Times*, 24 February 1989.

31. Communist China was only represented at foreign minister level in order to indicate Chinese anger over remarks to the Japanese Diet on 18 February by then prime minister Noboru Takeshita denying Hirohito's responsibility for atrocities committed by the Japanese in China during the Second World War, *Keesing's Record of World Events* (1990) p. 37 341.

32. PRO, British Embassy (Ankara) to FO, 24 March 1953, FO371/106516.

33. PRO, FO minute, 27 March 1953, FO371/106516.

34. On Mrs Thatcher at Andropov's funeral, see Howe, *Conflict of Loyalty*, pp. 352–4.

35. R. Cohen, *Theatre of Power: The Art of Diplomatic Signalling* (London and New York, Longman, 1987) p. 158.

36. HCDeb., vol. 154, 9 June 1989, col. 262(w).

37. *Financial Times*, 14 and 16 March 1985.

38. 24 February 1989.

8 Commonwealth Heads of Government Meetings

James Mayall

Unlike most of the other organizations which hold summit meetings represented in this volume, it is not obvious that if the Commonwealth did not exist it would be necessary to invent it. The Commonwealth lacks a strategic, regional or functional rationale, and few if any of the issues that appear on the agenda of its Heads of Government meetings (CHOGMs) can be resolved there. Yet, judging by the numbers who attend these two-yearly summits – they fluctuate but seldom fall below 35 out of a membership of 50 – loyalty to the Commonwealth remains high. In recent years there has been some pressure from the larger member countries to reduce the length of the summit from its traditional and leisurely week-long format, but no serious suggestion that Commonwealth summitry itself should be abandoned.

The Commonwealth thus confronts us with a paradox: an organization without a specific or obvious role in contemporary international society to which nonetheless its member states remain deeply attached; or at least sufficiently committed for the majority of their leaders to block off a sizeable chunk of time every other year to attend the CHOGM. How is the paradox to be explained? To some extent the answer to this question will emerge when we consider the uses to which Commonwealth meetings are actually put, under a series of headings which will, hopefully, allow comparison with other summit-prone international associations. However, the explanation also lies in the unique history of the Commonwealth and its peculiar status amongst international organizations. Since the origins of its summit meetings are to be found in this history, it will be helpful to start with a brief review of the relevant background.

The Commonwealth was originally the British Commonwealth and Empire, a formulation which lasted until after the Second World War and which symbolized that it was both an extension – and in large measure a basis – of British world power, and a system of hierarchical stratification amongst British colonies and former possessions that remained linked constitutionally to the mother country. It was the latter, the old white dominions, that formed the first Commonwealth. 'At the widest reaches of optimism,' Dennis Austin wrote, 'when the Commonwealth was seen not only as important but permanent, it was argued that the relationship between Britain and the Dominions should be viewed teleologically. In the beginning was its end – a reconciliation of empire and liberty, or more classically expressed *imperium* and *libertas*.'[1] In this sense, indeed, the old Commonwealth was often represented as an international civil society of considerable power.

The description is apt on both counts. Australia, Canada, New Zealand and South Africa were linked with Britain through numerous family, regional, economic and professional associations and networks which existed independently of their governments, but the governments themselves were also linked in ways which differed significantly from imperial relations between the metropolitan power and its colonies on the one hand and the normal relations between sovereign states on the other. The dominions were independent, but on questions of imperial defence or the sterling area, Britain was accepted as *primus inter pares*.[2] Modern Commonwealth summits developed out of the periodic meetings of the British Prime Minister with his dominion counterparts. These early summits bequeathed two important legacies to the modern Commonwealth, although, as we shall see, both have been considerably modified and, some might say, diluted with the passage of time.

The first legacy was the informal nature of the summits. The prime ministers met without a formal agenda, in private and with a bare minimum of official advisers and paraphernalia. The second was the familiarity of leaders with constitutional and administrative practices in each other's countries. All were parliamentary democracies; all were constitutional monarchies under the same monarch; and English was the language of government and administration in them all, and, except in South Africa and the Canadian province of Quebec, the language of the majority of the population also.

Since 1945 the Commonwealth has undergone two major metamorphoses. The first challenge to the old Commonwealth came in 1947 with the independence of India and Pakistan. India became a republic but remained within the Commonwealth by recognizing the monarch as its head. From now on republicanism was not an obstacle to Commonwealth membership, even though Ireland left in 1949 when it adopted a republican constitution and South Africa left in 1961, ostensibly over the same issue.[3] The second challenge was the transformation of the Commonwealth by the admission of black African, Caribbean and Oceanic island countries from 1957 onwards. It was this change from a predominantly white to a predominantly African and Asian association that was the real reason underlying South Africa's withdrawal.

The combined effect of these changes was gradually to shift the central focus of the Commonwealth from the preservation of British interests, and their reconciliation with those of the old dominions, to the promotion of the interests of the majority of new members and the articulation of their mostly anti-Western demands for international reform.[4] The creation of an independent secretariat in 1966 – the Commonwealth had previously been serviced by the British Commonwealth Relations Office – symbolized the demotion of Britain from its formal leading role in Commonwealth affairs, although of course it remained the most powerful member. The enlargement of the membership and its increasing cultural heterogeneity inevitably affected the character of both the organization and its periodic summit meetings. The Commonwealth continues to pride itself on the informality of its meetings, and the commitment of its members to democratic values; but in practice it has evolved into a fairly conventional intergovernmental organization, in which the members jealously guard their sovereignty over domestic affairs, and still include amongst their number several blatantly non-democratic regimes.

Against this background, let us turn to the summits themselves by looking first at their pattern and purpose and then at other ways in which they are used by member governments and their likely future trajectory.

SYMBOL AND SUBSTANCE

The CHOGM meets every other year in a different Commonwealth country. Over the past ten years the conferences have been held in Nassau, Bahamas (1985); Vancouver, Canada (1987); Kuala Lumpur, Malaysia (1989); Harare, Zimbabwe (1991); and Limassol, Cyprus (1993).[5] Special meetings have been held at other times to deal with special problems; thus there was an extraordinary summit in 1966 in Lagos in an abortive attempt to prevent the disintegration of Nigeria and its slide into civil war, and a mini-summit in London in 1986 to review the report of the Commonwealth Eminent Persons Group on South Africa.[6]

The migratory pilgrimage of Commonwealth leaders around the world suggests that the meetings are primarily valued for what they symbolize rather than for what they do. (One is reminded of the one time the Security Council met in Addis Ababa in a show of solidarity with African opposition to South Africa, rather than as a demonstration by the major powers that they were willing to change their policies, which they were not.)

There is some force in this somewhat cynical criticism, the essence of which was captured by the Harare taxi driver who translated the acronym CHOGM in 1991 as 'Cheap Holiday On Government Money'. But the Commonwealth remains – and this is perhaps its chief value – one of the very few organizations that straddles the North–South divide and where leaders from both sides can meet in a cooperative rather than confrontational setting.

It is also an odd fact that despite the republican ethos of the new Commonwealth, the popularity of the Queen as its head has grown rather than diminished. Whether it is the Queen herself or the office which commands respect and affection remains unclear, but certainly at the 1989 CHOGM in Kuala Lumpur, when the President of Bangladesh suggested that the Queen's role was anachronistic, most other leaders went out of their way to rebuff him. It would be wrong, in any case, to underestimate the practical importance of symbolic reinforcement for the authority of the organization in its day to day work. The major substantive task for the heads of state is to approve the agenda of work for the secretariat for the ensuing two years. Compared with most multilateral or regional organizations the Commonwealth is a low-cost affair.[7] The question is how much value does it add in return for this modest investment? For the smaller member countries it provides valuable diplomatic services, and technical and financial assistance; and the larger members, who are the major contributors also get good value for money in relation to the amount they spend.[8] Yet for very few, if any, Commonwealth countries is the organization the primary focus of their foreign policy and relations. Most countries are more deeply involved in regional organizations of various kinds and in bilateral relations with the major powers. There is, therefore, an understandable anxiety that the Commonwealth may suffer from neglect unless it can succeed in periodically capturing the political high ground and the public and media attention that goes with it.

For the past 30 years the problems of white minority rule in Southern Africa, and between 1985 and 1991 the debate over sanctions imposed on South Africa, provided the Commonwealth with its political sex appeal. There is no doubt that, for much of the time, many non-African countries were frequently frustrated at the way in which Southern African issues crowded out other items on the Commonwealth agenda which they considered equally important. The relentless pressure on Britain to change its policy towards South Africa throughout the 1980s also drove the Conservative government under Mrs Thatcher to question the validity of Britain's continued membership, as it had done under her predecessor, Edward Heath, at the Singapore CHOGM in 1971. Yet British withdrawal was never seriously contemplated, and while it was Southern Africa – first Rhodesia and then South Africa itself – which pulled in the world's media and captured the headlines, the Secretariat, particularly under its second Secretary General, Sir Sridath Ramphal, skilfully exploited the summits to carve out a special role for the Commonwealth in North–South relations over a much wider range of issues. The weekend retreat – an invented tradition designed to re-create the relaxed and informal atmosphere of the old Commonwealth prime ministers' meetings – was used to gain support for the setting-up of expert groups whose work was intended to build consensus on intractable North–South issues, such as the integrated programme on commodities at the end of the 1970s or the Uruguay Round of multilateral trade negotiations a decade later.

Recent CHOGMs have sometimes threatened to deteriorate into a media circus, with set-piece speeches, photo-calls carefully timed to allow homeward transmission by satellite, and the press themselves sniffing around for a story which will command public attention over what is, by international standards, an extended period. The Commonwealth is not the G-7, let alone the G-3, so finding a story and sustaining the plot for the best part of a week calls for ingenuity and inventiveness. Even then, it does not always succeed: at Vancouver in 1987, despite the dramatic possibilities created by Mrs Thatcher's confrontation with almost all her colleagues, the summit moved steadily down the front pages of the Canadian press as the week progressed. None the less the leisurely timetable, and the fact that the big story acts as a kind of smoke-screen, probably means that behind it more useful business gets done, of both a bilateral and a Commonwealth-wide variety, than is the case with many other summit meetings. Public interest in the Commonwealth can be predicted to last at least through 1995 when South Africa will attend the CHOGM in New Zealand for the first time since rejoining following the multi-party elections in April 1994. Thereafter how the Commonwealth can generate a new big story, or whether it can hold together without one, remains to be seen.

PREPARATION AND PERSONALITIES

It would be impossible to organize a meeting of the size and complexity of a CHOGM without a considerable amount of pre-planning and agenda control. In a sense the existence of a Permanent Secretariat,[9] with experience stretching back over a period of 30 years, means that the Commonwealth has available a corps of sherpas on whom they can rely to ensure that the CHOGM runs smoothly. The fact that there is now a fairly standard format to the meetings – executive sessions of the heads of government interspersed by the retreat and accompanied by parallel meetings of senior officials and second-tier politicians in the Committee of the Whole (the CoW) – also goes some way to rendering the proceedings predictable. Typically the Secretary General takes soundings amongst governments as the date for the next summit approaches on the priority issues for discussion and these will be followed up by the Secretariat in an agenda letter during the summer. The editor of *The Round Table* noted of the Cyprus summit in 1993 that the aim of this letter is 'to encourage constructive discussion in three substantive areas: (i) an up-to-date global review (political and economic); (ii) on special issues (such as South Africa and a "new world order"); (iii) to review and make recommendations regarding Commonwealth functional activities'.[10]

However, despite such 'pre-cooking' and perhaps because very few major decisions result from Commonwealth negotiations, CHOGMs are probably less predictable than many other summits. If a major arms control treaty is to be concluded, or the European Union deepened or widened, the stakes are high and the role of the sherpas in confining the final assault to that of ceremonial flag-planting correspondingly enhanced. But the Commonwealth straddles substantially lower terrain than this. The paradoxical consequence is that particular leaders are often able to put their personal stamp on the proceedings, and even sometimes on the outcome. There are many examples. The Commonwealth was quicker than most international organizations to grasp the futility of pursuing the collectivist agenda of the 1970s campaign for a new international economic order, a fact which may have something to do with the influential advocacy of Lee Kuan Yew at successive Commonwealth summits. At Vancouver he threw down the gauntlet, stating his conviction unambiguously that communism had failed as both an economic and political system, and asking whether Third World Commonwealth leaders would have the courage to embark on their own '*glasnost*', analyse their shortcomings and put them right, or whether they would prefer to face further decline. The Vancouver Declaration on World Trade, innocuous in itself, was the first of a series of Commonwealth initiatives which continued through to the Limassol CHOGM in 1993 and which put the Commonwealth as a whole, and not just its developed members, behind the effort to bring the Uruguay Round to a successful conclusion.

The Fiji crisis also coincided with the Vancouver CHOGM in 1987, and might have been resolved differently, from the Commonwealth's point of view, had it not been for the intervention of the Indian Prime Minister,

Rajiv Gandhi. Colonel Rabuka's *coup* was directed against an elected government, but one which primarily represented the population of immigrant descent rather than indigenous Fijians. Many governments, including the British, and more surprisingly given the obvious parallels with South Africa, most of the Africans, had hoped that the crisis could be passed over in silence – it was not in any case on the agenda. The British also warned against precipitate action and suggested that the Commonwealth should not abandon a member as soon as it ran into difficulties, a fair point which was presumably not lost on the Africans. But Rajiv Gandhi, strongly supported by the Canadian Prime Minister, insisted that the Commonwealth could not condone the emergence of a regime which threatened to permanently disenfranchise the population of Indian descent. In the event, Colonel Rabuka declared a republic, and the Commonwealth had little alternative but to concede that Fiji's membership had lapsed.

Throughout the 1980s, however, it was the British Prime Minister, Margaret Thatcher, who dominated Commonwealth summits and gave to the organization a certain notoriety, albeit not one which its supporters would have wished. The conventional wisdom within Commonwealth circles is that by isolating Britain from the Commonwealth over South Africa, Mrs Thatcher cut the umbilical cord linking all other members to Britain, and proved the independent viability of the organization and its capacity for action with or without British participation.

There is some truth in this version, but not much. Mrs Thatcher was certainly unyielding in her refusal to have British policy dictated by other Commonwealth countries, and she frequently defied the evidence by insisting that the other members were coming round to her own point of view. But however much she disliked having to listen to lectures on international morality, she recognized that there were limits to how far she could go without damaging British interests.

In a kind of corkscrew way the Commonwealth also provided her with opportunities for pursuing her own policies. Before taking office in 1979 she had threatened to lift sanctions against Rhodesia and accept the internal settlement worked out by Ian Smith and Bishop Muzorewa. The Foreign Office persuaded her that since it would not end the war this would solve nothing and would alienate independent Africa into the bargain. But the threat was taken seriously within the Commonwealth and it was at the Lusaka CHOGM that the tacit alliance emerged between the British and the Front Line States that led eventually to the Lancaster House conference and Zimbabwe's independence.[11] Each needed the other: Mrs Thatcher could not extract herself from the crisis without a political settlement, and nor could Tanzania and Zambia for whom the price of supporting the insurgency had by 1979 assumed crippling proportions. At Lusaka Mrs Thatcher promised to have one more go at reaching a constitutional settlement, while Presidents Nyerere and Kaunda promised to use their influence with the leaders of Zimbabwe's Patriotic Front. In the end they threatened Mugabe and Nkomo that they would close down the war unless they attended the constitutional conference. The circumstances were certainly propitious, but the summit was necessary to achieve the breakthrough.

The Commonwealth also provided opportunities for Mrs Thatcher and her Commonwealth opponents to lock horns over South Africa. Within the Commonwealth, which broke with Britain in deciding to impose an escalating set of sanctions on South Africa in 1986 and 1987, there is a widespread belief that this action hastened the collapse of apartheid. Mrs Thatcher believed otherwise, insisting throughout that sanctions harmed those they were intended to help and that quiet diplomacy to reinforce existing pressures for reform within the country, was likely to prove more effective. To the extent that outside powers and interests contributed to the historic transition to multi-party democracy in South Africa, it is possible that both were right; the Commonwealth majority in understanding that rational argument alone was unlikely to bring about change in Pretoria, but also Mrs Thatcher who was able to hint to President de Klerk that unless there was a demonstrable quickening of reform, she might not be able to hold the line against Commonwealth demands for pulling the economic noose ever tighter. We cannot know for sure how effective this pincer movement actually was, but what seems certain is that Commonwealth summitry featured in South African calculations. In 1989, de Klerk allowed Mrs Thatcher to carry the message to the CHOGM in Malaysia that the South Africans were releasing Walter Sisulu and five other prominent ANC detainees, in part no doubt a reward for British help in persuading the IMF to roll over South Africa's debt. Two years later Nelson Mandela attended the Harare CHOGM as a free man and a guest of the host, President Robert Mugabe.

HIGH AND LOW POLITICS, DOMESTIC PRIORITIES AND FOREIGN GOALS

If Mrs Thatcher's abrasive style introduced an unusual, and for many, unwelcome *frisson* into Commonwealth summits, her performance was generally popular with the party faithful at home. Commonwealth-bashing, particularly around conference time – the CHOGM usually follows close on the heels of the annual party conferences – is a favourite sport of the Conservative right wing, and Mrs Thatcher's press secretary, Bernard Ingham, was always careful to portray his mistress as standing robustly and often alone against the serried ranks of bleeding-heart liberals. The British tabloid press stood to attention and cheered.

Britain was certainly not alone, however, in using the CHOGM to pursue domestic political goals and play to a domestic audience. It is often remarked that Commonwealth summits take on the atmosphere of the city in which they are held. To some extent, no doubt, particular places weave their spell, a process which is encouraged for reasons of national honour and prestige as well as for baser motives by the determined efforts of the host government to create a carnival mood surrounding the proceedings.

On a more mundane level each CHOGM provides opportunities to the host government and its regional neighbours to press their own concerns. Whether these are matters of high or low politics will depend on time and place. What is low politics for one of the major countries may also be of great political significance for the small island countries of the South Pacific. But it will also depend on whether a government sees domestic advantage in cutting a figure on the world stage, or views the CHOGM as a way of solving a local problem. Thus in 1985 the Prime Minister of the Bahamas, who was widely believed to have been implicated in drug-trafficking, deflected the charges and made much of the need for protection of vulnerable island countries who could not alone avoid being used as staging posts in the illegal trade. In 1987 Canada, for whose fragile national identity the Commonwealth has always been important, concentrated on the South African issue with the tacit purpose of challenging Britain and building up credit in Africa and the Third World. In 1989 Dr Mahatir, the prime minister of Malaysia, used the conference to announce his conversion from Commonwealth critic to enthusiastic supporter, while the proximity of the CHOGM to Hong Kong allowed the local media to campaign vigorously on behalf of the democracy movement there. In 1991 Robert Mugabe sought to move the summit away from its single-issue preoccupation with South Africa, and arguably to deflect criticism of Zimbabwe's *de facto* one-party state by championing the new Commonwealth enthusiasm for monitoring democratic elections and protecting human rights. In 1993 the Cyprus government was clearly interested in hosting the conference as a way of reminding the world of its unresolved conflict with Turkey, which has occupied the northern part of the island since 1974. It is difficult to know how effectively the Commonwealth serves these and other domestic policy goals of its members, although since there is never a shortage of volunteers to host the next CHOGM the exercise is presumably held to be worthwhile.

In two other ways the CHOGM allows Commonwealth member states to pursue domestic and foreign policy goals simultaneously. First, the summit provides opportunities for bilateral lobbying and 'behind-the-scene' talks. Both the heads of government and their foreign ministers spend much of their time outside the plenary sessions closeted with their opposite numbers from countries with which they are either in conflict or share a particular common interest that they wish to promote. For example, while India has always refused to have the Kashmir dispute, which it regards as an internal matter, become the subject of Commonwealth debate, the CHOGM has sometimes provided useful cover for informal discussions with Pakistan, and the passing of messages between the two governments without risking a domestic backlash. South Pacific island countries have used the Commonwealth to build coalitions at the United Nations and elsewhere for pressing the case for controls on dragnet fishing; as have Caribbean countries, led by Prime Minister Manley of Jamaica, in urging the wider international community to create a drug-monitoring facility.

Secondly, participation in summits is a source of domestic legitimacy, particularly for fragile democratic governments. Since the end of the cold war the major Western powers have been much less hesitant than previously in seeking to promote democracy, for example by attaching political conditions to the provision of economic and financial assistance. The implications of this trend for the future of the Commonwealth will be returned to shortly; here the point to note is that, where they are successful, restored democratic governments can look to the Commonwealth to buttress their legitimacy against their domestic opponents. Benazir Bhutto went out of her way to use the CHOGM in this way, both after her initial victory in the Pakistan elections of 1989 and again in 1993.

THE FUTURE TRAJECTORY

What conclusions can be offered on the basis of these reflections about the likely future development of Commonwealth summits? Two seem likely to prove uncontroversial. First, Commonwealth summits will continue. The Commonwealth cannot seriously pretend to be a regime (in the sense that this word is customarily used in the academic literature), but it is certainly an institution, an association of states which are not necessarily like-minded but which find the historical accident that has brought them together useful for a wide variety of continuing reasons. Moreover, the compromise between ritual and routine which is almost certainly a pre-condition of survival for any modern institution, seems sufficiently well balanced to give the Commonwealth an underlying stability. If the CHOGM was called upon to play a more central role in world affairs, its continuing stability might be in doubt, but it is supported by the fact that the Commonwealth costs so little compared with other international organizations; that acting through its Secretariat, it does useful if unspec-tacular work, and that the bureaucratic absurdities and inefficiencies of which it is sometimes accused, pale into insignificance when compared with the Byzantine proliferation, inflation and rigidity which characterizes the United Nations and its agencies.

The second conclusion – already borne out in the preparation for the New Zealand CHOGM in November 1995 – is that the summits will be adjusted downwards, from the original leisurely week-long format, to three to four days, essentially a long weekend. This relative downgrading reflects the increasingly crowded official diaries and changing priorities of the larger Commonwealth countries. The consequence of shorter summits will almost certainly be more intensive preparation by the com-mittee of officials and the enlargement of the scope of routine business which does not have to be brought to the summit. The corollary will be a strengthening of the symbolic over the substantive functions of the CHOGM.

It is less easy to predict with confidence whether Commonwealth summits, scaled down in this way, will suffer from the absence of a high profile political issue to focus their discussions. Now that South Africa need no longer dominate the agenda, what is to take its place? There is, of course, no shortage of issues – for instance, the environment, Third World debt or drugs – on which high-level international dialogue, particularly North–South dialogue, is urgently required. The trouble is that it is not obvious that the Commonwealth, as an organization, has a comparative advantage in dealing with them. It may indeed be able to bring together a useful cross-section of relevant expertise and interests on all these issues, as it did during the 1970s in the debates over the feasibility of creating a New International Economic Order, but there must be some doubt as to whether this will be sufficient to engage the interest of heads of state and so create the mandate for the Commonwealth's functional work. The problem is compounded by the fact that while the capacity to act on these issues exists independently of Commonwealth summit meetings, it can probably only be mobilized at them.

The fashionable answer to the question about the post-South Africa agenda of Commonwealth summits is that future CHOGMs should devote themselves to the reconstruction of a genuine Commonwealth civil society. In calling for a 'new multilateralism' as a necessary solution to the functioning of international society and the dissolution of the 'peace dividend' following the end of the cold war, the Secretary General has suggested that the Commonwealth is well placed to play a strong supporting role to the United Nations.

We are also an organization which operates on the basis of great intimacy and camaraderie. This is made possible by the informality of our organization, its minimalist structure, a common language and a shared commitment to values such as democracy, human rights and the rule of law. These characteristics are useful in a world where there is an increasing realization that security, democracy and development are inextricably linked.[12]

Indeed they would be were these common values as securely grounded as the Secretary General suggests. Were there a genuine international civil society rather than an international society of states, some of whose organizations such as the Commonwealth share some aspects of civility, the summits would be the official counterpart of, say, the regular transnational meetings that take place between European social democrats and Christian democrats – in other words, between like-minded political parties. In these circumstances the CHOGM would be a celebration by a group of liberal states of their joint faith.

Unfortunately this is not an accurate description of the contemporary Commonwealth. It does have significant achievements to its credit: the fact that only two (when the Secretary General wrote) now alas three of its 50 members have military governments may not be quite a gilt-edged assurance of a post-communist world made safe for democracy, but is certainly better than a Commonwealth in which a third or so of its member states were governed by men who gained power by the use or threat of violence. The good offices of the Commonwealth have also been regularly sought for both the preparation and monitoring of multi-party elections. While governments from both North and South were unenthusiastic when the Secretary General called for a new humanitarian order at the Cyprus CHOGM, peer pressure may nonetheless impose some restrictions on unrepresentative leaders. Certainly those with a questionable record on human rights tend to stay away.

At the same time there are dangers in positing a value consensus for such a heterogeneous collection of states. A number of Commonwealth governments – Singapore, Malaysia and India – have made no secret of their attachment to Asian values rather than universal rights. If too public an attempt is made to make the CHOGM a forum for the debate of international standards an inevitable consequence will be that Commonwealth summits will become targets for non-governmental organizations and opposition groups who wish to mobilize international support against their own governments.

Even the Commonwealth commitment to democracy is problematic. If only democratic states are eligible for membership – and with the conditions set for the entry of the Cameroons, a step has already been taken in this direction – what is to happen if and when a democratic government falls from grace, or if the transfer of power from a military to a democratically elected civilian government is aborted, as in Nigeria in 1994?[13] It may be too logical to demand that conditions for membership should be matched by sanctions for non-compliance, but if it is to survive the Commonwealth will require not merely intimacy and camaraderie based on common values, but delicacy of judgement when applying them. This is a traditional function of diplomacy, and one that the Commonwealth has generally discharged well. It should not be lost sight of in the search for new directions.

NOTES AND REFERENCES

1. Dennis Austin, *The Commonwealth and Britain, Chatham House Papers, 41* (London, Routledge and Kegan Paul, 1988), p. 19.
2. The constitutional position in this regard was formalized in the Statute of Westminster in December 1931. For the text see A.B. Keith (ed.), *Speeches and Documents on the British Dominions, 1918–1931: From Self Government to National Sovereignty* (Oxford, OUP, 1938), pp. 303–7. This volume also contains a valuable series of documents (pp. 311–51) relating to the external relations and defence of the Empire (1923–31).
3. The developments leading to the withdrawal of South Africa from the Commonwealth are documented in Nicholas Mansergh (ed.), *Documents and Speeches on Commonwealth Affairs, 1952–1962* (Oxford, OUP, 1963), pp. 306–400.
4. See Peter Lyon, 'The Commonwealth and the Third World' in Robert O'Neill and R. J. Vincent (eds), *The West and the Third World* (London, Macmillan), pp. 173–207.
5. Much of the period surveyed in this chapter has been dealt with in greater detail by Stephen Chan in Jonathan Alun (ed.), *Twelve Years of*

Commonwealth Diplomatic History: Commonwealth Summit Meetings (Lewiston/Queenstown/Lampeter, The Edward Mellen Press, 1992).

6. For the text of the communiqué, see Austin, *The Commonwealth and Britain*, Appendix D, pp. 70–4.
7. Details of the Contributions to the Secretariat, the Commonwealth Fund for Technical Cooperation (CFTC), the Commonwealth Youth Programme (CYP) and the Commonwealth Science Council (CSC) are published in the Reports of the Commonwealth Secretary General to the Heads of Government. In 1993 the total was approximately £35m, of which the CFTC share was £22m.
8. Britain provides 30 per cent, Canada 15.07 per cent and Australia 8.07 per cent of the assessed contributions.
9. See Stephen Chan, *The Commonwealth in World Politics: A Study of International Action, 1965–85* (London, Lester Crook Academic Publishing, 1988), chapter 3.
10. *The Round Table*, October 1993, p. 372.
11. See Chan, *Twelve Years of Commonwealth Diplomatic History*, pp. 29–33.
12. Chief Emeka Anyaoku, *The Commonwealth and the New Multilateralism*, The Centre for the Study of Global Governance, LSE, Public Lecture no. 4, 1994.
13. Nigeria's membership was suspended at the Auckland summit in November 1995 after the military government had refused to respond to the unanimous request of the Heads of Government that it should refrain from executing Ken Sara Wiwa and eight other human rights activists. See James Mayall, 'Judicial murder puts democratic values on trial', *The World Today*, vol. 51, no. 12 (Dec. 1995), pp. 236–8.

9 African Summitry
Richard Hodder-Williams

I

The role of summits in the international politics of post-colonial Africa must be seen within a context dominated by five factors. The first derives from the very process of decolonization itself. As the colonial flags came down and the new flags of the independent states rose to replace them, the formal powers and institutions were transferred from European states to the African states themselves, but this inheritance consisted of precisely those arrangements and links which had hitherto served the imperial states. Few involved long and well-developed understandings between countries, and the African states had little actual physical presence, in the form of embassies or High Commissions, in other sovereign states within the continent. Existing lines of communication were overwhelmingly limited to those between what was now an independent country and the former metropolitan power, because virtually the last responsibility to be handed over in the extended process of transferring power was control of foreign relations.[1] Hence, the new states of Africa had to construct their foreign relations (as well as their foreign policies) *de novo*. What forms these would take and who would dominate them were initial questions of major importance to be resolved.[2]

The second factor was the paucity of trained diplomats. Colonial governments turned to this aspect of the governmental apparatus late in their hasty preparations for independence, although the training of diplomats became one of the most conscious aspects of the government-sponsored aid programmes in the 1960s and early 1970s.[3] The lack of experienced diplomats had several consequences. The first generation of ambassadors and high commissioners were patronage appointments, often reflecting an individual's contribution to the ruling party's success in acquiring power. This tradition, more American than British, continued in most countries so that it developed into a convention; sometimes appointments were rewards, sometimes strategic ways of removing difficult political opponents in a civilized manner. The results were, inevitably given the large numbers of people and countries involved, varied. Essentially, however, this convention strengthened the hand of executive presidents, who often used their representatives in foreign countries either as personal emissaries or merely as guardians of diplomatic niceties. When important policy questions arose or crises blew up, the norm was for the diplomats to be bypassed.

Third, most of the new states of Africa lacked clear goals in the area of foreign relations. Some, it is true, were concerned to alter inherited borders (such as Somalia) and all were determined to make real their independence. But little thought had been given to specific policies even in these areas. Given the nature of African nationalism, this was hardly surprising.[4] The struggle for independence had been governed by three factors: a determination to replace foreign rulers with indigenous rulers (which united the peoples of the new states), a competition to control the new state between rival parties (which divided the peoples of the new states), and a rivalry between the aspiring party leaders as to who would best symbolize the newly won independence. Although arguments over alignment and non-alignment divided the intellectual leadership in some countries, they barely resonated with the people and found little place in any detailed planning of foreign policy needs and priorities.[5] These arguments would emerge after independence, mostly in the crucible of crises and the instrumental context of immediate domestic needs. While it would be an exaggeration to say that foreign policy was initially made entirely 'on the hoof', it tended to be made at the highest level as and when necessary.

In the fourth place, there was widespread determination to express the newly acquired sovereignty in a clear and visible manner. This necessitated proactive statements and actions and required the new state to introduce policies independent of, and different from, those of their colonial masters. Quiet diplomacy, although it might be the most effective way of ensuring flows of suitable aid and other support in the international community, did not strike the right kind of stance, one appropriate to a sovereign state. It was important that a country's leader be seen to be an international figure in his own right, listened to in the capitals of the world, and apparently active on urgent business in concert with fellow African heads of government. Pageantry confers status; bilateral meetings resulting in concords suggest action and progress; conferences give evidence of sovereignty. Beneficial results did sometimes occur, but the emphasis on action was in itself an important part of asserting independence.

Finally, there was the need to show competence. The transfer of power had not been universally supported in the metropolitan countries and African leaders were aware that they were to some extent on trial before the court of international public opinion. More immediately, they were determined to find African solutions to African problems, to show that political leaders could be statesmen in resolving continental conflicts, and to move forward the pan-African ideals which had been so important (differently though they may have been interpreted) during the movement towards independence.[6] This was, of course, linked with the need felt to express sovereignty, but it was something more than that; it was a determination to wrest from the European powers the dominant role in mediating between warring factions in Africa and imposing solutions, as it was also a determination to take the initiative in locating Africa's position within the world. Whether the superpowers would permit such aspirations remained to be seen.

This, then, is the context in which the new states of Africa began their international politics. The problems to which answers were needed were both entirely predictable (such as the difficulties posed for development by the continent's position on the periphery of the world economic system and its essentially competing, rather than complementary, economies) and often the logical consequences of the imperial powers' unfinished – or ignored – business (such as the disintegration of the Congo or the border disputes between Kenya and Somalia).[7] The means to cope with these issues were either inherited (and largely inadequate) or had to be constructed. The context which I have sketched out here almost inevitably ensured that the means would be a series of *ad hoc* meetings of heads of government. There were as yet no alternative structures, no continent-wide mediating organization (especially between anglophone and francophone countries), no long-established channels of diplomatic communication, no tradition of interstate transactions such as dominated the European experience. What made summitry virtually inevitable, however, was an additional factor, the political culture and decision-making process of the new African states themselves.

II

The constitutions which Britain and France bequeathed to Africa were highly centralized ones.[8] Power was concentrated in both systems, either through the presidential model associated with France or the sovereign parliament with disciplined majority party associated with Britain. Exaggerating the institutional forces tending towards the centralization of power was the status, and in consequence the authority, of the national leader. Personal rule aptly describes the norm in Africa.[9] There were variations, ranging from the highly authoritarian to the more consensual, but the empirical reality was that people and activists expected, and permitted, the leader to dominate policy-making. Within a short while, those leaders accepted the expectation and acted accordingly. Despite the fact that personal rule was the norm, rather than the exception, the 'people' – so frequently elevated as the fountain of wisdom and legitimacy, yet as frequently ignored – appear to operate schizophrenically by supporting a powerful leader when in office, but quickly excoriating him when fallen.[10] However, it is not of great importance that many African leaders' legitimacy had shallow roots; the reality was that they exercised enormous powers.

In foreign affairs, this was particularly true. I draw attention to just two instances. In West Africa, Nkwame Nkrumah and Modibo Keita were committed rhetorically (and, indeed, ideologically) to an Africa undivided by 'artificial' colonial boundaries and decided to create, as a first stage towards a United Africa, a union between their two countries, Ghana and Mali. But the federation was effectively stillborn, a memorial to ambition and hubris for which both men later suffered. More successful was the union of Tanganyika and Zanzibar into the United Republic of Tanzania. But this was the work of Julius Nyerere and Abeid Karume operating with virtually no consultation and without any obvious sense of obligation to their parties or legislatures.[11] Both felt that they had the right, and the necessary authority, to go ahead unilaterally. In each of these examples, the leaders judged correctly that there would be no recriminations from their supporters.

These were occasions when African leaders could operate unilaterally. For the most part, however, they could only advance their nations' interests by reacting to the behaviour of others, or bargaining with stronger states. Their objectives and conventional resources were small. Among the tropical African states, only Nigeria and Ethiopia had substantial populations; none of the states independent in the 1960s had major mineral resources; oil was not exploited in any quantities until the middle 1970s; the strategic significance of most states was minimal (and the cold war tended to be more an excuse for external interference than an opportunity to bargain profitably); and none was strong militarily. There may be a few instances where individual states did temporarily enjoy the resources to influence directly the thrust of the developed world's policy in Africa (Nigeria's relations with Britain over Southern Rhodesia are a case in point), but the general rule has been that African states acting individually have carried little weight.[12]

Quite naturally, therefore, African leaders emphasized those organizations which, for the most part, weighted states equally, regardless of population, economy or military strength. The United Nations was consequently employed as a forum in which an African view could be expressed and in which votes could regularly be taken to embarrass the Great Powers. By operating as a bloc, often with other post-colonial states, individual weakness could be translated into a certain degree of collective influence. Similarly, and some might argue more beneficially, African members of the Commonwealth used the annual heads of government meetings to exploit their numerical advantage and bring pressure to bear upon British governments.[13] These were, in effect, summits. The passions evident at the Singapore meeting left such an indelible mark on Conservative politicians that Lusaka could thrust a doubtful Mrs Thatcher into the Lancaster House negotiations from which Zimbabwe was born.[14] In these high-profile occasions, African leaders could ensure that their perspectives were at least heard, if not always accepted.

It can be seen, therefore, that for the majority of African states, summits would inevitably become central to their foreign policy performances. The status and aspirations of leaders, the need for collective action, the psychological attachment to the ideal of pan-Africanism, the lack of alternative and developed structures for exerting influence, all together provided a cumulative pressure which made summits essential resources for political leaders. Only a few mavericks, such as Malawi's President Banda, shunned such occasions and even he found it necessary to employ summitry from time to time.[15] Being so central to international politics does not, of course, ensure success and the history of summitry in post-independent Africa is a story of failures as much as of successes.

III

In the immediate aftermath of independence, however, leaders sought to create an organizational structure which would be uniquely African and which would provide the opportunity for continent-wide policies to be made at the highest level. Some leaders wanted a powerful, even federal structure, so that the pan-Africanist ideal might be translated into policies binding over all its members; others, the majority, favoured something less ambitious. In July 1963, perhaps the most important of all African summits took place in Addis Ababa where 27 heads of government ultimately agreed on the establishment of the Organization of African Unity, an association of sovereign states pledged – but not bound – to the acceptance of politics emanating from the organization.[16] Its most powerful body, indeed the only body with the authority to make decisions in its name, was the Assembly of Heads of State and Government. Each year (except for 1982 when Libyan intransigence kept enough states away to deny the occasion its quorum) there has in effect been a summit of African heads of government.[17]

A good deal can be learned about individual countries from observing their leaders' treatment of these occasions. Some used them very much to posture and display power and wealth; thus President Mobutu's entourage was consistently larger and more obvious than other delegations. Initially, there was competition to host the annual gathering, because it indicated status within the continent. But the experience of Libya's turn as host, together with the costly expectation that the host country covered many of the costs, resulted in a decision to meet always in Addis Ababa. This created some embarrassments during the later part of Mengistu's rule, but it obviated the need to choose a chairman who both met with the approval of the great majority of leaders and headed a country with sufficient resources to manage a major international conference, which more and more countries became eligible to attend. By 1995 there were 51 members. Over time, the choice of chairman was more carefully taken, for the Assembly's agenda and tone are largely set by the chairman for the year and the policy proposals emanating from the Council of Ministers. And the chairman has become the continent's voice in the wider international community. Notwithstanding the dominant position of each current chairman, there has been a number of occasions (for example, at the time of the Nigerian civil war or the aftermath of the Portuguese evacuation of Angola) when the substantive outcomes of meetings have been due entirely to the arguments and positions of the leaders at the summit.

There had been many groupings of African leaders before the creation of the OAU, both in East Africa (such as PAFMECA – the Pan-African Freedom Movement for East and Central Africa; later PAFMECSA – the Pan-African Freedom Movement for East, Central and Southern Africa)[18] and in West Africa; and the pan-Africanist movement, whose origins go back at least to 1918, had brought together individuals (rather than states) from much, but by no means all, of the continent, alongside supporters from outside the continent altogether. The genesis of the Addis Ababa conference was quintessentially personalized diplomacy in which a limited number of high-profile leaders, through their direct contacts and the commitment and status of the Emperor Heile Selassie of Ethiopia, were the dominant movers. There was no consensus about the fundamental principles and goals that should underpin the new organization, some following Nkwame Nkrumah in an idealist commitment to a united states of Africa, others following Julius Nyerere in a pragmatic realization of the limitations imposed by the sovereignty of new states. The more cautious faction prevailed and the OAU was established with broad aims and a constitution which enshrined the inviolability of borders and the principle of non-interference in member states' internal affairs. These principles created problems which, as I shall show, the leaders had difficulties in resolving.

However, so far as African summitry is concerned, the critical principle was that the annual Assembly of the Heads of State and Government was the most significant body both in constitutional theory and in practice, because it was only in that forum that the leaders of the sovereign states met with the authority – backed by the culture of dominant executive presidents – to commit those states to action. For all the excellent work that sections of the OAU undoubtedly performed, when hard decisions had to be made, the responsibility lay clearly with the heads of government.

Just as the press has tended again and again to predict the demise of the Commonwealth, it has also regularly expressed surprise at the continuation and vitality of the OAU. For sure, it is not difficult to find deep tensions and failed policies. The OAU has failed to manage all the continent's border disputes. It took 20 separate votes at the Mogadishu meeting in 1974 to choose a new secretary-general. The recognition of the Saharawi Arab Democratic Republic led first to a boycott of the 1982 summit in Tripoli, and then to the resignation of Morocco (the only country to have left the OAU) and the temporary withdrawal of Zaire. The bitter disputes over the Libya–Chad border caused the rescheduled Tripoli summit to be inquorate again and resulted in the decision to hold all Heads of State and Government Meetings in Addis Ababa (although the enormous cost for host countries was an added reason). Policies over the isolation of Israel following the 1967 Arab–Israeli War, the breaking of economic relations with Britain over her failure to cope with Rhodesia's Unilateral Declaration of Independence, the refusal by some states to boycott apartheid South Africa, the inability either to resolve or even address civil wars (Nigeria and Sudan in the first case, Eritrea in the second), and the refusal to impose sanctions on the most tyrannical of governments, are all used to illustrate the weakness and ineffectiveness of the OAU.

Such an undilutedly negative evaluation sets absurdly high standards for an international organization of sovereign states. There are, as with all such organizations, lines of fission within its membership. Lines of cleavage can be geographical (Southern African concerns contrasted with those of West Africa, the Mahgreb with sub-Saharan Africa); linguistic (especially between francophone and anglophone countries); religious (the Muslim-majority states feeling more involved in the Arab–Israeli conflict than others); or ideological. These lines of fission are cross-cutting, not cumulative. And they become salient at different times, as issues – both within the continent and outside it – wax and wane. However, the fact of their existence should not obscure the powerful forces for fusion and unity. That there is still the annual Assembly of the Heads of State and Government of the OAU is a symbol of a genuine commitment to the idea of an Africa distinct from, and hopefully largely independent of, the rest of the world. This pan-African ideal is strong; indeed, its strength can be divisive precisely because so many Africans hold the ideal sacred and so dispute with passion how that ideal can be translated into reality. Nevertheless, the conception of a distinct Africa can hold countries together to face external threats, while at the same time embracing internal disagreements.

However, the OAU is more than a symbol. Its institutions, less reported and less visible, function across a wide spectrum of issue areas. Despite recurrent financial problems, networks of specialists proliferate (as in the Commonwealth), the Council of Ministers regularly meets to carry the heaviest burden of policy-making, specialist institutions (such as the Pan-African News Agency) seek to limit continental dependence upon the North. And the permanent secretariat, for all its weaknesses of poor nomi-nations, unreliable finances and lack of authority, is occupied in putting together composite resolutions, briefing the chairman, attending multilat-eral conferences and representing the continent in many international fora. Nor should the African Development Bank be forgotten. Despite its imperfections, it has contributed both directly and indirectly to economic development within the continent. At the level of 'low politics', then, the OAU (and this is true of the regional organizations as well) performs a wide range of extremely useful functions; it is easy to criticize and there must be doubts about cost-effectiveness, but the aggregate interest of the continent has been enhanced by these activities.

Above all, however, the summits enable the continent's leaders to coor-dinate their activities at other gatherings such as the United Nations. Orchestrating attacks on the colonial powers, especially over Southern African issues, or agreeing upon nominations for important UN positions (for example, heads of relevant agencies like UNESCO or even the secretary-generalship itself) significantly enhance the effectiveness of Africa as a whole and, through bloc-voting, the individual states within it. It is relevant that the OAU funds permanent missions in New York and Geneva as well as in Addis Ababa and Lagos. The current chairman represents the continent not only at formal meetings of the United Nations but as a world ambassador in European capitals. For 'high politics', where the votes of African states are needed in international organizations, the annual Assembly of Heads of State and Government is invaluable; it can harmonize actions in the wider world. And the ideological determination to ensure that Africa's political problems are resolved by African politicians has, notwithstanding some involvement by the superpowers in limited parts of the continent and the French as supporters of special domestic factions, been largely successful; there may have been some Cuban soldiers and Russian advisers in Angola and Ethiopia in the 1970s, and Western support in the more conservative states, but, for good or ill, the continent's leaders have largely succeeded in keeping outsiders out. This is not to say that Africa managed to exclude the Great Powers from exercising influence, especially in the economic sphere, but it has ensured that their physical presence was kept to a limited number of diplomats and advisers.

While the failures to which I have alluded are real, the successes, especially mediation between states, are far more numerous. Normally, mediation is carried out through *ad hoc* summit meetings at which OAU nominees attempt to broker solutions. A random selection of these might include President Eyadama's mission in 1969 to heal the rift between the two Congos; President Kaunda's chairing of meetings (with Nyerere and Obote as observers) between Kenyatta and Egal over Kenya–Somali border problems; the endorsement at the 1975 meeting in Kampala that the presidents of Tanzania, Zambia, Botswana and Mozambique (the original Front Line States) should negotiate with South Africa over Rhodesia; the successful mediation of the Mali–Burkina Faso border dispute in 1985; as well as the time-consuming – although ultimately unsuccessful – mediation work of President Bongo in the Libya–Chad dispute and the Consultative Commission in the Nigerian civil war.

The most tangible success of the OAU has been the elimination of white minority rule in Southern Africa. A multi-faceted strategy contributed to this. Central has been the Liberation Committee, based in Dar es Salaam, which has funnelled resources to selected liberation movements (recognition for which usually followed summit gatherings between aspiring leaders and major heads of state within the OAU) and overseen much training. The Lusaka Manifesto, approved by the 1968 Heads of State and Government Meeting, set out a continental policy towards decolonization which was largely followed.[19] The establishment of another *ad hoc* group of countries, the Front Line States, closely involved in combatting apartheid in South Africa ensured that the generalized support expressed at full OAU meetings was infused, often through individual membership of other international groupings such as the Commonwealth, into a wider community. The cumulative impact, expressed largely through heads of government either severally or together, was substantial and undoubtedly contributed significantly to the collapse of the Portuguese Empire, to a more robust British policy over Rhodesia than would otherwise have been the case, the peaceful decolonization of Namibia and the constellation of forces which was responsible for the transition to majority rule in South Africa. Other pressures and other actors were necessary to ensure the collapse of white minority rule, but the OAU – and related groupings of heads of government – played an important part.

While the 1960s and 1970s were dominated by intra-continental conflicts and the commitment to continental liberation, the 1980s were devoted much more to economic and social concerns. The 1980 Lagos meeting may be seen as something of a turning point in this respect. By then, the optimism of the 1960s (shared by North and South alike) had dissipated and given way to the pessimism underlying World Bank reports or Willy Brandt's call for a North–South dialogue.[20] At Lagos, the meeting approved a plan of action which set out an ambitious programme of economic reconstruction for the continent and envisaged an African common market by the year 2000. Thereafter, one of the very rare extraordinary meetings of heads of state and government, in late 1987, was devoted exclusively to the debt problem; discussions increasingly took the problems of women and children, for example, far more seriously; attention was paid to the African Economic Recovery Programme, although the central importance of non-African actors (such as commercial banks, multilateral organizations like the World Bank and International Monetary Fund, and government aid agencies) made the leaders' discussions largely ineffective; the 1981 Nairobi gathering approved a Charter of Human and People's Rights which had, by 1986, received the ratification of the necessary two-thirds of the membership to come into force and the African Commission on Human and People's Rights was approved in 1987 (to be located in Banjul) and to be composed of 11 eminent Africans 'known for their high morality, integrity and impartiality'; in June 1991 a treaty was signed to create the African Economic Community, to come into force after the normal two-thirds ratification rule had been met, which would establish a common market within 34 years (in other words, by 2025) building first upon regional cooperation.

This reflects the ongoing debate which had divided Nkrumah and Nyerere more than 30 years earlier. It revolves around two strategic issues. One disputes the rival priorities of the political and the economic. For Nkrumah and his supporters, political unity and political power were the prerequisites for any genuine economic or social development in the continent; for Nyerere and his supporters, economic development was of such immediate and central importance that it had to take precedence over more ideological – though desirable – goals such as continental unity. The Nkrumah view is still held by some, especially former secretaries-general like Edem Kodjo, who have experienced how the dead hand of sovereign interests and the tied hands of boundary immutability impose a conservative dominance over possible solutions. Paradoxically, Nyerere was prepared to impose economic costs on his own Tanzania for the sake of political purity. By the 1980s, however, the great majority of African leaders were committed to solving economic problems at home (even if that meant accepting Structural Adjustment Programmes and instituting more democratic forms of governance). OAU summits were important in legitimizing, and encouraging, this development.

The second strategic issue disputes the relative advantages of regional economic blocs and a single African market. Nkrumah feared, and with justification, that the emphasis on regional groupings would dilute a sense of continental unity; Nyerere believed that no other form of cooperation was feasible. The 1991 Assembly of Heads of State and Government explicitly lent its support to regional groupings as the basis for a common market a generation away in the future. Certainly, there has been a resurgence of interest in regional associations, and their root problems – sovereignty and pride, competitive rather than complementary economies, tradition and existing lines of credit and markets – have at least been addressed, if rarely resolved. But innovation, in Africa as elsewhere in the world, is a great deal more difficult to achieve in bad economic times than when economies are growing. Nevertheless, the diplomatic timetable for heads of governments in Africa is a congested one. The calendar has to make room – just to select some of the more significant gatherings – for meetings of the Economic Community of West African States (all the more important with its military commitment to Liberia), the Afro-Malagasy Joint Organization, the East African Community and Preferential Trade Area, the Regional Summit of East and Central African States, the East and Central African Security Summit, the Southern African Development Co-ordination Conference, not to mention the wider groupings such as the Commonwealth, the Non-Aligned States and the United Nations.

The attention to economic cooperation, transport, communications and trade, refugees and rights, women and children has spawned a large number of bilateral and regional gatherings. But it remains the case that it needs the authority of the heads of governments to iron out differences and impose uniform policies, things which bureaucratic negotiation cannot achieve by itself. Indeed, it is expected that the critical choices and bargains will be made at summits, with the most important issues being considered at the Assembly of Heads of State and Government, or even at a specially called extraordinary meeting. While it is hard not to conclude that these occasions have failed to resolve all Africa's problems (indeed, it would be odd if they could have done), it is almost certainly the case that many problems that were solved would not have been solved without the institution of the summit in its various forms.

IV

Summits may be regular, as with the OAU or other regional organizations, or *ad hoc*, as with attempts to settle the Nigerian civil war or advance independence in Southern Africa. They are necessary because the dominant, even domineering, players in the game of international politics are heads of state. They are also often successful precisely because the same individuals carry so much weight in their own countries' policy-making process. The ideology which underpins this is the presumption that the state's coercive powers are available and sufficient to settle disputes internal to a country and that political will is normally enough to achieve goals. The principle of personal rule is built upon a very simple concept of power, in which authority can be used with virtually no constraints to impose rational policy preferences on a people. This belief in the primacy of politics and of power was a natural consequence of the nationalist movements' successes before independence and the centralized constitutional structures which were inherited. It made good sense at the time; and it seemed to reflect reality as the heads of government made, and unmade, international organizations and resolved the initial conflicts with which they were faced.

As the years passed, however, the bilateral, personal diplomacy which dominated in the 1960s began to be less effective and less appropriate. Two developments account for the change in emphasis (for it is a change in *emphasis* rather than a break with previous practice). In the first place, the sense of unity engendered by the nationalist phase and symbolized by the creation of the OAU slowly broke down. The first generation of leaders did share a good deal and they respected each other, even when they disagreed (although Hastings Banda soon became a solo maverick). But the onset of military involvement after 1965 not only removed distinguished members of 'the Club', as it were; it also brought to power individuals who lacked political skills (or interest) and who governed in ways which forfeited respect. Julius Nyerere's refusal to be associated with Idi Amin doomed the East African Community (in trouble though it already was) and its demise, despite talented and committed civil servants, was certain once there was no possibility of holding summits. It certainly lends further weight to the argument that foreign policy initiatives depend overwhelmingly on the heads of government and their readiness to do business with one another.

The second development relates to the changing context in which African leaders operated. The conditions which effectively determined the limitations of actions in the early years of independence naturally altered over time and, as an inevitable consequence, both the agenda and the means of international politics changed. The issues concerned border disputes less and became broader, more concerned with economic matters than the control of the state, and demanded different means of prosecution. Thus the bureaucrats became more significant players, negotiating over time with the European Union in successive Lomé Conventions; with the IMF over structural adjustment programmes; with the metropolitan departments concerned with development aid over funding projects and debt adjustment; and with NGOs and UN agencies over refugees. The summit became less important, less appropriate, indeed less available. The structure of relationships was governed by the dominant partners in these negotiations and the dominant partners, overwhelmingly from the North, limited *their* summitry to states and issues far distant from African concerns. The OAU's heads of state asked for a special meeting with donor countries and organizations to discuss debt problems, but they were firmly told that other fora, both bilateral and multilateral, were perfectly adequate for the purpose.

While summitry may have diminished in significance, this must be seen as a matter of emphasis. Within the African continent itself, and where the issues remain distinctly African in content, the logic of personal rule and presidentialism prevails and the cultivation, indeed need, for summits increases. Taking 1994 alone, African presidents were busy meeting, not only in the standard set pieces (at the OAU, or SADCC, or ECOWAS gatherings) but also in the dyadic summits which are still at the heart of intra-continental diplomacy. The presidential entourage *en route* from airport to international hotel still demands the patient acquiescence of many ordinary folk by the roadside to cheer the visiting dignitary; and the meetings, which generated this disruption of the ordinary folk's lives, still remain as the primary method of resolving interterritorial disputes, or establishing bilateral policies of cooperation, often more cultural than economic. The domestic imperatives of individual political systems almost all press in this direction; and, until the dominance of personal rule is ended, they will continue to do so.

NOTES AND REFERENCES

1.   The paucity of diplomatic development is well caught and measured in David H. Johns, 'Diplomatic exchange and inter-state inequality in Africa: an empirical analysis', in Timothy M. Shaw and Kenneth A. Heard (eds.), *The Politics of Africa: dependence and development* (London, Longman, 1979), pp. 269–84. See also the same author's 'The "normalization" of intra-African diplomatic activity', *Journal of Modern African Studies*, vol. 10 (1972), pp. 597–610.
2.   See, generally, I. William Zartman, *International Relations in the New Africa* (Lanham MD, University Press of America, 1987) and Olajide Aluko, *The Foreign Policies of African States* (London, Hodder and Stoughton, 1977).
3.   The University of Oxford continues to provide a course for diplomats, despite the establishment of similarly targeted courses in places like the University of Nairobi.
4.   See Richard Hodder-Williams, *An Introduction to the Politics of Tropical Africa* (London, Allen and Unwin, 1984), pp. 69–76 for an overview of the complexities associated with this term and the references cited there.
5.   A classic exception to this was the competition between Tom Mboya and Oginga Odinga in Kenya in the late 1950s and early 1960s. See Tom Mboya, *Freedom and After* (London, Andre Deutsch, 1963) and Oginga Odinga, *Not Yet Uhuru* (London and Nairobi, Heinemann, 1967).
6.   See Colin Legum, *Panafricanism: a short political guide* (New York, Praeger, 1961).
7.   Catherine Hoskyns (ed.), *The Organisation of African Unity and the Congo Crisis 1964–65: case studies in African diplomacy: 1* (Oxford University Press for the Institute of Public Administration, University College, Dar es Salaam, 1969) and Catherine Hoskyns (ed.), *The Ethiopia–Somali–Kenya Dispute 1960–67: case studies in African diplomacy 2* (Oxford University Press for the Institute of Public Administration, University College, Dar es Salaam, 1969).
8.   See Hodder-Williams, *An Introduction to the Politics of Tropical Africa*, pp. 84–5.
9.   Robert H. Jackson and Carl G. Rosberg, *Personal Rule in Black Africa: prince, autocrat, prophet, tyrant* (Berkeley CA, University of California Press, 1982).
10.   See, for example, the remarkable transformation in Ghana at the overthrow of Nkwame Nkrumah, as reported in Jack Goody, 'Consensus and dissent in Ghana', *Political Science Quarterly*, vol. 83 (1968), pp. 337–52.
11.   Martin Bailey, 'Zanzibar's external relations', *International Journal of Politics*, vol. 4 (1974–5), pp. 35–57.

12. M. Tamarkin, *The Making of Zimbabwe: decolonization in regional and international politics* (London, Frank Cass, 1990), pp. 250–1.
13. The 1966 meeting in Lagos was called especially to discuss Rhodesia. See also two articles by Derek Ingram: 'Commonwealth Prime Ministers, 1969: the end of disenchantment?', *The Round Table*, no. 232 (1968), pp. 357–64 and 'The Commonwealth Meeting in Lusaka', *The Round Table*, no. 271 (1979), pp. 204–10.
14. Martyn Gregory, 'Rhodesia: from Lusaka to Lancaster House', *The World Today*, vol. 36 (1980), pp. 11–18; Tamarkin, *The Making of Zimbabwe*, pp. 247–67.
15. Carolyn McMaster, *Malawi: foreign policy and development* (London, Julian Friedmann, 1974).
16. See, generally, Zdenek Cervenka, *The Organisation of African Unity and its Charter* (London, C. Hurst, 1969).
17. An excellent review of the OAU's activities normally appears in the annual volume of *Africa Contemporary Record*.
18. Richard Cox, *Pan-Africanism in Practice: PAFMECSA 1958–1964* (Oxford University Press, for the Institute of Race Relations, 1964).
19. The Lusaka Manifesto can be found in *Africa Contemporary Record*.
20. For example, W. Brandt et al., *North–South: a programme for survival* (London, Pan Books, 1980) and World Bank, *Accelerated Development in sub-Saharan Africa* (Washington DC, World Bank, 1981).

10 Three Non-Aligned Summits – Harare 1986; Belgrade 1989 and Jakarta 1992
Sally Morphet

INTRODUCTION

The last three non-aligned summits before Cartagena (1995) cover a period in which non-aligned countries have had, like other political movements, to adapt their concerns to the post cold war era. It seems sensible therefore to consider all three. Harare in 1986, the eighth in the series of summits, which began in 1961, was the last one to be held before the cold war ended. The participants at Belgrade in 1989 were, by contrast, already beginning to discuss questions about the non-aligned movement in a changing world order, whilst Jakarta in 1992 was concerned with problems stemming from the end of the cold war as well as showing one way of achieving domestic economic growth. Indonesia gave up its leadership of the non-aligned late in 1995 when it handed over the chairmanship to Colombia at the eleventh summit which unusually, for reasons connected with the fiftieth anniversary of the UN, was held in October.

The number of non-aligned countries[1] has grown from 25 at their first summit in 1961 to 113 in late 1995. Since the 1961 summit at Belgrade, summits have been held at Cairo (1964), Lusaka (1970), Algiers (1973), Colombo (1976), Havana (1979), New Delhi (1983), Harare (1986), Belgrade (1989), Jakarta (1992) and Cartagena (1995).[2] The non-aligned have usually held these in late August/early September so that they can discuss the range of subjects which they will face (and introduce) at the forthcoming UN General Assembly (and also in the Security Council), and decide how best and at what level they should deal with them, both in these arenas and elsewhere, in the context of their common interests and aspirations in the foreign policy arena. As the non-aligned noted in the final paragraph of the 1992 Jakarta Message, 'A Call for Collective Action and the Democratization of International Relations':

> Since Bandung 37 years ago, we have consistently struggled for the realisation of our fundamental principles and objectives. As we chart our course for this decade and beyond, the Movement is committed to the shaping of a new international order, free from war, poverty, intolerance and injustice, a world based on the principles of peaceful coexistence and genuine interdependence, a world which takes into account the diversity of social systems and cultures. It should reflect global not separate interests. And it should be sought through the central and irreplaceable role of the United Nations. We, the members of the Non-Aligned Movement, holding fast to the principles and ideals as originally articulated by our founding fathers, do hereby affirm the fundamental human rights to development, social progress and the full participation of all in shaping the common destiny of humankind. Through dialogue and cooperation, we will project our Movement as a vibrant, constructive and genuinely interdependent component of the mainstream of international relations. Only then, can a new international order take shape on a truly universal basis, ensuring harmony, peace, justice and prosperity for all.[3]

The non-aligned movement has been the focal point for Third World discussion of their collective view of major global political and economic issues since the Belgrade summit in 1961. Established through the efforts of Tito, Nasser and Nehru, the movement was designed to find ways for weaker countries to influence the major powers, break down the bloc system and to further their foreign policy interests on such issues as disarmament, decolonization, apartheid, Palestine, Great Power military bases, natural resources and economic development in the context of UN Charter principles. The non-aligned countries continue to find their summits useful and relevant.[4] They, like other world actors, have attempted to adapt in the changing post cold war climate. They have adjusted to the demise of the Soviet Union[5] and, more recently, were glad to welcome South Africa as a member of their movement at their foreign ministers' conference in Cairo in June 1994. This represented a major triumph after long years of campaigning. A number of countries, the most important of which is China,[6] play a role as Observers in the movement (this means that they have access to most of the conference and could, if all agreed, become full members of the movement). Guests of the movement now include 10 out of 15 members of the EU. Guests cannot become members of the movement since they are members of Great Power alliances. Like the Observers, they also have some access during the conferences, as do a number of Guest organizations such as the International Committee of the Red Cross (ICRC). A number of Eastern European countries and countries stemming from the former Soviet Union are now Guests. Russia, itself, sought admission as a Guest at the Cairo foreign ministers' conference in May/June 1994. The non-aligned decided to postpone their decision about its application, and Russia became a Guest at Cartagena.

The non-aligned have always worked to some extent through regional groups. These groups are similar to those now in operation at the UN except in the case of Europe. These include Africa, Asia, Europe[7] and Latin America. Liberation movements have also been represented at non-aligned meetings. Meetings of other groupings (Mediterranean members of the non-aligned and labour ministers, for example) have also been set up when appropriate. The non-aligned have, deliberately, never been exclusively regional in their decision-making. This arrangement has helped certain members of regional groups, such as the PLO, who have not always been given total regional support; they have therefore had to rely on support from other groups, which has been more consistent overall. The non-aligned share much of the same membership as the larger Group of 77,[8] founded in 1964. This deals exclusively with economic issues and is based on UN regional groupings. A Joint Coordinating Committee of both bodies has been in operation since the end of 1994. New ideas have usually moved from the non-aligned to the Group of 77 (indeed some of these ideas can also be found in the communiqués agreed at Commonwealth Heads of Government meetings) rather than vice versa.

Each summit, like other non-aligned meetings, produces a number of lengthy documents outlining non-aligned positions on a number of political and economic issues. The Harare[9] documents were 391 pages long. The Belgrade[10] documents were deliberately designed to be much shorter: they cover 153 pages. The Jakarta[11] documents were 141 pages. Most of the subjects discussed are dealt with in the Political and Economic Committees which are set up at the beginning of each major meeting. Summits are preceded by meetings of senior officials and foreign ministers. The chairmanship is handed over to the incoming country during the foreign ministers meeting. At Jakarta these latter meetings were held from 29–31 August 1992. The summit itself lasted from 1–6 September. One hundred of a possible 108 members (over 60 at head of state level) attended, as well as 8 Observer countries and 8 Observer organizations, and 21 Guest countries and 21 Guest organizations.

The following discussion of the questions raised can be no more than illustrative. Non-aligned summits usually touch on all the significant policy questions of the day and include both high and low politics. The non-aligned can perhaps be compared to the G-7 in the sense that they discuss major global political and economic issues.

To what extent are summits mainly symbolic and to what extent are they substantive? Are they just an opportunity for a photo-call or are they more often than not the venue and opportunity for substantial dialogue?

All non-aligned summits have attempted to be both symbolic and substantive. They have always dealt with substantive questions. Some have had much more symbolic content than others.

Harare 1986   The summit at Harare was deliberately chosen as the venue of the eighth summit at the non-aligned foreign ministers' meeting at Luanda in 1985 for symbolic reasons. The location was designed to focus the attention of the world on the continuing intractable problem of South Africa. This remained one of the two major regional political problems of concern to the non-aligned – the other being Palestine/Israel. And the meeting did indeed succeed in focusing increased symbolic attention on the issues of Southern Africa, particularly those of South Africa. But there was also, as usual, tremendous concern with substance. The choice of Zimbabwe as summit host ensured a realistic approach to the problems within Southern Africa. The Indians, who wished for a tougher line, were unable to break the cohesion of the Front Line States on the need for a careful approach to the question of sanctions. Their initiative in setting up the AFRICA Fund to help the Front Line States was, however, welcomed.

Belgrade 1989   The choice of Belgrade to provide the next chairman of the non-aligned at the Nicosia foreign ministers' meeting in 1988 did not have the symbolism that had been so important in the case of Harare. Both Yugoslavia and Cyprus were put in the running as compromise candidates after the two official candidates, Nicaragua and Indonesia, were asked to withdraw their bids for 1989 on the understanding that the summit would go to a candidate representing the European group. Belgrade was a more substantive summit in that the Yugoslavs pressed through changes in order to help the movement adapt to the changed international climate. This included an attempt to make the movement more understandable to non–non-aligned countries by producing a short Declaration[12] covering the main concerns of the non-aligned besides giving greater priority to human rights and the UN.

Jakarta 1992 The south-east Asian setting for Jakarta was, in a different way, as symbolic for the non-aligned as Harare had been. The credentials of the non-aligned, particularly Indonesia, had been strengthened by Indonesian participation as one of the co-chairman in the negotiations leading to the Agreements on Cambodia which had finally been reached in October 1991.[13] These efforts signalled the new determination by groups of non-aligned countries to participate even more actively in the solution of long-standing regional problems including South Africa and Palestine. The symbolism of action not words was also enhanced by the increasing significance given to the economic development of the main south-east Asian participants – Indonesia, Malaysia and Singapore.

This symbolism was also expressed in substantive concerns. The non-aligned countries' resolve to exert more influence on the UN system was expressed in their commitment to strengthening their UN coordination, and their decision to establish the high-level Working Group on UN restructuring, as well as in their decisions concerning the establishment of a Joint Coordinating Committee with the Group of 77 and the reactivation of the Ministerial Committee for Economic Cooperation. They also decided to continue to use the South Commission as a think-tank and to establish an *ad hoc* advisory group of experts to suggest policy guidelines on the debt problem.

To what extent is the substance of the summit negotiations largely concluded before the meeting takes place? Are they 'pre-cooked' or free-ranging? How much scope is there for individual participants to make a difference as a result of summit meetings?

The non-aligned have always covered many political and economic foreign policy issues. The range can be roughly illustrated by counting the main headings used in the summit documents which, at these three summits were, respectively, 70, 45 and 56. The first draft of the documents is prepared by the incoming non-aligned country in the chair. Since the early 1980s the drafters have usually tried to steer a middle course between right and left so that one cancels out the other as they battle between themselves. This has meant that the final documents remain in the moderate mainstream mould. The incoming chairman sends the first draft to members some six weeks before the meeting is due to take place. A second draft is sometimes circulated just before the meeting.

Participants then put in numerous amendments (usually about a hundred to each) to the Political and Economic Committees. The major issues are dealt with at the summit itself if disagreements have not been resolved at either senior official or foreign minister level.

Harare 1986   The first drafts of the Political and Economic Declarations by the Zimbabweans were well drafted both in terms of content and tactically: they were designed to appeal to the sophisticated mainstream of the movement (Yugoslavia, India, Algeria, Indonesia, Egypt etc.). This meant, as turned out to be the case, that amendments from the left (Cuba, Nicaragua etc.) could be played off against those from the right (Saudi Arabia, Singapore etc.) particularly in relation to the Political Declaration.

At the senior officials meeting new items were suggested by the left – non-aggression and non-use of force in international relations (Iran); state terrorism and US threats against Arab states (Syria); and US aggression against Libya (Libya). None of these was accepted although the senior officials had undertaken to consider written suggestions. These points were remade at the next foreign minister level meeting and then referred separately to the summit. Ultimately both these final Declarations were changed less than the drafts prepared for the previous two summits (Havana 1979, and New Delhi 1983).

The most controversial subject remaining to be decided at the end of the conference was the decision on the locations for the next foreign minister and summit meetings. The decision to postpone the decision on the site of the next summit was relatively easy. The decision as to the site of the next foreign ministers' meeting at which North Korea was the only formal candidate, Libya having withdrawn, was much more difficult. In the early hours of the morning Argentina, Saudi Arabia, Qatar and Iraq led the fight to ensure that the North Korean bid did not succeed. The final agreed outcome was that Cyprus (despite some Arab misgivings) was chosen to host the conference.

Belgrade 1989   Once again the summit documents could not be 'precooked'. But, as at Harare, the Yugoslavs were determined to keep as much control as they could at all stages of the development of the documents which, in this case, deliberately reflected the mainstream concerns to adapt the movement to an already changing world. The conference was held in September 1989, two months before the Berlin Wall fell.

The driving force behind the concern to modernize the movement was the Yugoslavs; their main allies were Egypt, Algeria and, on the whole, India, as well as the silent majority. The desire of the mainstream non-aligned to take a less confrontational and more cooperative global approach was particularly noticeable in the short, ten-page, new-style Declaration covering all major issues which the Yugoslavs hoped would serve as the updated non-aligned credo of the 1990s. This was adopted almost unaltered (as was the Cypriot document on the modernization of the movement which had been called for at Nicosia) after some fierce battles with a disparate band of old-fashioned countries of the left such as Cuba and Ghana. In fact other countries which opposed some aspects of the new style often opposed it for conservative reasons. Zimbabwean pique at the fact that the Yugoslavs had not used language taken from the May 1989 ministerial meeting in their draft Southern Africa resolutions seems to have been a major factor in the African drive to ensure that some (though not all) of the language agreed on Southern Africa was old style rather than new style.

Jakarta 1992 The fact that important parts of non-aligned documents cannot always be decided on in advance was dramatically demonstrated at Jakarta in the context of the intense internal debate over the question of how the movement should deal with the break-up of Yugoslavia. The main supporters of the Federal Republic of Yugoslavia were a number of black African countries whose main underlying concern was territorial integrity (in other words, the sanctity of existing boundaries). Many of the non-aligned were also concerned about the precedent that would be set if the Federal Republic were to be expelled from the movement; this was not normal non-aligned practice.[14] Against them were ranged nearly all the 44 members of the Islamic Conference who made sure that the subject of Bosnia and the Federal Republic remained a focus of attention at all the levels of the conference.

The Indonesian first draft of the proposed summit document (over 60 pages) which was circulated in early August, deliberately did not mention the Yugoslav conflict. The first mention came in the first revision of this draft which had been circulated by the Indonesians just before the conference was due to begin. This first revision contained an Indonesian draft on Bosnia expressing grave concern over the tragic situation 'arising mainly from the acts of violence perpetrated by Serbian irregular forces'. The battle over the content of the text of the final document then continued, primarily in the Political Committee, chaired by Ghana. Islamic states led by Malaysia submitted a draft amendment on 31 August to the first revision. This demanded that aggressor forces be withdrawn immediately from Bosnia and called for peace-keeping forces on the Bosnia–Serbia border as well as the lifting of the arms embargo on Bosnia. The Yugoslavs countered with an amendment which, *inter alia,* condemned attempts to gain territory by force and ethnic cleansing. The Indonesian chairman's compromise text was reopened, not only at foreign minister level by the Malaysians, but also at heads of state level on the evening before the final closing ceremony was due to take place. Final agreement on a text was not reached until a meeting of heads of delegation two hours after the summit had been due to close.

The eventual compromise solution included a strengthened text in the Final Document strongly condemning 'the obnoxious policy of ethnic cleansing by Serbs in Bosnia' but no mention in the shorter Jakarta Message and no separate statement. The non-aligned called for the speedy withdrawal of all external forces from Bosnia and the deployment of UN peace-keeping forces along the border as well as expressing support for the London Conference. The Yugoslavs formally reserved their position on the text in a final, closed, plenary session. In the final, open, plenary session President Suharto made a point of reiterating the condemnation of human rights atrocities, especially against Muslims, and of ethnic cleansing.

To what extent is the format of a summit meeting best suited to high as opposed to low politics? How practical are summits as fora to influence and shape international events? Are they a useful institution and are they more successful for certain subjects under certain circumstances than for others?

Non-aligned summit meetings concentrate on determining non-aligned positions on the major questions on the agenda of the UN General Assembly and Security Council. Thus they have always covered both high and low political issues. Their success in shaping international events is particularly related to their consistency and continuity and their determination to keep issues of concern to them both agreed upon within the non-aligned movement, and on the global agenda, often for decades, until the time is ripe to deal with them. They also try, with a certain amount of success, to keep the movement free from internal dissension. Both Harare and Belgrade were relatively free of this. By contrast extremely difficult and protracted negotiations over former Yugoslavia had to be dealt with at Jakarta.

Harare 1986   The non-aligned movement's continuity of focus on certain issues can be illustrated by looking at certain of the documents produced at Harare. These included a special Declaration on Southern Africa and on

India's AFRICA fund, as well as a special appeal on the independence of Namibia. The non-aligned also stressed the need for continuity in their declaration on the strengthening of collective action, as well as sending a letter to President Reagan and Mr Gorbachev urging them to take steps to prevent the outbreak of nuclear war and calling for an immediate moratorium on nuclear testing. The non-aligned also approved what was then the non-aligned Action Programme for Economic Cooperation. All these ideas echoed material in the 1961 summit documents. The ideal of non-alignment was also asserted by Mugabe in his closing speech. He noted even-handedly how Great Power interference had 'exacerbated local conflicts in Southern Africa, in Central America and South-West Asia'.[15] He appealed yet again to Iran and Iraq, both non-aligned members, to put an end to their tragic conflict. He noted too that 'the interrelated issues of money, finance, trade, external debt and development' had been highlighted by the summit 'as some of the most pressing problems of our time' which require 'urgent and concerted action on a global scale'.

These could be said to be among the high political issues of 1986. However the Political Declaration also touched on Mayotte and New Caledonia besides the right to development, the right of nations to preserve their culture and national heritage, and the new international information and communication order. The Economic Declaration also discussed less important issues such as UNCTAD; telecommunications; transnational corporations; environmental and other qualitative aspects of development; and the international year of shelter for the homeless.

Belgrade 1989   This summit was much more concerned with modernization and bringing into more prominence such issues as human rights and the environment, both then moving from low politics to high politics. The Yugoslavs were able to strengthen human rights language in the final draft of their short declaration which called for, *inter alia*, 'the right of every individual to fully enjoy civil, political, economic, social and cultural rights'. A resolution on the environment noted that the increased deterioration of the environment in developing countries was a 'consequence of the widening gap in development levels between the North and the South'. Environmental protection in developing countries had to be viewed as an integral part of development. The non-aligned were ready to intensify and promote international cooperation on environmental issues; the primary responsibility for global environmental protection, including the provision of additional resources for developing countries, belonged to the developed world however. The resolution recommended, *inter alia*, the convening of a special non-aligned ministerial meeting to coordinate policies for the 1992 Conference on the Environment as well as supporting the Brazilian offer to host the Conference.

Jakarta 1992   This summit was notable for President Suharto's determination to emphasize economic issues – again an issue moving from low to high politics. In his opening speech to the summit the President gave prominence to problems arising from protectionism, debt and commodity prices; the need for appropriate North–South negotiations; and the importance of intensifying and strengthening South–South cooperation. The final, short, Jakarta Message called, *inter alia*, for reform and restructuring of the world economic system. 'Never before,' it noted, 'have the fate and fortunes of the North and South been so inextricably linked.' It suggested reactivation of constructive dialogue between North and South 'based on genuine interdependence, mutuality of interests and of benefits, and shared responsibility'. Intensified South–South cooperation was also imperative both for 'promoting our own development and for reducing undue dependence on the North'. In discussion of both North–South and South–South, much emphasis was laid on the need for constructive action-oriented results. Indonesia subsequently took steps to establish a G-7–non-aligned dialogue through its relationship with Japan. At the subsequent General Assembly Suharto called, amongst other things, for a new North–South 'compact on development and a new democratic partnership in fashioning global solutions' to global economic problems. He subsequently attended the third Group of 15 Summit in Senegal in November 1992[16] and has continued, unavailingly on the whole, to try to find ways of bringing about more cooperation with the North.

To what extent do summits serve domestic as well as foreign policy goals? Has the relationship between these two functions evolved in a particular direction and if it has what factors have driven this trend?

One involved Yugoslav, writing about the Belgrade Summit in 1992,[17] noted that the movement had previously 'upheld the strategy of non-integration in the world in order to avoid being sucked into the vortex of the Cold War'.

[Now] the Movement instituted a new strategy of the integration in the world in order not to be left out from the mainstream of economic and technological development. Instead of the unsuccessful concept of the New International Economic Order, priority was given to various forms of regional linkages with developed countries. Similarly, significant changes were effected in the order of priorities, the realisation of which the Movement is striving to achieve, so that the action to promote human rights and protection of the environment were added to peace and development, the Movement's traditional goals. A more flexible attitude was also taken *vis-à-vis* the United States and the West not only in deterrence [deference] to the once despised shibboleth that 'might is right', but also in the realisation that no major task or goals of the Movement can be solved without establishing a dialogue and cooperation with the centres of political, economic and military might in the notorious triangle Europe–USA–Japan.

The Yugoslavs were also concerned to re-emphasize non-aligned commitment to human rights and the UN, and to ensure that non-aligned concerns were understood by both Western and former Eastern bloc countries. This meant that they were less able to ignore the effect that their internal policies had upon their credibility in foreign policy. This is perhaps the vital change that has taken place in this context. By 1989 they had recognized that foreign policy and domestic issues, particularly those dealing with economic questions, were becoming more and more interdependent as the world became a global village. This too was one theme of the Jakarta Message which, *inter alia*, called for reform and restructuring of the world economic system. 'Never before,' it noted, 'have the fate and fortunes of the North and South been so inextricably linked.'

The increased concern with domestic policies could also be seen in the concern shown by the non-aligned over the question of humanitarian intervention following the invasion and annexation of Kuwait by Iraq (both members of the non-aligned) in August 1990. These concerns were reinforced at their foreign ministers' meeting in Ghana in 1991 by the new non-aligned commitment to encourage and sustain political pluralism. The non-aligned subsequently included new material in the Jakarta Final Document noting that the 'violation or abuse of human rights should not be condoned under any circumstances'. They reaffirmed the universal validity of basic human rights and fundamental freedoms and welcomed the trend towards democracy and the protection of human rights in both texts. They asserted the need for a balance between individual and community rights, while reaffirming non-aligned commitment to respect civil, political, economic, social and cultural rights, and their indivisibility. However, they also stated in the Message that 'no country ... should use its power to dictate its concept of democracy and human rights or to impose conditionalities on others'. They rejected any human rights–aid linkage – development and human rights were mutually supportive – and asserted the competence and responsibility of national governments in the implementation of human rights.

To what extent are these particular summits now firmly institutionalized as part of a fixed regime? Are they still evolving or are they unlikely to change substantially? Is their importance being diminished by the increasing frequency of less formal personal diplomacy (telephone calls between heads of government, for example) or by the growing numbers of specialist advisers who are in more regular diplomatic contact?

Summits have served the non-aligned well over the years. They have provided an arena for discussing foreign policy issues and for resolving some of the major disputes which Third World countries have faced. Their continuity of approach to major questions, combined with adaptability in a changing world has paid slow dividends and outlasted the demise of one superpower. The movement has, as one commentator has noted, provided 'a framework and form of expressing the common interests and aspirations of the countries of the so-called Third World' comprising two-thirds of its sovereign states and two thirds of its population. 'The root causes [the economic situation of developing countries and the inequitable position of a large number of countries from Asia, Latin America and Africa in the international community] which led to its formation have not disappeared.'[18]

The summits, besides continuing to press an agenda relating to common interests, have also acquired an internal, institutional momentum. In this respect, the non-aligned summits have much in common with the Commonwealth summits[19] which have shown a 'surprising capacity to respond to changing circumstances and a resilience to internal stress. Continuity is perhaps made more likely because the association has acquired characteristics of other international organizations … it … provides a kind of club within which views can be expressed, ideas shared and advice sought and given on a confidential basis. And it offers a multilateral framework within which bilateral links can be readily cultivated.' It is arguable that all this is true of the non-aligned.

The overall shape of summits is likely to remain, though possibly constrained by considerations of cost. The latest wave of adaptation to new circumstances stems from discussion in the Ministerial Committee on Methodology which was set up under the Cypriot Foreign Minister at Nicosia in 1988. This sought to devise the best mechanisms for the achievement of non-aligned goals at the UN, and ways of dealing with the problems that had been encountered during the Yugoslav chairmanship.

The Committee recommended, *inter alia*, the provision of a back-up committee and *ad hoc* groups for the Coordinating Bureau at the UN, and of a Joint Coordinating Committee with appropriate guidelines to facilitate the exchange of views between the non-aligned and Group of 77. Both these were agreed at Jakarta, as was the proposal to reactivate the non-aligned Ministerial Committee for Economic Cooperation (first set up at the Harare summit). The participants also decided to set up the high-level committee on UN restructuring proposed by President Suharto and asked the Coordinating Bureau to study further the question of a mechanism for peaceful settlement of disputes between its members.

CONCLUSION

The contribution non-aligned summits have made to the shaping of international events between 1961 and the present day has, it can be argued, been more profound than many commentators realize. The combination of continuity of focus and the non-aligned countries' overall concern with major economic and political subjects has paid slow but sure dividends, particularly in the political sphere. At a basic level the non-aligned have been able to ensure that subjects of concern to them have remained on the political agenda until the time became ripe to deal with them. Namibia and South Africa are two such examples. The use of the UN as a place where justice meets power politics has also proved eminently useful. Certain UN resolutions agreed both in the General Assembly and the Security Council have shown the path which needs to be traversed to ensure a long-lasting peaceful settlement in a particular area. It is not surprising that US diplomacy was able to succeed in Southern Africa in the 1980s since they decided in 1981 'to operate within a UN framework and to retain Resolution 435 as the basis and pivot for a settlement' which provided 'indispensable credibility'.[20] They have, so far, proved less good at dealing with economic issues on either a practical or theoretical level.

Non-aligned summits (as well as other less important meetings) have also been used both as a focus for attempting to resolve internal disputes and as a background for the resolution of bilateral disputes between members. They have provided new countries with an opportunity to learn about global politics on the world stage. Non-aligned countries still provide nearly two-thirds (124 countries) of the membership of the UN General Assembly (113 out of 185 countries). More importantly they have paved the way for agreed resolutions, such as SCR 435 on Namibia, which can provide the basis for a just settlement of a particular issue according to

UN Charter principles. The symbolism of summits is sometimes as important as their substantive conclusions. They cannot be 'pre-cooked' in all respects. They serve domestic goals in so far as they contribute to the prestige of the host state. It is, however, difficult to predict their future as they are so tied up with the UN. If global multilateralism becomes less important, they too may become less important. The overall position of those attending non-aligned summits was well summed up by the Indian Prime Minister in his speech at Jakarta when he said that there was a feeling that the non-aligned were faced with a power structure which allowed them little room for manoeuvre. He disagreed.

When our movement was relatively young, we had even less room for manoeuvre. Our economies were weak and our trade, cultural and even intellectual dependence on the metropolitan powers, was stronger than today. Over the past three decades, we have developed our own economic, technological and, above all, human resources. Our experience in international diplomacy is certainly richer. We are better placed than before in many respects. What is needed, I believe, is the over-arching solidarity and adherence to a shared vision which gave our Movement its original strength and mission.

Ultimately the institution of the summit is as good as the shared vision of those who have set it up. Only if there is a shared vision will there be an incentive for non-aligned countries to continue the long struggle to attempt to make some of their policies a reality.

NOTES AND REFERENCES

The opinions expressed in this chapter are the author's own and should not be taken as an expression of official government policy.

1. The non-aligned movement has included among its members certain liberation movements, including SWAPO, now replaced by Namibia, and the Palestine Liberation Organization (the PLO), since the end of 1988 known as Palestine.
2. The six-year gap between 1964 and 1970 reflected the battle between Sukarno (Indonesia) who espoused militant struggle against the West and was overthrown in September 1965, and Tito (Yugoslavia) who championed active and peaceful coexistence and cooperation through the United Nations. Iraq was due to hold the summit in 1982. This had to be cancelled because of the Iran–Iraq war. The postponed summit was subsequently held in New Delhi in February 1983.

3. Tenth Conference of Heads of State or Government of Non-Aligned Countries Jakarta, 1–6 September 1992, A/47/675, 18 November 1992, p. 11. The Bandung Conference of 1955 was not a non-aligned summit, the first of which was held in 1961, but it contributed much to the development of non-aligned ideas.

4. The summits are underpinned by a system of other meetings including meetings at foreign minister level two years after each summit (the last such meeting was held in Cairo in May/June 1994 – it would normally have been held in August/September but was held early as Cairo was hosting the UN Population Conference at that time) and yearly meetings at ministerial level in New York in late September at the beginning of the General Assembly. Non-aligned members of the Security Council often vote together as a group. See my article, 'The Influence of States and Groups of States on and in the Security Council and General Assembly, 1980–94', *Review of International Studies*, vol. 21, no. 4 (October 1995).

5. This meant that their name became less relevant. Countries in the movement considered changing it at their foreign ministers' meeting at Accra in 1991. They decided that this would be too complicated and have retained the current name.

6. China became an Observer in the non-aligned in 1992. India was opposed to its involvement before the fragmentation of the Soviet Union.

7. There have always been European members of the non-aligned. Cyprus and Malta are both European members. The Federal Republic of Yugoslavia (Serbia and Montenegro) was not asked to the non-aligned foreign ministers' meeting at Cairo in June 1994. It remains a European member. The UN has a Western European and Others Group and an Eastern European Group.

8. The Group of 77's membership in 1995 was 131. This includes such countries as Brazil which remains an Observer in the non-aligned,

9. See UN document A/41/697 and S/18392 of 14 October 1986.

10. See UN document A/44/551 and S/20870 of 29 September 1989.

11. For UN document reference see note 3. A more detailed account of the summit can be found in my article, 'The Non-Aligned in the New World Order: The Jakarta Summit, September 1992', *International Relations*, vol. XI, no. 4 (April 1993).

12. This idea had been tried successfully at the Nicosia foreign ministers meeting in 1988. See also my article 'The Non-Aligned Movement and the Foreign Ministers' Meeting at Nicosia', *International Relations*, vol. IX, no. 5 (May 1989).

13. A useful account of the negotiations leading up to these is given in 'The Singapore Symposium: The Changing Role of the United Nations' in *Conflict Resolution and Peace-Keeping*, 13–15 March 1991, pp. 65–79. The Head of State of Cambodia, Norodom Sihanouk, in his speech to the summit stressed that 'Indonesia has played a very important role in the search for, and the achievement of, peace in favour of Cambodia'.

14. The nearest precedent was the attempt to expel Egypt at the 1979 Havana summit over the Camp David Agreements. This did not succeed. In this case the Federal Republic of Yugoslavia remained a member of the movement. The decision as to what to do was, sensibly, postponed until the General Assembly had an opportunity to consider the question.

15. This was, of course, a shorthand reference to the Soviet Union's occupation of Afghanistan, a member of the non-aligned.
16. The Group of 15 was set up at the 1989 Belgrade summit to increase South–South cooperation in quantity and quality.
17. Dr Ranko Petkovic, 'The Non-Aligned in Jakarta', *Belgrade Review of International Affairs*, 1007–8, 1992, pp. 7–8.
18. Ibid., p. 7.
19. Margaret Doxey, 'The Commonwealth in a Changing World: Behind the Headlines', Canadian Institute of International Affairs, Summer 1992, p. 13.
20. Chester Crocker, *High Noon in Southern Africa – Making Peace in a Rough Neighbourhood* (New York, Norton & Company, 1993), p. 454.

Part III
One-Off or *Ad Hoc* Summits

11 The Western Summit at Bermuda, December 1953

John Young

On 20 May 1953, the American President, Dwight Eisenhower, was interrupted, during a round of golf, by two White House officials with an urgent message. The French Prime Minister, René Mayer, had asked Eisenhower to arrange a three-power conference with the British Premier, Winston Churchill, in the near future. The President was forced to return to Washington to consult his foreign policy advisers. It was soon decided in principle to agree to Mayer's request and Eisenhower immediately telephoned his old friend Churchill, suggesting a venue for the conference at Presque Isle, Maine. Churchill agreed to the conference proposal, but not the venue: instead of Presque Isle, he successfully pressed for the meeting to be held on the British territory of Bermuda. He made much of this success when obtaining Cabinet approval for his decision the following morning.[1] Thus was born the idea of a conference among the Western 'Big Three', a meeting which – despite the events of 20 May – became identified with the person of Winston Churchill.[2] Bermuda was, arguably, the most powerful gathering of world leaders since Potsdam, and its story reveals much about the difficulties in holding successful summits, even among allies.

That the Bermuda conference became identified with Churchill was doubly ironic, since René Mayer originally requested the meeting in order to restrain the British Premier's recent forays into world affairs, particularly his eagerness for talks with Russia following Stalin's death on 5 March 1953. Before this date relations with Russia were deeply lodged in the mutual suspicion and distrust of the cold war. After the outbreak of the Korean War in 1950, East–West divisions (which had grown in the 1940s) became rigid; in America McCarthyism was rife; and there was a massive Western rearmament effort. Though the Russians avoided involvement in Korea, contact with them stagnated. In particular there was no progress on the peace treaties with Germany and Austria, left unfinished after the Second World War. But this period had also seen divisions *within* the Western camp. The most divisive issue brought on by

Korea was German rearmament. Coming so soon after Hitler's defeat this idea (pressed by Washington after September 1950) terrified Germany's traditional enemies, the French, and led them to put a counter-proposal: Germany should only be rearmed within a 'European Defence Community' (EDC). This would allow German forces to be raised, but only within a federal European Army, without their own independent command structure. France, West Germany, Italy and the Benelux states began talks which led to an EDC treaty in 1952. But the problem by then was that the French themselves had had second thoughts about rearming Germany under any conditions. Indeed, the Paris government shrank from putting the new treaty for ratification for fear the National Assembly would reject it. Instead France tried to induce America and Britain to give solid military guarantees to the EDC, in the hope of 'buying' support in the Assembly for the new body. But neither Washington, nor London, was willing to restrict their own military independence.[3]

Thus in early 1953 there was a complex situation, both globally and within the Western alliance. An East–West meeting was not out of the question at this time. Churchill had, intermittently, been urging a meeting since February 1950 when, in a speech in Edinburgh, he first used the word 'summit' to apply to a leader level conference.[4] In February 1953, Eisenhower, who had just become president, expressed a willingness to meet Stalin if 'there was the slightest chance of doing any good'.[5] But in many quarters even Stalin's death a short time later did not make a meeting with the Russians very attractive. In the United States some of Eisenhower's staff believed that a positive approach should immediately be made to the new leadership in Moscow, offering foreign ministers' talks; but the State Department, under John Foster Dulles, was more cautious, arguing that Washington should await events. Eventually Eisenhower made a speech, on 16 April 1953, calling for 'a peace that is neither partial nor punitive' with Moscow whilst also demanding clear evidence of Soviet good faith.[6] In London meanwhile, despite some initial optimism from the Foreign Secretary, Anthony Eden, the Foreign Office argued in a policy paper of early April that what changes there seemed to be in Russian policy (notably a more promising line on Korean peace talks) might be 'tactical' moves to dupe the West.[7] The Quai d'Orsay quite agreed with this analysis, and the French foreign minister, Georges Bidault, expressed horror at the possible effect of talks with Russia on the EDC – for if the West and Russia began at last to draw up a German peace treaty the French Assembly would have an excellent reason to delay the EDC and German rearmament.[8] The general Western reaction to Stalin's death was thus a reluctance to hold discussions with Russia and a determination that any relaxation of tension should not weaken the West. In particular there were suspicions that Stalin's successors might merely be trying to sabotage German rearmament.

Already, however, it was clear that Churchill's approach to talks between the Western 'Big Three' and Russia was very different. And his views became even more important when on 6 April he took over the running of the Foreign Office after Anthony Eden was forced into temporary retirement by illness. As early as 10 March, the Prime Minister had suggested to Eisenhower that contacts should be opened with Stalin's successors. Undaunted by the President's cautious reply[9] in late March, Churchill had raised the idea with Eden of a personal message to the Soviet Foreign Minister, Molotov. Eden was able to steer the Prime Minister towards a different course of action, that Britain should 'test the water' by seeing whether the Russians would make concessions on certain precise issues (notably a dispute over Anglo-Soviet fishing rights which had arisen).[10] Soon after Churchill became acting Foreign Secretary, Eisenhower sent him a copy of his 16 April speech, which made Churchill more enthusiastic about contacts with Russia. Recalling the war years, he was attracted to the idea of an Anglo–Soviet–American conference, with a wide agenda, on the lines of Yalta or Potsdam, as the way to resolve all the world's problems, and on 21 April sent another message to Eisenhower, in favour of an opening to Moscow. In early May he became even bolder, suggesting to the President that he – Churchill – should visit Moscow personally (another tactic he had pursued on occasions during the war). An increasingly incredulous Eisenhower continued to preach the need for caution and concrete advances.[11]

Churchill finally revealed his hopes for talks with Russia in a speech to the House of Commons on 11 May, which was the immediate cause of the Bermuda Conference. He called for 'a conference on the highest level ... between the leading powers without long delay ... confined to the smallest number of powers and persons possible'. Despite its importance, the speech was made without consulting the Cabinet and without giving the Foreign Office full time for consideration; predictably, Foreign Office officials were unenthusiastic about it.[12] It was not at all clear what would be discussed at such a meeting; Churchill simply seemed to hope for a general improvement in the international atmosphere. The least favourable response to Churchill came from across the Channel. In Paris, it appeared that Churchill was not only risking the chances of ratifying the EDC, but also that he wanted a great power conference from which France was excluded (as it had been excluded from the wartime conferences of Yalta and Potsdam). The French were unable to get a clear reassurance from the

Foreign Office that they would be included in the talks which Churchill proposed. It was as a result of uncertainty generated in Paris by these events that Mayer decided to try and arrange a three-power meeting with Eisenhower and Churchill on 20 May.[13]

Almost immediately the plans for the Bermuda conference faced serious problems. On 21 May, the very same day that the British Cabinet approved the conference proposal, Mayer's own government fell as a result of an adverse vote in the National Assembly; and France was plunged into a political crisis of extraordinary duration – even for the Fourth Republic. For almost a month there were attempts by one politician after another to form an administration, before an independent deputy, Joseph Laniel, successfully emerged with one on 26 June. Churchill, unsurprisingly, had little sympathy for the events in Paris. He was willing to go ahead with arrangements for Bermuda on an Anglo-American basis without a French premier being present. For a time Eisenhower resisted, but eventually he agreed to fix a date, 8 July, for beginning the conference. France, the main architect of Bermuda, had succeeded in delaying the conference for weeks and now seemed unlikely even to attend, except as an observer. Meanwhile Churchill became very enthusiastic about Bermuda, personally arranging that Eisenhower should be welcomed by a guard of honour from the Royal Welch Fusiliers.[14] He also sent a message to Molotov expressing the hope that Bermuda would lead to contacts between East and West.[15] Others however continued to see the conference as a way to control the Prime Minister. Eisenhower and the American government stated that Bermuda did not mean that talks with Russia would follow.[16] They were encouraged in this line by the West German Chancellor, Konrad Adenauer. Adenauer had based his whole policy in Germany on cooperation with the West and was terrified by the possible results of Churchill's ideas of talks with Russia (especially since it was an election year in Germany). Churchill's ideas gave priority to détente with Russia over the success of the EDC or Adenauer's electoral prospects. The future of Germany was bound to be a major subject in East–West talks, but the talks would take place over Adenauer's head and would give greater credibility to the Soviet aim of a united but neutralized Germany – a new state tied neither to East nor West. His fears were of great concern to the British Foreign Office. On 30 May the Foreign Office put a powerful memorandum to Churchill highlighting the dangers of a 'neutralized' united Germany: this would mean a reversal of Western policy on Germany, ruin NATO's defence strategy (based on a defence of the Elbe), weaken Germany in the face of Russia, undermine all the hopes of a lasting Franco-German *rapprochement*, upset the West Germans themselves, and perhaps even lead the Americans to leave Europe. In the face of such formidable arguments the Prime Minister tried to switch the blame for Europe's problems onto the French failure to ratify the EDC.[17]

By early June, doubts about Churchill's likely policy at Bermuda were growing in Washington and London. John Foster Dulles was deeply concerned about Churchill's 'incipient tendency ... toward a position of mediation between the US and the USSR'. Dulles and other senior policy-makers were determined to have a fixed agenda for Bermuda, to prevent it becoming a 'simple little party' with no substantive discussions.[18] On 29 May Anthony Nutting, a junior Foreign Office minister, argued in a long minute that Bermuda would raise enormous public expectations about a Russian meeting, but that the Americans were unlikely to allow these hopes to be completely fulfilled; so the best that could be expected was a 'qualified success' – possibly Russian talks based on a very precise (but not impossible) agenda. The British Embassy in Moscow still saw no reason to believe that Soviet policy had changed substantially since Stalin.[19] Pressure also built up in the Cabinet for a full discussion on foreign policy before Bermuda in order to prevent Churchill 'going it alone' with Russia.[20] The Foreign Office and the Western allies had their fears eased in late June, however, by Churchill's own misfortune. On the evening of 23 June the Prime Minister suffered a stroke. This left him mentally quite alert, but physically exhausted. The details were withheld from the public, the Cabinet and Eisenhower, but the President was asked to agree to a temporary deferment of Bermuda.[21] In fact, the Americans eagerly welcomed such a delay, given the current international atmosphere: armistice talks were now progressing in Korea (they reached agreement in July) and in Berlin there was a short-lived anti-Soviet rising, which caused consternation in Moscow and was quickly followed by a crisis in the collective leadership, when the secret police chief, Lavrenti Beria was arrested and shot. Churchill was despondent. 'I am as bad as the French,' he wrote to Eisenhower. It was quickly arranged that Lord Salisbury, who had become the new acting Foreign Secretary, should visit Washington, at the time when Bermuda should have been held, for talks with Dulles and Bidault.[22] Salisbury was despatched to Washington with instructions to seek a four-power conference (comprising Britain, America, France and Russia). However, a meeting should only be held *after* the EDC was ratified so that the French would be induced to approve, rather than delay, EDC and Russia would be prevented from obstructing German disarmament further.[23]

Once in Washington, on 11 July, Salisbury pressed British views but was opposed strongly by Bidault. The Frenchman wanted four-power talks to be disposed of swiftly – he expected them to fail – and *then* EDC could be ratified; the French Assembly, he argued, would never ratify EDC if a German peace treaty seemed possible. Unfortunately for the British approach, Dulles agreed with Bidault, after Adenauer sent a message to Washington favouring an early four-power meeting to end the uncertainty about Russian talks once and for all. Dulles and Bidault, in contrast to Churchill, were determined to have talks with Moscow based on a fixed agenda, centring around the still uncompleted German peace treaty, and they were unwilling to compromise Western policy in Germany in such talks. Also they wanted such talks to take place at foreign minister level, where their own experience could be brought to bear, not at a summit.

The Western powers would only talk to Russia on the basis of a reunified Germany with the freedom to join the Western alliance system. Churchill was bitterly disappointed with the events in Washington, but on 13 July the Cabinet had little choice other than to accept Dulles' and Bidault's line of an early foreign ministers' conference with a fixed agenda.[24] In a letter to Churchill Eisenhower made it clear that he would have pressed the same policy at Bermuda, had the conference been held.[25] Over the next few months there were belated attempts to arrange talks with Russia, but Moscow's reaction was disappointing. The Berlin Rising, though short-lived, had made the Soviets reluctant to provoke further speculation in East Germany about reunification. On 4 August, the Soviets rejected the Western proposals for the future of Germany and instead proposed a *five*-power conference (including China) to discuss general world problems. A few days later, apparently in an attempt to influence the German elections, Moscow offered to form a provisional all-German government immediately. Despite pessimism over these tactics, America, Britain and France decided to send a reply that kept the chance of talks open, though they delayed sending this to Moscow until 4 September, two days before the German elections returned Adenauer safely to power.[26] Churchill, as he recovered from his stroke, remained determined to retain office in the belief that he could yet bring peace with Russia.[27] Meanwhile the Bermuda conference continued to be delayed. In early October Churchill suggested meeting Eisenhower in the Azores, but the President, still uncertain about Soviet policy, was keen to invite France to any talks and, in any case, was facing a full timetable.[28]

That the Bermuda conference was held, at last, in December, was due to the next Soviet note, issued on 3 November, which laid down such firm conditions for a meeting that it was widely seen as making four-power talks almost impossible.[29] But what for others came as a blow, came to Churchill as an opportunity. 'The Soviet answer puts us back to where we were when Bermuda broke down,' he wrote to Eisenhower on 5 November, 'so why not let us try Bermuda again?' It was not at all clear what such a conference would discuss precisely and in Washington there were still doubts about encouraging Churchill's policies. But it was decided that Bermuda could not be put off forever. It had, after all, only been 'deferred' in June. So Eisenhower (in Dulles' absence) agreed to meet Churchill, though he also insisted on inviting the French. The conference would be held in early December. Churchill was delighted and in his messages to Eisenhower he even played down the importance of Russian talks. 'By all means let us announce that we are meeting to discuss matters of common interest', he wrote, 'we might both brace the French up on EDC'. He seemed far more interested in the 'special relationship', telling the President that 'I am bringing my paintbox with me as I cannot take you on at golf', and again taking pride in arranging for a guard of honour from the Royal Welch Fusiliers ('with their goat') to greet the President.[30] Privately, however, the Russians were still to the fore in Churchill's mind: 'There is a feeling', he told his doctor immodestly, 'that I am the only person who [can] do anything with Russia'.[31] Churchill's relations with the French – whom he would gladly have left out of Bermuda – were far less good than those with Eisenhower. Churchill invited Laniel to the new Bermuda conference on 8 November, in a personal message, and was deeply offended that this was accepted via diplomatic channels. Churchill's annoyance with Paris spilled over in a further message to Laniel on 12 November. 'I am glad to hear from various sources that you are coming to our meeting in Bermuda', he wrote; then, after inviting Laniel's party to be accommodated at British expense, he added, 'If I do not hear from you I should proceed on the assumption that you accept.' Churchill's staff tried to tone the message down but only succeeded in changing the words 'our meeting' to 'the meeting' before Churchill sent it off. Fortunately, the Ambassador to Paris, Sir Oliver Harvey, refused to deliver it; fearing 'a harmful misunderstanding', he managed to persuade Laniel to send a friendly personal message to Churchill. None of this augured well for Anglo-French relations at Bermuda.[32]

The detailed preparations for the conference showed that Britain, France and the USA had very different approaches to the subjects for discussion. On 3 November, Churchill had again told the Commons that there should be contacts with Moscow, but he was noticeably more subdued than in his 11 May declarations and Eden and the Foreign Office still had little faith in this policy: they hoped Bermuda would be primarily useful as a demonstration of Western unity. To achieve this they were even willing to ease pressure on France to ratify EDC. In a draft Cabinet memorandum, Eden declared that the Russians had done no more than make 'certain gestures, which have cost them little' since the death of Stalin, but Churchill would not allow this paper to go before ministers – instead all the Cabinet saw was a paper on communism in the Far East.[33] Nonetheless the British official briefing-papers for Bermuda took Eden's line: Germany must remain tied firmly to the West; pressure on France over EDC should be relaxed for a time; changes in Soviet policy should be treated as merely 'tactical'. The Foreign Office was determined that if talks *were* held with Russia they should deal with the precise question of Germany; Britain would not agree to Germany's 'neutralization' because it was vital to secure her role in Western defence, complete her reconciliation with France, and prevent any 'future German adventures'.[34]

Neither did the French plan any new policy departures at Bermuda. On EDC Laniel and Bidault continued to hope for Anglo-American guarantees to help ratification. In the Far East events were moving to a climax: General Navarre, the French commander in Indochina hoped to bring about a decisive battle with the *Vietminh* nationalists to force heavy losses on them and make them talk peace – Paris no longer hoped for absolute victory in the struggle. Bidault wanted to supplement these military efforts by opening talks with Peking, though he feared that this would enrage the Americans. On 24 November Laniel made a speech to the Assembly outlining his policy in the light of Bermuda, which concentrated on three subjects: on Russian talks he declared himself in favour of discussions about Germany only if there was reciprocation from Moscow; in the Far East he talked of including Peking in a general pacification; and on EDC he continued to demand a British military guarantee. The French Cabinet approved Laniel's line on 2 December.[35] Both Dulles and Eisenhower made it plain, even to the press, that they expected little from Bermuda beyond an exchange of views. And even this allowed wide scope for differences with Britain and France. Dulles, for example, was determined to use Bermuda to put pressure on the French over EDC; he was equally determined, in the Far East, to oppose communism in Korea and Indochina and to avoid talks with China.

To the Secretary of State what really mattered in the world was the preservation of a firm anti-communist front in the face of Moscow. It meant a strong stance in both Europe (hence the need for German rearmament) and East Asia (including opposition to both Russia *and* China on ideological grounds); and of course it meant no support for Churchill's belief in informal talks with Moscow.[36] It was clear in the light of these beliefs that Bermuda was in grave danger of becoming not a demonstration of unity but of disunity in the Western alliance, and of reaching no substantial agreements. It was a fortunate irony therefore that on 26 November, the Russians suddenly – at last – agreed to hold four-power foreign ministers' talks. This of course completely altered the situation from the time when Bermuda had been arranged. The Russians had now provided Bermuda with a substantive issue to discuss – something which, hitherto, it had lacked. It also provided the basis for a discussion about Russia at Bermuda based on specific issues rather than the generalities which Churchill would have preferred.[37]

On the long flight over to Bermuda, at the beginning of December, Churchill's staff tried to persuade him to read a few short documents on British policy – they did not attempt to make him read all the extensive Foreign Office briefs. But Churchill was uninterested, preferring to occupy himself with an historical novel, C. S. Forester's *Death to the French*. This merely ensured that his anti-French sentiments were reinforced: 'The French,' he declared, 'are going to be very difficult. They will want everything and give nothing.' It was an attitude which exasperated Eden who argued that 'the French are pretty hopeless, but ... a geographical necessity'. Churchill promised to hide the Forester novel before the French party arrived, but he made it plain that he was far more interested in talking to Eisenhower (with whom he was to have some long private conversations during the conference): talking to Frenchmen, according to the Prime Minister, was the Foreign Secretary's job.[38] The most important subject during the talks of 4–7 December was, of course, Russia, and it soon became clear that Churchill's ideas had no chance of being accepted. The foreign ministers, on 4 December, agreed on an ungrudging reply to the Soviet note of 26 November. At the first plenary meeting that evening, Churchill urged that contacts with Russia must be opened, but Bidault made an anti-Soviet speech and Eisenhower compared Russia to a 'whore' who had patched her dress, but still needed to be 'beat into the back streets'. Eisenhower (supported by the three foreign ministers) was determined that if the Berlin meeting achieved little, it should be brought to a swift conclusion. Surprisingly Churchill did not actually press for a meeting of Western and Soviet leaders – only for an opening of contacts using trade and personal links (which, in due course, might encourage a relaxation in totalitarianism in Russia). Illness and the strength of his opponents had apparently had their effect on the Prime Minister. The main debate about Russia effectively became one of timing the four-power conference which was to be held in Berlin: the French wanted to begin in late January, when their elections were over; but Dulles successfully pressed for 4 January, so as to settle the question as soon as possible.[39] Churchill was bitter about his failure, complaining to Eden on 7 December that there was 'nothing in [the] communiqué which shows the slightest desire for the success of the [Berlin] conference'; the communiqué declared that 'if the danger of aggression now appears less imminent we attribute this to the mounting strength of the free world and the firmness of its policies'.[40] Churchill saw that his failure to influence Eisenhower on the Russian issue had much to do with Dulles: 'This fellow preaches like a methodist minister and his bloody text is always the same. That nothing but evil can come out of meeting with Malenkov.... Even as it is I have not been defeated by this bastard. I have been humiliated by my own decay.'[41]

After Russia the other major topic was EDC, and this issue, as expected, proved divisive. In the foreign ministers' meetings, Dulles soon made it clear that unless EDC was approved in the New Year, Congress might not grant the next round of financing for the NATO alliance. Bidault quite agreed that EDC was the only way forward on German rearmament but insisted that the political problems in Paris were, as yet, insurmountable. His allies were not convinced. Eden, following the Foreign Office line, tried not to press the French too far, but Churchill warned Bidault that if America left Europe Britain would follow, and even upset Eisenhower by telling the French quite bluntly that Germany would be rearmed within a reformed version of NATO if EDC was rebuffed. (Eisenhower preferred to say the EDC *must* be passed, rather than talk of alternatives.) The arguments reached a climax in the closing session on 7 December when Bidault pressed for a statement to be included in the communiqué that the fulfilment of EDC 'depends on the solution of the problems with which France has long been faced'. Dulles especially opposed this for fear that France would demand all sorts of conditions before ratifying EDC, and the arguments went on beyond midnight into the early morning. To French annoyance, Eisenhower had to leave in the middle of this debate to return to the United States, but Dulles continued to threaten a major change in American policy if France did not act resolutely on EDC. Eventually, the French suggested a new draft, stating simply that 'the French [foreign] minister ... explained the problems facing his government in regard to the European Defence Community'. After further debate, and despite the clear weakness of this statement, an exhausted Churchill and Dulles accepted it.[42] The Far East did not emerge as the major issue at Bermuda as many had expected it would. Due to timetable problems (caused mainly by the concentration on EDC), all that occurred was a brief discussion of Korea and a rather longer outline, by Bidault, of the position in Indochina.

What became a much more important issue was, ironically, unforeseen by Britain and France. This was a proposal from Eisenhower for a rather different approach to cooperation with Russia: an attempt to bring about the international control of atomic energy. The President hoped to address the United Nations on this issue, on 8 December, but he decided to discuss it first with Churchill and Laniel. The British (though not the French) were actually shown the text of the speech, which suggested the creation of an International Atomic Energy Authority to foster the peaceful use of atomic energy for the benefit of more than the established nuclear powers. Churchill, hoping to have talks on Anglo-American atomic cooperation, had brought his scientific adviser, Lord Cherwell, and the latter approved Eisenhower's scheme whilst doubting that it would achieve much. But the British were concerned that during their conversations Eisenhower argued that there was little difference between conventional weapons and tactical nuclear weapons; he seemed quite willing to use atomic weapons should the war in Korea break out once more. Eden, especially, was despondent about this, but to their relief Eisenhower agreed to remove from the speech a statement that America was prepared to use its atomic weapons in Europe. Churchill accepted the speech with mixed feelings: it showed an American willingness to talk about cooperation with Russia, but only in a limited area, and he was only too aware that a major UN speech on 8 December would draw the world's attention away from the results of Bermuda.[43]

In bilateral talks behind the scenes, Churchill had some success in developing his friendship with Eisenhower. The President had not been enthusiastic about seeing the Prime Minister, who was felt by Americans to be too old, too arrogant – and too prone to doze off in meetings. Certainly, Churchill revealed his arrogant side at Bermuda (he arrived for all the plenary sessions, alone, exactly one minute late) but he went out of his way to charm Eisenhower (insisting that the President chair the sessions though he was not the host) and the President found Bermuda to be 'a sort of home-coming, a renewal of an old and close relationship'. Even so he rejected the idea of Britain and America 'ganging up', in the way Churchill wanted, to set the world to rights. The 'special relationship' remained essentially unfulfilled.[44] More interesting than the Churchill–Eisenhower meetings perhaps were the meetings of Eden and Dulles, both formally and on daily swimming expeditions. Contrary to the accepted view of their relationship they proved able to cooperate closely and exchanged views on the Middle East and policy towards China, among other issues.[45] The French experience at Bermuda, even apart from EDC, was a troubled one. At the first dinner, on 4 December, Laniel seemed to observers to be bored and the next day took to his bed with a temperature of 104°. There were suggestions (actually unfounded) that his illness was 'diplomatic'; certainly Bidault was none too pleased to have to face Churchill and Eisenhower, as well as Eden and Dulles, alone. Indeed, Laniel and his foreign minister were not on speaking terms. Eden had to act as an intermediary between them. Churchill, who referred to the French increasingly as 'bloody frogs', remained unenthusiastic about their presence, and both he and Eisenhower were enraged when, on the opening day, a French spokesman gave a graphic (partially verbatim) account of the first plenary session to newsmen, which included the President's likening of Russia to a 'whore'. And yet, at the end of the conference, the Prime Minister seemed to relent so far as France was concerned: he invited the still ailing Laniel to fly back in his RAF Canopus.[46] The French press and public were less kind to Laniel's performance at Bermuda, accusing him of harming national prestige by allowing the Anglo-Americans to humiliate him and by using illness as an 'excuse' to avoid discussions. The Premier tried with little success to counter both these accusations: in the mid-December elections, in which he had had high hopes of being elected President, René Coty was chosen instead to be head of state.

In its aftermath, Bermuda was widely seen as a failure. The press, which had looked forward to it with expectation, was disappointed to find itself separated from the delegates by extraordinary measures (especially after the French-inspired leaks of 4 December): even Laniel and Eisenhower had to carry identity cards at the conference meetings! Churchill refused to do so.[47] Unsurprisingly the press response was critical. The *New York Times* was typically dismissive, stating that Bermuda was 'magnificently comprehensive' in its *tour d'horizon* 'but did not arrive anywhere'. In London, *The Times* conceded that such meetings were useful for letting the Western leaders gain 'a better knowledge of each other' but felt that 'the imprecise ... communiqué ... raises the question whether the three-power conference ... was worthwhile'. The French press was also contemptuous: a 'spectacular meeting to exchange banalities' was one description.[48] At the dawn of post-war summitry, the leaders present certainly cannot be accused of using the meeting as a 'photo opportunity'. They made little impression on domestic audiences except in a negative sense – which was particularly damaging to Laniel. For those present at Bermuda the situation seemed no better. It was referred to as 'Winston's conference' or 'Winston's baby', and except for the Soviet note of 26 November was seen as purposeless. Ismay, the NATO representative, was appalled to find that there was no fixed agenda, no secretariat, not even any agreed minutes. At one of the meetings on 7 December, Dulles went so far as to query the communiqué's reference to a 'full accord' between the three powers. 'He was not sure that our views were in such close harmony' noted the British records blandly.[49] Even the main discussions at Bermuda had little result. Thanks to Russian delays, the Berlin conference did not start until 25 January and came to nothing. The discussions on EDC at Bermuda, on the other hand, were immediately forgotten when, at a NATO meeting in Paris the following week, Dulles made public his warning about an 'agonizing reappraisal' of American foreign policy if German rearmament did not come soon. Unimpressed, the French continued to cause delays before finally rejecting EDC in a parliamentary vote in August 1954. By then there had also been decisive events in Indochina, where the French were defeated at Dien Bien Phu. As a result, at a five-power conference of foreign ministers (including China) in Geneva in 1954, the fateful decision was taken to divide Vietnam between the communist North and pro-Western South – the latter increasingly supported by the United States.

On the surface Bermuda appeared to be the most powerful international gathering since the last meeting of three Great Power leaders at Potsdam. Since 1945 there had been meetings of the British, French and American leaders, but only on a bilateral basis. And there would not be such a gathering as Bermuda again until the Geneva Summit of July 1955, also attended by the Soviet leader, Nikita Khrushchev. Another Western summit was held in December 1959 (prior to the ill-fated summit with Khrushchev in 1960). Of course, it is arguable that, even in 1953, a conference that included Britain and France was no longer a meeting of 'Great Powers': that title should perhaps be reserved for meetings of the Soviet and American leaders. None the less, a meeting of the three major Western leaders in 1953 provided at least an opportunity for important decisions, and the real reason for its failure should be sought in the ideas of the man with whom it was identified, Winston Churchill. It was the Prime Minister's wartime experience of personal diplomacy (especially the three great conferences of Tehran, Yalta and Potsdam) which encouraged him to believe in the kind of open forum for discussion which Bermuda was meant to be. But the wartime conferences, which Churchill had hoped to recreate, had been held at a time of East–West cooperation and even then they had spawned as many problems as they solved. If a meeting with the Russian leader, Georgi Malenkov, *had* been held in 1953 it is of course impossible to say what would have resulted; but when a summit was finally held in 1955 it led to little, and in retrospect it is clear that long-term 'détente' could only succeed when both America and Russia had learnt, over a long period, that there could be gains from conversation rather than cold war and that each had strong interests in pursuing such a course. Bermuda itself represented a diluted attempt at personal diplomacy on a three-power basis; but the problem here was simply that the Western powers had little to discuss among themselves in such a setting. The only substantial issue (the Russian note) could have been decided through ordinary diplomatic channels, and elsewhere the wide agenda tended to produce divisions, rather than friendly discussion, especially over EDC. Thus, although Bermuda was intended to deal with substantive issues, it was too poorly prepared in advance and too much at the mercy of disagreements between those present to achieve a great deal.

Neither Churchill nor anyone else achieved what they hoped for at Bermuda. The Prime Minister's search for a radically new approach to Russia never really had much chance of success. The original Bermuda conference was called in May with the hope of controlling him; and although (by his enthusiasm for such a meeting) he made Bermuda his own in December, it did not alter the fact that the Americans, French and even his own Foreign Office disliked his ideas. Thus there were disagreements between delegates, not only on the issues discussed, but also on the form that discussions should take. Churchill favoured a free-ranging discussion, which he believed he could dominate, but the professional diplomats preferred a fixed agenda. In any case, when the decisive meetings came at Bermuda Churchill himself, due to his ill health, failed to press his ideas with verve. There were really two problems with his policy. Most obvious was the belief of the State Department and Foreign Office that Russian policy remained substantially unchanged after the death of Stalin: men like Dulles saw any signs of 'moderation' from Moscow as signs of the rectitude of Western policy – if they interpreted them as 'moderation' at all. Western foreign ministries were determined to negotiate with Moscow only from a position of strength: they were determined to create the EDC, for example, *before* talking to Russia. The second reason for Churchill's failure – and one that is too often minimized in importance – was the danger his policy entailed for Western unity, especially for the success of EDC. By raising the spectre of a German peace treaty, Churchill gave the opponents of German rearmament an excellent excuse for new delays. Arguably Churchill's greatest mistake in 1953 was not his naïvety regarding the Russians, but his cavalier attitude towards the Western alliance which had more tensions within it in the 1950s than is usually admitted. It was not at all ridiculous at this time for the West to suspect that the only reason for Soviet moderation was to divide the allies among themselves; the effect of Churchill's ideas was to achieve just that. The primary aim of Churchill's opponents at Bermuda, apart from countering the idea of a Russian summit, was in fact to demonstrate Western unity. But in this they clearly failed. The communiqué revealed divisions on EDC, and there were disagreements on the timing of the Berlin conference, the question of openings to China, and (on an Anglo-American level) the 'special relationship'. It would be wrong to exaggerate the extent of this; the three powers did agree on a meeting with the Soviets and did agree to maintain their established policies in Germany (which helped to ensure the failure at Berlin). But divisions there certainly were, and they were not only visible between nations, but also *within* each of the three governments. Laniel and Bidault differed openly at Bermuda. Eisenhower's 'Atoms for Peace' speech was prepared by the White House rather than the State Department, and represented a rather more positive outlook on relations with the East than that evinced by Dulles. And Churchill's differences with the Foreign Office on the possibility of talks with Russia, concessions to the Soviets over Germany, and the importance of France to the Western alliance, were obvious. Bermuda was the first major gathering of world leaders since the term 'summit' was coined by Churchill. But it was also an excellent example of how summit diplomacy can fail, almost completely, even when close allies meet. In future leaders would learn the need to impress journalists on such occasions, to iron out major problems in advance of a meeting, to give at least the appearance of making substantial agreements and to agree in advance too on the purpose and form of their discussions.[50]

NOTES AND REFERENCES

1. R. J. Donovan, *Eisenhower: the inside story* (London, 1956), pp. 201–2; R. J. Cutler, *No Time for Rest* (Boston, 1965), p. 316; Public Record Office (PRO), Kew, CAB. 128/26, CC (53) 33rd (21 May).
2. Certain accounts treat the conference as being Churchill's from the outset: H. Macmillan, *Tides of Fortune, 1945–55* (London, Macmillan, 1969), p. 512; and Churchill's own account in *House of Commons, debates, fifth series* (HCDeb., 5s), vol. 522, cols 577–86.
3. On EDC see especially R. Fursdon, *The European Defence Community* (London, Macmillan, 1980); S. Dockrill, *Britain's Policy for West German Rearmament* (Cambridge, Cambridge University Press, 1991).
4. R. R. James, *Winston S. Churchill: his complete speeches, Vol. VIII, 1950–63* (New York and London, Chelsea House, 1974), pp. 7936–44; and see A. Seldon, *Churchill's Indian Summer* (London, Hodder and Stoughton, 1981) pp. 396–7.
5. *Public Papers of the Presidents of the United States, Dwight D. Eisenhower, 1953* (Washington, 1960), pp. 69–70.
6. Ibid., pp. 179–88; and on the debate leading to the speech see W. W. Rostow, *Europe after Stalin* (Austin, Texas, 1982).
7. PRO, FO 371/125030/9 (7 April).

8.   Vincent Auriol Papers, Archives Nationales (AN), Paris, 4 AU 116 (circular telegram, 8 April); Georges Bidault Papers, AN, box 45 (notes of 16 and 20 March).
9.   P. Boyle, *The Churchill–Eisenhower Correspondence, 1953–5* (Chapel Hill, NC, University of North Carolina Press, 1990), pp. 31–2.
10. E. Shuckburgh, *Descent to Suez: diaries, 1951–6* (London, Weidenfeld and Nicolson, 1986), pp. 82–5; Lord Avon (Anthony Eden) Papers, University of Birmingham Library, AP 20/1 (diary, 28 and 29 March, 2 and 3 April); PRO, PREM. 11/422 (28 March, 3 and 4 April).
11. Boyle, *Correspondence*, pp. 36–8, 41–4 and 46–53.
12. 515 HCDeb., 5s, cols. 883–98, especially 897; Seldon, *Indian Summer*, pp. 399–401.
13. René Mayer Papers, AN, 363 AP 22, file 6 ('Conditions dans lesquelles a été preparé … Bermudes', n.d.).
14. Boyle, *Correspondence*, pp. 61–8 and 73–8.
15. Ibid., p. 64.
16. Ibid., pp. 56–7; *Public Papers, 1953*, p. 326.
17. FO 371/103660/34 (30 May); PREM. 11/449/30 and 31 May.
18. US National Archives (USNA), Washington DC, State Department, Record Group 59, decimal files, 396.1 (4 and 7 June).
19. FO 371/106538/110 (29 May); PREM. 11/420 (25 May).
20. PREM. 11/428 (9–12 June).
21. M. Gilbert, *'Never Despair': Winston S. Churchill, 1945–65* (London, Heinemann, 1988), chapter 45.
22. Boyle, *Correspondence*, p. 81.
23. CAB. 128/26, CC (53) 39th (6 July).
24. Ibid., 42nd (13 July). For full records of the Washington conference see: CAB. 21/3073; *Foreign Relations of the United States (FRUS), 1952–4* (Washington, 1983), pp. 1607–96.
25. Boyle, *Correspondence*, pp. 87–8.
26. D. Folliot (ed.), *Documents on International Affairs, 1953* (1956), pp. 77–8, 81–91.
27. See, for example, Macmillan, *Tides of Fortune*, pp. 524–5.
28. Boyle, *Correspondence*, pp. 89–91.
29. Folliot, *Documents*, pp. 100–6.
30. Boyle, *Correspondence*, pp. 93–7.
31. Lord Moran, *Winston Churchill: the struggle for survival* (London, Constable, 1966), diary of 10 November.
32. PREM. 11/418 (11–12 November).
33. 520 HCDeb., 5s, cols 28–31; PREM. 11/418 (19 November); CAB. 129/64, C (53) 330 (24 November).
34. FO 371/103694/771, 103695/792 and 103985/8.
35. *Journal Officiel, Débats, Assemblée Nationale 1953*, pp. 5484–7; V. Auriol, *Journal du Septennat, Vol. VII, 1953–4* (Paris, 1971), pp. 537–9.
36. Cyrus L. Sulzberger, *A Long Row of Candles* (Toronto, 1969), pp. 921–2, 927–8 and 930–31; *FRUS, 1952–4*, V, 1729–31; USNA, lot files, CFM M-88, box 83 (16 and 28 November, 1 December).
37. Folliot, *Documents*, pp. 107–9.
38. Moran, *Churchill*, 2, 3 and 7 December; PREM. 11/418 (1 December).

39. *FRUS, 1952–4*, V, 1754–61, 1763–7, 1774–91; PREM. 11/418 (records of all formal meetings).
40. PREM. 11/418 (7 December); Folliot, *Documents*, pp. 110–11.
41. Moran, *Churchill*, 7 December.
42. *FRUS, 1952–4*, V, 1740–44, 1763–7, 1769–86, 1794–1806, 1834–7 and 1843–4; PREM. 11/418 (7 December).
43. *FRUS*, ibid., 1722, 1739–40, 1750–54, 1767–9 and 1786; for background to the speech see S. Ambrose, *Eisenhower, the President, 1952–69* (London, Allen and Unwin, 1984), pp. 145–7; for the text see *Public Papers, 1953*, pp. 813–22; and regarding British doubts see J. Colville, *The Fringes of Power: Downing Street Diaries* (London, Hodder and Stoughton, 1985), pp. 683–5.
44. *FRUS*, ibid., 1739–40, 1767–9, 1786; D. D. Eisenhower, *Mandate for Change* (New York, Doubleday, 1963), p. 249; Ambrose, *Eisenhower*, pp. 146–7.
45. *FRUS*, ibid., 1807–9; Sulzberger, *Candles*, pp. 933–5; I. McDonald, *Man of the Times* (London, 1976), p. 134.
46. Moran, *Churchill*, 4–8 December; Colville, *Fringes of Power*, pp. 689–90; G. Elgey, *La République des Illusions* (Paris, 1968), p. 331.
47. Elgey, *La République*, p. 332.
48. Reports on the Press in FO 371/103529/9 and 107447/44 and 45.
49. Sulzberger, *Candles*, pp. 930–33 and 935; PREM. 11/418 (7 December).
50. A version of this essay was originally published in the *English Historical Review*, 101 (1986), pp. 889–912. I am grateful to the British Academy for providing financial support for the research involved.

12 'Oh Don't Deceive Me': The Nassau Summit[1]
Mark Smith

The Anglo-American summit at Nassau in December 1962 has acquired the status of one of the defining moments in Anglo-American relations. The meeting was bookended on one side by a schism between the two governments surpassed only by Suez in the post-war years, and on the other by an agreement described as 'almost the bargain of the century': the sale of Polaris (then a state-of-the-art submarine-launched nuclear missile system) to Britain on terms that remain unparalleled to this day.[2] Although the summit was not solely concerned with Polaris – indeed the issue did not even appear on the original agenda – it has become, incontestably, the 'Polaris summit'. The weeks preceding the meeting saw the character of both the Anglo-American political relationship and British nuclear policy thrown into genuine question, but after two days of threats, emotivism and brinkmanship at Nassau, both were restored with striking thoroughness.

This achievement has led to close examination of the summit as a case study in 'special relationship' dynamics: the unprecedented nature of the final agreement, which was much more acceptable in its terms to the British than to the American delegation, seems to underline the unique nature of Anglo-American relations. The summit personnel were primarily politicians rather than professional diplomats or military specialists, and a particular emphasis has been placed on the role of the British Prime Minister, Harold Macmillan, and his friendship with President Kennedy. It has been argued that Macmillan's eloquent and affecting speeches at the summit, and a personal warmth between himself and the President (described as 'the most astonishing Prime Minister–President relationship in modern times') decisively swung the final decision Macmillan's way.[3] This account of Nassau, and by implication of summitry, clearly argues that the individual personalities present had a significant and possibly critical effect on the outcome; in other words, that different personnel would have produced a different result. They also carry, more implicitly, the assumption that a summit, as opposed to normal, lengthier diplomatic

182

channels, is the most appropriate occasion for the personal factor to be brought into play. The role of professional politicians in the evolution of summitry has been sharply criticized, notably by Eubank, who describes them as 'neophyte diplomats', and also by George Ball, who was a participant at the Nassau summit and whose jaded view of the summit process in general, and Nassau in particular led him to describe the summit as 'the ill-fated Nassau Conference'.[4] Both Ball and Eubank centre their criticism around, firstly, a lofty portrayal of politicians as ham-fisted amateurs irrevocably in thrall to partisan politics; and secondly a view of the concentrated atmosphere of summit meetings *per se* as fundamentally unsuited to major political decisions.[5] Ball argues: 'Not only do summit meetings exaggerate the role of personal chemistry ... but the sense of theatre they engender cannot help but color the judgement of the participants.... It is not an atmosphere that makes for cool judgement.'[6]

This leads to the questions that need to be addressed in the light of old and new evidence: firstly, was the summit largely symbolic with much of the substance decided beforehand, or was it the venue for substantial and free-ranging dialogue? In the case of Nassau, this focuses on how much of the eventual agreement was struck *at* the summit, and therefore the scope that existed for Macmillan's diplomacy to make a genuine difference to the outcome. Secondly, was a summit the most suitable venue for the issues under discussion? This can be divided into two issues: whether dealing with the matter at a summit meeting had a significant effect on the outcome, and whether a summit meeting was the appropriate setting for a decision on the future of Anglo-American nuclear relations. The third question concerns the role and importance of domestic politics at a summit primarily concerned with foreign and defence policy issues. A clear understanding of the outcome of the Nassau summit requires a brief prior examination of the nature of Anglo-American relations in the nuclear field, and the breakdown in this relationship in the weeks just before the meeting; both had a significant impact on the nature of the summit. Therefore this chapter will begin with an analysis of these issues, followed by an examination of the conference itself.

ANGLO-AMERICAN RELATIONS AND THE SKYBOLT AFFAIR

That wider and important political considerations were inescapably bound up in the issue of Polaris, and therefore with Nassau, is something that needs to be kept in mind from the outset; very little of what follows can be understood without a firm grasp of the prevailing orthodoxy in the British government that surrounded the nuclear programme and the Anglo-American relationship. The British nuclear weapons project and the relationship with the US both enjoyed strikingly iconic status in post-war British politics, but particularly so during Macmillan's tenure as Prime Minister. He put the two at the heart of his foreign and defence policy, and the increasing Anglo-American cooperation in the nuclear field over this period drew closer two strands of policy that were always, at least in British eyes, inextricably linked. In Clark's words, 'the effects of the nuclear rapprochement with the US, which is the critical occurrence of the years 1957–62 … go well beyond the realm of nuclear strategy and impinge upon the entire foreign policy architecture of the British government'.[7] It is important to note here that, in spite of the deepening Anglo-American nuclear relationship, it was a fundamental principle of the British programme that the nuclear force *must* retain some 'independence' outside of its more obvious role in the NATO military machine; this concept was to be a crucial obstacle to agreement at Nassau.[8] The climax of the growing Anglo-American *rapprochement* came in 1960, with US agreement to sell an air-launched nuclear missile called Skybolt to the British; this agreement also contained two implicit though never fully stated clauses that were to resurface two years later as tools in British diplomacy at Nassau. The first was a British – but not necessarily American – understanding that Polaris would be a contingency item should Skybolt fail to arrive.[9] Second, a tacit bargain existed to the effect that the provision of Skybolt was a quid pro quo for British agreement to allow Holy Loch in Scotland to be used as a base for US Polaris submarines.[10] Both these, but in particular the latter, were to be invoked at the Nassau summit as moral, if not legal, obligations on the US. The defining topic at the Nassau summit developed two years later, when the US government decided to cancel the Skybolt programme in late 1962.

Domestically, 1962 had been a difficult year for Macmillan, and by the autumn the public popularity of the government had reached an all-time low. Ongoing economic difficulties and dwindling public popularity had led him to sack a third of his Cabinet in July; the British EEC entry application was also suffering setbacks, and unemployment was approaching a post-war high. A series of by-election disasters further deepened his predicament.[11] On 7 November, the US Defense Secretary, Robert McNamara, informed the British government by telephone that the Skybolt programme was in severe and possibly terminal difficulty, although he stressed that no final decision had been taken.[12] This was clearly a grave blow: with the administration already in serious difficulties, two of the most resonantly emblematic elements in Macmillan's foreign and defence policy – the nuclear programme and the Anglo-American relationship of which it was a vital part – abruptly became a cause for serious concern. Hence, as the crisis unfolded and the summit approached, Macmillan was playing for very high stakes in terms of both his foreign and defence policy, and also, possibly, his political future.[13]

The view from Washington was a different one, in which internal divisions rather than domestic difficulties were important. The Skybolt affair, and more precisely the debate over its replacement, exposed a division within the Kennedy administration. Schlesinger, a well-placed observer, pin-points the problem: a resolution of the problem 'compelled the President to choose between those in his own government whose main interest lay in transforming Western Europe, including Britain, into a unified political and economic entity, and those whose main interest lay in guarding the Anglo-American special relationship and integrity of the deterrent'.[14] The former included the 'Grand Design' advocates in the Kennedy administration, who felt, probably correctly, that Britain's possession of a unilateral nuclear force was a barrier to entry into the EEC, and by implication to greater West European unity in the cold war; the cancellation of Skybolt offered an opportunity to end this and facilitate increased British participation in Europe.[15] Moreover, at a time when many in the US were uneasy at possible nuclear ambitions on the part of France and Germany, to provide the British with an American-produced weapon ran the risk of setting a precedent, or at least legitimizing unilateral nuclear forces; the new US strategy embodied in the McNamara Doctrine emphasized tight presidential – in other words, US – control of NATO's nuclear forces and deplored 'independent' nuclear programmes.[16]

In opposition was a second, more disparate group that voiced grave concern at the political consequences in Britain if Skybolt should be canceled without a suitable replacement being offered. A briefing-paper prepared for President Kennedy only five days before the summit argued that this would mean the end of the Macmillan government, and stated the possible consequences in stark terms:

> The alternative is a Labour Government which would be equivocal on the subject of the EEC, would persist in dangerous illusions regarding East–West relations, would wish to spend more on social welfare and less on defence, and would allow the British ship of state ... to drift towards the Scandinavian position of part-participant, part-spectator with regard to the Atlantic community.[17]

The arrival of a Labour administration in the following year showed these fears to be largely illusory, but the fact that they were being expressed so bluntly is significant in understanding the position of the US delegation at the Nassau conference. The Kennedy administration was caught between the logic of its own nuclear and European policies, and the potentially serious effect on a major ally if the logic of those policies was followed through.

Clearly, there were strong incentives on both sides of the Atlantic for relations to be repaired, and a mutually satisfactory resolution found. Whilst the concept of a 'special relationship' might have had more immediate political resonance in Britain than in the US, the quid pro quo over the use of Holy Loch and the highly Atlanticist stance of the Macmillan administration seems to indicate that fractured Anglo-American relations would have considerable repercussions in Washington as well as London. Given this, it is odd that there seems to have been little or no intergovernmental discussion on the issue prior to the summit. The only direct contact appears to have been a meeting between McNamara and Thorneycroft on 11 December, when formal notice of Skybolt's demise was given. This was probably the last time, prior to the summit, that meaningful discussion at Cabinet level was possible. The next step up for this from the British point of view was the Prime Minister–President link, as Thorneycroft made clear to Macmillan shortly before the talks with McNamara.[18] The meeting was not a success: Skybolt seemed doomed, and the only viable replacement – Polaris – was only offered as part of a NATO force under alliance control.[19] The meeting is also notable in the respect that curtailing the use of Holy Loch was explicitly threatened. Thorneycroft, dismayed at the fate of Skybolt and rebuffed on Polaris, told McNamara that the Skybolt sale was 'intimately related' to British agreement to the use of Holy Loch, and therefore a cancellation of Skybolt would 'present the UK Government with gravest difficulties in maintaining desired US–UK relations'.[20] This meeting failed to provide any kind of consensus on possible replacements, and so when the summit began there was still much to be decided. The extent to which *unilateral* decisions were taken on what was required is important, since it should provide some indication of how far the two delegations at Nassau were in accord when negotiations began, and thus how far the personnel at the summit were genuinely able to affect the outcome.

The fact that the only direct consultations seem to have been those just mentioned has led some analysts to conclude that the British government deliberately maintained a silence, preferring to let an atmosphere of mistrust and betrayal build up in order to increase the pressure on the Kennedy administration (whose views on unilateral nuclear forces were well known) to provide an alternative to Skybolt.[21] It is worth taking time to examine this question, since its implications for summitry should be clear. A close reading of the available records does not bear out this thesis, but does none the less shed some interesting light on summitry and Nassau.

The summit meeting itself was arranged on around 17 November; although the precise date of Skybolt's inclusion on the agenda is not clear, it was raised by the British government on 25 November, and agreed between London and Washington by 4 December.[22] Clearly then, the implications of McNamara's phone call in early November had sunk in sufficiently for the British government to want to discuss it with the President. The British Ambassador in Washington, David Ormsby-Gore, advised the Foreign Secretary, Home, on 8 December that 'if ... Skybolt cannot be saved, this [the summit] is certainly the moment for us to put forward whatever alternative demands we may wish to make'.[23] Other minutes also indicate that the summit was seen as potentially a fruitful option, but express caution over how far to rely on the Prime Minister–President link.[24] It seems that the British were waiting for the US to provide some indications of replacement options for the cancelled Skybolt. Moreover, there appears to have been a distinct lack of consensus within the British government over what they themselves favoured. Thorneycroft opted for Polaris from an early stage,[25] whilst Macmillan was still arguing on 9 December that 'our best plan would be to try and play Skybolt along for another year to eighteen months in order to avoid political difficulties at home'.[26] Apart from indicating that Polaris was not a universally favoured choice, this position as expressed is hard to square with the argument that Macmillan deliberately allowed Anglo-American discord to become so heated and so public that a high-level summit became the venue for the matter to be resolved.

On balance then it appears that the British government failed to give a clear indication to their US counterparts of what they required, due to lack of agreement among themselves and a latent feeling that it was incumbent on the US to state the available options. From this it follows that the US government must have had little clear idea of British goals at the Nassau summit, and therefore that any proposals drawn up prior to the meeting were formulated with the US *perception* of British require-ments in mind. Moreover, with little or no input from London, the potential scope for American priorities to affect the outcome was corre-spondingly higher. The problem of how to resolve the Kennedy adminis-tration's foreign policy with an arrangement drawn up by the previous administration was tackled at a meeting held in Washington a few days before the summit.[27] The key participants at this meeting – Kennedy,

McNamara, McGeorge Bundy, George Ball and David Bruce (US ambassador to Britain) – were also at the summit; moreover these personnel were representative of the intra-administration dispute over Skybolt. Ball saw the US-sponsored British nuclear programme as an inhibitor of British entry into the EEC, whilst McNamara and probably Kennedy himself voiced concern at the political consequences of cancelling Skybolt with no replacement. The dilemma was summed up by Bundy as 'grave political risks for Mr Macmillan if we should not help him, and serious risks also for our own policy in Europe if we should help him too much'.[28] The proposal adopted was therefore an attempt to reconcile two conflicting areas of policy which met in the issue of Skybolt, and the significant part ran as follows: '1. We would offer appropriate components of Polaris missiles to the British. 2. It would be a condition of this offer that the British would commit their eventual Polaris forces to a multilateral or multinational force in NATO.'[29]

The second clause of this proposal was to be the focus of negotiations at the summit, but a further episode added a significant facet to the US negotiating position. *En route* to the summit, the President and David Ormsby-Gore, two good personal friends, drew up an alternative programme under which the US and Britain would continue with the Skybolt programme and split the costs fifty-fifty, although only Britain would actually deploy the missile.[30] Thus Kennedy had agreed to two different offers in as many days. A clue to the reasoning behind this can be found in the minutes of the Washington meeting. David Bruce, the US ambassador to Britain, in pointing out the political consequences in Britain of cancelling Skybolt, had argued that 'the old question was what would satisfy the Prime Minister's needs for this hour, and he [Bruce] thought that only the Prime Minister could answer this question'.[31] The fact that Kennedy was receptive to this logic seems to indicate that to 'meet the Prime Minister's needs' was what fundamentally had been decided at the meeting; he very likely assumed that Ormsby-Gore was acting with at least the tacit blessing of London when he drew up the deal. The implications for Nassau and summitry are twofold. Firstly, this development suggests that it was the immediate political (rather than military) requirements of the Prime Minister that were uppermost in Kennedy's mind, and therefore that any arrangement would have to be sanctioned through this channel. In short, the time when the Skybolt affair could have been resolved through low-key diplomatic or bureaucratic channels seems to have passed. Secondly, the fact that Kennedy agreed to two separate and different arrangements so close together suggests that he was unsure of what the Prime Minister's 'needs for this hour' actually were, and is therefore a further indication that little or no discussion took place between the two governments prior to the summit.[32] Clearly then, a substantial amount of discussion had yet to take place as the summit negotiations opened.

THE SUMMIT MEETING, 18–22 DECEMBER 1962

The make-up of the two delegations at Nassau is significant both for an understanding of negotiating positions and for the character of what was to follow. The British delegation consisted almost entirely of politicians – Macmillan, Home and Thorneycroft – and professional civil servants (mostly private secretaries). Most of the negotiations described in the minutes of the meeting were carried out by the politicians of the party, but the role of their advisers in drawing up the various drafts around which much of the discussion took place is less clear.[33] The highly political nature of the British party is evidence of the wider importance of the Skybolt issue: at stake was considerably more than a piece of military hardware. Baylis also suggests that the omission of any military advisers from the Chiefs of Staff was a deliberate attempt on the part of the Prime Minister to marginalize the military, whose interminable infighting over the nature of the British nuclear programme had bedevilled his tenure at the Ministry of Defence in the 1950s.[34] The composition of the US delegation is equally significant, since it was similar to that of the Washington meeting and thus represented almost a microcosm of the divide within the administration itself. This division, it is important to note, was not so much over Polaris itself as the *conditions* of such an offer. Ball had argued at the pre-summit meeting in Washington that 'a decision in favour of a national force in this range of weapons would change our entire policy and would represent a major political decision'.[35] The operative word in this sentence is 'national': Ball favoured a nuclear force under NATO control, and was thus keen to avoid any offer of Polaris under the same terms as the Skybolt offer. This effectively meant that the apparatus for such a system would have to be drawn up prior to offering the actual hardware, and thus that any offer to the British *at* Nassau was to be avoided; what *was* required was British assent to such a system.

The reasons behind the British failure to consult with the US over Skybolt have already been described as a mixture of diplomatic paralysis and lack of agreement over what was required. This latter problem seems to have existed until very shortly before the summit, but by the time the delegation actually arrived in Nassau, Polaris had emerged as the only acceptable option; Ormsby-Gore was informed that the agreement he had drawn up with Kennedy *en route* was no longer satisfactory, and Macmillan himself informed Kennedy of this in informal talks the evening before negotiations began.[36] Several writers have noted the resentful mood of the British delegation as it arrived in the Bahamas, and there has been some debate over whether this was deliberately exaggerated in order to encourage a satisfactory offer in what promised to be a difficult summit. Nunnerley admits that some State Department officials certainly felt that the British had encouraged the atmosphere to become colder than events merited, and cagily acknowledges that it would have suited the British if this were the case.[37] At any rate, it has been remarked on more than one occasion, and with varying degrees of good humour, that the (British) choice of welcoming tune to be played as Kennedy got off the plane at Nassau – 'Oh Don't Deceive Me' – seemed a little too apposite to be a coincidence.[38]

As the discussions opened on 19 December, Kennedy was aware, possibly for the first time, of what the British required, and it has been shown that he had already prepared a draft offer on Polaris. Therefore, the real issue to be decided at Nassau was not *whether* Polaris would be offered, but rather the *terms* on which such an offer might be agreed. Macmillan's opening remarks at the summit show his grasp of the principal obstacle to a satisfactory outcome for his delegation. After some remarks expressing regret at the way in which the summit meeting had been overshadowed by Skybolt but stressing that 'the question had blown up and must be resolved'[39] (in other words, it must be resolved *at* the summit), he went on to say that he 'fully appreciated the feelings which President Kennedy and his Government had about the dangers of doing anything which might be obnoxious to European countries'.[40] He tried to counter this by arguing that the history of Anglo-American nuclear cooperation made Britain a special case; the NATO allies, 'and especially President de Gaulle', were fully aware of this and thus there was no danger of either setting a dangerous precedent or jeopardizing moves towards European integration. The Prime Minister then censured the NATO nuclear force, favoured by Ball, as premature, and wound up by requesting 'a switch from the lame horse, Skybolt, to what was now the favourite, Polaris'.[41] This was a well-briefed and highly perceptive opening gambit on Macmillan's part: he was attempting to answer the State Department arguments on European cohesion and the British EEC application before they were actually put, and invoking Anglo-American nuclear cooperation subtly underlined the link between the Skybolt agreement and US use of Holy Loch. In contrast to Thorneycroft's blunt pre-summit threat to McNamara, Macmillan trod carefully around the Holy Loch issue at Nassau: he stated that the US would be able to keep these bases even if the Skybolt issue remained unresolved. Thus Macmillan's playing of the Holy Loch card aimed at invoking a sense of moral obligation rather than a threat.

Kennedy's reply to this is intriguing, given what had been agreed in Washington immediately prior to the summit. The fifty-fifty deal on Skybolt, which he had drawn up with Ormsby-Gore *en route* to the summit, was reiterated, although the President should have been aware that this was no longer acceptable. It seems likely that Kennedy was conscious of his own internal concerns here. The Skybolt arrangement would be more favourably received than Polaris in the State Department, and moreover would only be an adjustment to an existing arrangement and so would not go against Kennedy's own policies on Europe and national nuclear forces. In other words, to offer Polaris straight away would have been politically very tricky. This proposal was therefore very much along the lines favoured by George Ball and the State Department. The President then produced a draft communiqué outlining his opening offer of either Skybolt, or a joint study on 'assigning' a possible British Polaris force to NATO. Later that day, however, a highly significant addition was submitted by the US delegation. The important part of this ran as follows: 'Only in the event of a dire national emergency ... would Her Majesty's Government be faced with a decision of utilizing such forces on its own.'[42] This sentence represented an American attempt to provide the kind of opt-out clause that would enable the British government to claim that the nuclear force was, at the last resort, fundamentally independent rather than simply a component of a NATO multinational force; the American delegation, like its British counterparts, was clearly very aware of the concerns of their opposite numbers. In presenting this document, Kennedy then, in response to a query from Macmillan regarding the use of the phrase 'assigned to NATO', put his finger on the real problem that would have to be resolved at Nassau: 'For their different reasons, the UK wanted the word "assign" interpreted as loosely as possible and the US wanted it interpreted as tightly as possible.'[43]

The discussions that ensued were characterized by competing redrafts submitted by each delegation, with the concepts of 'independence' and 'assign', and the public meaning attached to them, the focus of dispute. At the heart were two notions of the British nuclear programme that were substantially at odds. The conflicting concepts clashed in the form of a pair of fundamentally irreconcilable foreign/defence policies which could not coexist explicitly in the same agreement – this was the dilemma facing the negotiators at Nassau. The state of play after a day's negotiations can be judged from a despondent cable Macmillan sent to Rab Butler (Deputy Prime Minister) in London:

I am afraid things are not at present going very well.... So far the Americans have felt unwilling to offer us the Polaris missile on terms that are acceptable to us. They wish us to assign the whole of the British Polaris force to NATO or a multilateral force. Such an arrangement would not give us an independent contribution to the nuclear deterrent in any real sense of the word, since under the American proposal we would only be able to withdraw the force from NATO in the event of a dire national emergency. It would therefore not be available outside the NATO area or play a role in strengthening our foreign policy.... I am sorry to send you such a depressing report, but I still feel the Americans do not like the idea of ditching their old friends. Unlike his highbrow advisers, the President is a political animal and senses the dangers ahead.[44]

In 'highbrow advisers' Macmillan probably included George Ball, who throughout the summit continued to press the State Department case for a multilateral force. Ball has since become a prominent critic both of summitry and Nassau; this is hardly surprising since the final agreement that was drawn up was considerably more satisfactory to the British delegation than to the US. The British Polaris force would be used for 'international defence of the Western alliance' (a much broader term than that of 'defending the NATO area'), with an opt-out clause when 'supreme national interests were at stake'; the multilateral force was relegated to a bland and isolated paragraph promising 'best endeavours to this end'.[45] Kennedy's efforts to produce a tightly worded set of conditions were therefore largely thwarted, as the indistinct terms of the agreement testify. In Nunnerley's words, 'Kennedy had been reluctant to consider an unconditional offer of Polaris'[46] – the operative word in this sentence being 'unconditional' – and the conditions that were eventually agreed were far more imprecise than he or his administration would have wished. Macmillan's emotively put case that it would have to be Polaris without strings, or nothing, clearly had the desired effect. The nature of a summit meeting as such and the short time-frame it imposes had only a limited effect on the outcome of this particular summit. It is true that the submitted drafts and the final agreement were put together in a hurry, but this is only partly to blame for the vagueness of the terms: these terms were also vague by design. This was primarily a British aim, as Kennedy's earlier point about the British wanting terms defined as loosely as possible makes clear, but the ambiguities also served to bridge the gap between two policies; the President had acknowledged that 'the difficulty was that in the next few weeks [the two governments] might be saying different things'.[47] Therefore the gap between the US and British positions, even given the considerable ground conceded by the American delegation, was papered over with vagueness.

CONCLUSION

The agreement at Nassau played an important role in repairing a potentially damaging problem in Anglo-American relations; by the end of the meeting the status of the Atlantic relationship and the British nuclear programme had been restored to their former place in British foreign policy. A critical factor in this was the concessions granted by the US delegation at the summit; that these concessions were substantial is indicated by the criticisms of the agreement voiced by George Ball. The topic to be addressed now is the extent to which the nature of the agreement was decided *at* the summit, and affected *by* the summit atmosphere.

The first and most obvious factor in this assessment is that of how far the substance of the agreement was arranged prior to the meeting itself. It seems clear that in the case of the Nassau summit little was actually discussed, much less concluded, beforehand. In the first place, the lack of communication between London and Washington, particularly in the month or so after McNamara's telephone notification in November, meant that there was little or no opportunity for any kind of preliminary draft to be drawn up in time for the summit. It has been argued above that this silence was due more to political uncertainty and ineptitude than to a deliberate wish to decide matters at the summit itself. Therefore, while both sides had discussed negotiating options among themselves before the meeting, there was little interadministration contact to draw up any drafts to discuss. This has clear and direct implications for the question of how far the summit was the venue for substantial dialogue, rather than a symbolic exercise in public relations. The summit was certainly symbolic (this will be returned to below) but the negotiations did show a genuine amount of progress, as might have been expected given the lack of discussion beforehand. The US meeting in Washington is clear evidence that the delegation came to Nassau prepared to *offer* Polaris; the British arrived at the summit having decided, eventually, to *request* it. The axis of negotiation was the terms on which this could be agreed, and most accounts of the summit demonstrate that reaching this agreement was no mean task. At the heart was a fundamental and largely irreconcilable difference in foreign policy architecture. Neither could accede to the demands of the other without compromising an important element of its foreign policy (for the British, the concept of an essentially independent nuclear force; for the

US, its European policy, the multilateralist idea and the basic ethos of the McNamara Doctrine) and yet alliance politics and the importance of the Anglo-American axis to both governments exerted strong pressure for some sort of compromise to be devised.

Therefore the negotiations at Nassau were a genuine dialogue between conflicting foreign policy priorities, which produced a substantive, if necessarily vague, agreement. The extent to which domestic politics affected the outcome can now be assessed. It has been shown that both parties were acutely aware of the domestic political scene in their respective states. This was particularly true in the British case: the importance of the British nuclear programme and the Anglo-American relationship of which it was an integral part were of critical importance to Macmillan's foreign and defence policy, but the domestic difficulties of the British government lent the Skybolt affair an added gravity. Whether an unsatisfactorily resolved crisis might have proved fatal for Macmillan's government is a hypothetical question, and a difficult one to answer, but it can safely be said that an unsatisfactory resolution of the Skybolt problem would have had serious implications for the government's credibility; moreover, the fact that this view was being expressed at the time suggests that these fears were genuinely felt, even if they may have been illusory. This helps to explain why the British delegation was not interested in the study of Polaris offered by Kennedy at Nassau: for the sake of his domestic position, the Prime Minister had to return from the summit with a tangible gain. The domestic influences on the US delegation were less serious. It is true to say that the Kennedy administration was divided on the issue of what to offer the British, but this was not the kind of home front crisis confronted by Macmillan. Rather, the US delegation was attempting to reconcile different priorities within its foreign policy, as opposed to facing possibly serious knock-on effects of an unsuccessful summit on its domestic position.

Finally, there is the matter of whether the summit itself was the appropriate venue for this particular matter to be settled. As previously indicated, this question can be divided into two parts: (a) did the fact that the issue was dealt with *at* a summit meeting have a significant effect on the final decision – in other words, did the venue affect the outcome?; and (b) was a summit meeting the appropriate setting for a decision on the future of Anglo-American nuclear relations? Several factors argue for an affirmative answer to both these questions. Firstly, the nature of this particular summit had a clear effect on the outcome. The atmosphere of suspicion that had built up by the time of the meeting itself has been noted previously, as has the British argument that the Skybolt issue needed resolution *at* the summit. Thus the need to settle the issue within two days lent a sense of urgency to the proceedings, and the inability to consider the matter at length, coupled with the fact that at the heart of the dispute was a deeper conflict in nuclear policy, had a clear effect on the document that was eventually cobbled together. This raises Ball's critique of summits and the negative effect of 'the sense of theatre they engender'.[48] This was particularly clearly the case at the Nassau summit, as the breach in Atlantic relations lent an added dimension to the crowded and very high-profile ambience of the summit itself. Moreover, the subsequent Anglo-American dispute over British obligations to the proposed NATO nuclear force suggest that the Nassau summit had not resolved the fundamental differences, but had only repaired relations sufficiently for an agreement to be worked out. The vagueness of the document itself is further evidence both of this, and of the fact that the issue needed to be resolved in large part at the summit. A trickier question to answer is whether the personnel at the summit affected the outcome. Ball and others clearly imply (critically or otherwise) that Macmillan's relationship with Kennedy was the decisive factor at Nassau, but this can be questioned or at least qualified. It has been shown that Kennedy was already prepared to offer Polaris – on terms – to the British delegation when he arrived at Nassau; the basis of this seems to have been the domestic position of a loyalist administration and still pivotal NATO ally. It has also been shown that the terms on which this draft offer was predicated were substantially withdrawn at the summit. However, it seems hard to believe that this took place on the grounds that Kennedy simply 'liked' Macmillan, as Ball claims; alliance pressures and priorities are not operative only on certain individuals. This is not to say that Macmillan's summit diplomacy was not critical, since it clearly was so; rather his achievement was to impress the seriousness of his domestic position and the crucial importance of the nuclear programme to his foreign policy, as opposed simply to invoking his friendship with the President.

The question of whether the summit was the appropriate venue for this matter to be dealt with can now be tackled. The two considerations to bear in mind in answering this question are the nature of what was at stake at Nassau, and the state of Anglo-American relations at the time of the summit. In the case of the former, a fundamental key to understanding the British position at Nassau is the foreign policy role that was assigned to Skybolt/Polaris which went well beyond its utility as military hardware. The potential cancellation of the US Skybolt sale had implications for the entire shape of British foreign and defence policy, and therefore merited resolution at the highest level. The failure of Thorneycroft and McNamara to find a solution at their meeting was possibly the last chance of resolving the problem before the summit. Moreover, the US government was faced with a conflict within its administration, a contradiction forced into the open by the failure of the Skybolt programme. That this intra-administration dispute reached the level of McNamara and Ball suggests that it would have to be the President who made the final decision. The second factor at work here is the state of Anglo-American relations at the time. Both the very public role and emblematic character given to the Atlantic axis by the British government, and the importance of alliance politics in both governments, dictated that the atmosphere could not be allowed to remain so visibly soured for long; the air not only needed to be cleared, but had to be *seen* to be cleared. Thus, while the summit at Nassau was not drawn up with Skybolt in mind, it became the most opportune venue for the matter to be considered. In summary then, the implications of Nassau for the study of summitry are fourfold. Firstly, despite the limited available time and the high-profile atmosphere of an international summit, it is nevertheless possible for substantial dialogue to take place and for important agreements to be reached *at* the summit itself. To a certain extent, the urgency imposed by time and profile can themselves create pressure for progress to be made, although wider political circumstances will also play a key role. This has both positive and negative aspects: on the positive side, the atmosphere of a summit meeting can help to force participants to cut through political deadlocks, thrash out their differences face to face, and patch up fractured relationships in a very public fashion. On the other hand, these same pressures created by summits can also lead to agreements which are ill-considered and badly thought through; in other words, by creating unrealistic expectations and imposing undue haste, summitry as a politico-diplomatic process can produce agreements that give the illusion of full agreement where only partial accord actually exists. The Skybolt crisis merited high-level, high-profile resolution and a summit meeting is thus an attractive venue, but the pressures created *by* summits make proper consideration difficult (although it should be borne in mind that considerable pressure had already built up *before* the meeting). Secondly, the scope for individuals to make a difference to the outcome may be considerable, given the small numbers of personnel, the face to face discussions and the limits on time. However, this should be qualified: a key argument in this chapter has been that the personal friendship between Macmillan and Kennedy had only a limited effect on the outcome. Of greater importance were the former's eloquent and forceful diplomacy, and the latter's own doubts about a NATO nuclear force and concern over the state of Anglo-American relations. The personal beliefs and diplomacy of individuals thus have a prominent role. Thirdly, it is clear that domestic politics can impinge on summit negotiations to a significant degree: the domestic popularity (or otherwise) of an administration is always likely to have a significant bearing on the aims of one delegation, but of additional importance is the strength of the link – if any – between domestic position and the subject under discussion. At Nassau, as has been shown, this link was strong and thus created additional pressure on both delegations to produce a helpful result.

Finally, the nature of summit meetings lends itself to the stuff of 'high politics'. The image of top-level politicians in a very high profile atmosphere, especially given the media-driven nature of modern politics, means that summitry is a naturally attractive process for high level discussions on important issues in foreign and defence policy, despite the problems which are unavoidably engendered by the use of summits to deal with such topics. This is particularly true of a summit involving two close cold war allies, and more so when the summit involves allies whose relations were as intertwined as those between Britain and the US. In these circumstances, the potent symbolism of a meeting at the highest level to repair a breach in relations is likely to provide a strong incentive for employing this channel of diplomacy.

NOTES AND REFERENCES

1. I would like to thank Professor John Baylis and Dr Len Scott of the Department of International Politics, University of Wales Aberystwyth, and Dr David H. Dunn of the University of Birmingham, for encouragement, advice and comments on earlier versions of this piece.
2. J. Dickie, *Special No More* (London, Weidenfeld & Nicolson, 1994), p. 124.
3. D. Nunnerley, *President Kennedy and Britain* (London, Bodley Head, 1972), pp. 30, 33; A. Horne, *Macmillan Vol. 2* (London, Macmillan, 1989), pp. 437–9; G. Ball, *Diplomacy for a Crowded World* (London, Bodley Head, 1976), p. 32.
4. K. Eubank, *The Summit Conferences 1919–1960* (Oklahoma City, University of Oklahoma Press, 1966), p. vii; Ball, *Diplomacy for a Crowded World*, p. 32.
5. See Eubank, *The Summit Conferences*, p. 201; Ball, *Diplomacy for a Crowded World*, pp. 30–5.
6. Ball, *Diplomacy for a Crowded World*, pp. 33–4; Eubank, *The Summit Conferences*, p. 198
7. I. Clark, *Nuclear Diplomacy and the Special Relationship* (London, Oxford University Press, 1994), p. 28.

8.   Despite this rhetorical stress on independence, by the time of the Nassau summit Britain was effectively dependent on the US for crucial components of its nuclear programme; moreover, the blend of independence and interdependence with the US in British nuclear strategy was blurred and sometimes contradictory. See Clark, *Nuclear Diplomacy*, pp. 14–17.

9.   D. C. Watt, 'Demythologizing the Eisenhower Era' in W. R. Louis and H. Bull (eds), *The Special Relationship* (London, OUP, 1986), p. 67.

10.   See R. Neustadt, *Alliance Politics* (New York, Columbia University Press, 1970), pp. 33–4.

11.   Horne, *Macmillan*, pp. 428–9.

12.   McNamara had in fact recommended that the President cancel the programme. See A. Schlesinger, *A Thousand Days* (London, Andre Deutsch, 1965), p. 732.

13.   See Clark, *Nuclear Diplomacy*, pp. 409–10; Nunnerley, *President Kennedy and Britain*, p. 151; J. Baylis, *Anglo-American Defence Relations 1939–84* (London, Macmillan, 2nd edn, 1984), p. 101.

14.   Schlesinger, *A Thousand Days*, p. 731.

15.   Ibid., p. 734.

16.   See L. Freedman, *The Evolution of Nuclear Strategy* (London, Macmillan, 2nd edn, 1989), p. 307.

17.   Clark, *Nuclear Diplomacy*, p. 410.

18.   See Thorneycroft to PM, 7/12/62, DEFE 13/410 Public Record Office (PRO).

19.   McNamara was himself under pressure. He had been handed a State Department letter, signed by Secreatry of State Dean Rusk, instructing him not to offer Polaris to Thorneycroft under any circumstances. See Neustadt, *Alliance Politics*, pp. 45–8.

20.   See Bruce to Secretary of State, 11 December 1962, RG 59, 741.5612/12–11–62, US National Archive, Washington DC.

21.   See for example S. Zuckerman, *Monkeys, Men and Missiles* (London, Collins, 1988), p. 252. Baylis, more cautiously, comments that 'If the British were as Machiavellian as this, and they may well have been, the need to do so may have stemmed from their belief that the United States was deliberately trying to force Britain out of the nuclear club.' Baylis, *Anglo-American Defence Relations*, p. 102. In the case of George Ball et al., this assessment by the British was an accurate one; in the case of Kennedy it is less clear. The President had described the British nuclear programme as 'a political necessity, but a piece of military foolishness'.

22.   Horne, *Macmillan*, p. 428. See de Zulueta to PM 25/1/62, and Ormsby-Gore to Foreign Office 4/12/62; both in PREM 11/4229 PRO.

23.   Ormsby-Gore to Home 8/12/62, PREM 11/4229 PRO.

24.   See Fraser to Thorneycroft 2/11/62, 9/11/62, 14/11/62, DEFE 13/409 PRO; Harris to Hockaday 9/11/62, DEFE 13/409 PRO.

25.   Clark, *Nuclear Diplomacy*, p. 355.

26.   Ibid., p. 357.

27.   Copy of original record kindly provided by Dr Ian Clark, Selwyn College, University of Cambridge. The original is 'Memo of Conversation by Bundy, 16/12/62', R. E. Neustadt Papers, Box 19, Government Consulting,

Skybolt/Atlantic Affairs, 12/62 Skybolt/Nassau (Classified) Folder 3, Kennedy Library, Boston.

28. Ibid.
29. Ibid.
30. Neustadt, *Alliance Politics*, p. 51.
31. 'Memo of Conversation by Bundy'.
32. Although Thorneycroft clearly did prefer Polaris and had said as much to McNamara, the Prime Minister had made no such preference clear. See note 26.
33. The minutes of the Nassau summit are contained in 'Prime Minister's Talks with President Kennedy and Mr. Diefenbaker', PREM 11/4229 PRO.
34. See J. Baylis, *Ambiguity and Deterrence* (London, Oxford University Press, 1996).
35. 'Memo of Conversation by Bundy'.
36. See Neustadt, *Alliance Politics*, p. 51; Nunnerley, *President Kennedy and Britain*, p. 155.
37. Nunnerley, *President Kennedy and Britain*, pp. 148–9.
38. See ibid., p. 153; Horne, *Macmillan*, p. 437; G. Ball, *The Past Has Another Pattern* (New York, Norton, 1982), p. 266.
39. 'Prime Minister's Talks', p. 7.
40. Ibid.
41. Ibid., p. 8.
42. Ibid., p. 21.
43. Ibid., p. 17.
44. PM to First Secretary of State, 20/12/62, PREM 11/4229 PRO.
45. 'Prime Minister's Talks', pp. 37–8.
46. Nunnerley, *President Kennedy and Britain*, p. 158.
47. 'Prime Minister's Talks', p. 33.
48. See previous reference, note 6.

13 'A Family Affair': the Lancaster House Agreement

Edmund Yorke

The great 'indaba' held at Lancaster House, London, which successfully achieved the final constitutional settlement of the Rhodesian problem, represented the political culmination of nearly 15 years of bitter and protracted military conflict which had virtually ruined one of the strongest economies in Africa and cost the lives of over 10 000 black and white Rhodesians. As one of the last great 'Colonial Conferences'[1] it was very much a one-off summit in terms of post-war international conference diplomacy. Nevertheless, this marathon conference which took place over three tortuous months between 10 September and 15 December 1979, incorporating over 47 plenary sessions, did exhibit some parallels with the conduct of the great superpower and economic summits of the post-war period. Moreover, it may yet be seen to have bequeathed important political legacies of direct relevance to the current Ulster peace talks in London and Dublin.

In this chapter the Lancaster House Agreement will be used as a platform for discussion of several processes or techniques, some of which typified the conduct of post-war Western summitry. Firstly, the question of how far Lancaster House was itself pre-determined by the deliberations and results of earlier summit meetings will be addressed. In this context the Commonwealth Heads of Government Summit held in Lusaka, Zambia in August 1979 and the Non-Aligned Summit held in Havana, Cuba in September 1979 will form a central focus of discussion. Secondly, stress will be laid upon the timing and location of this particular summit as a significant factor in its success. The importance of domestic factors, especially military imperatives, will also be emphasized as both an integral part of the pre-summit negotiations and of the actual processes of Lancaster House itself. These last two aspects will themselves be deployed to advance the argument that both facilitated the widespread use of 'dominant third party mediation'; and even coercive diplomatic tactics by the

200

host country, Britain, in order to achieve a solution to the Rhodesian problem. Finally (and this will reveal the untypical aspects of the Lancaster House Summit), there will be an attempt to highlight the vitally important role of the Commonwealth institution or 'family' and, in particular, the individual members of that family in determining both the processes and results of the summit.

Before embarking upon a detailed discussion of the techniques of summitry revealed at Lancaster House it is, however, important to review briefly the historical background to what has become one of the most successful post-war summits.

Since November 1965, when Ian Smith's Rhodesia Front Government had illegally proclaimed a Unilateral Declaration of Independence (UDI),[2] after repeatedly rejecting British proposals for a democratic multiracial constitution, the problem of the Rhodesian rebellion had haunted successive Labour and Conservative administrations. It was to be a prolonged international crisis largely due to Harold Wilson's early decision not to use force. In the words of R. Good:

> Formidable logistical problems, the kith and kin factor and negative advice from military commanders helped shape the decision but, underlying all else, was the economic and parliamentary crisis which gripped Britain at the time. For a brief moment, Wilson seemed to believe indirect measures would achieve the objectives. Sanctions would galvanise an effective opposition to the rebel regime in Rhodesia and Britain would be able to work with a reconstituted moderate government.[3]

In fact economic sanctions proved a miserable failure, largely due to Portugal and South Africa's collaboration with the Rhodesian authorities. Both South Africa, via Beit Bridge, and Portugal, via Mozambique, provided a route to the sea for oil imports. British government policy was reduced to numerous political initiatives ranging from Harold Wilson's 'Fearless' and 'Tiger' talks of the later 1960s,[4] to the Vance and Owen Anglo-American talks or proposals of 1977–8,[5] all of which had foundered on the obduracy of a white supremacist regime which opposed any concept of black majority rule based on the British government's 'six principles'. These principles, which originated mainly from Harold Wilson and were later endorsed by the United Nations were: firstly, unimpeded progress to majority rule; secondly, guarantees against retrogressive amendments to the constitution; thirdly, an immediate improvement in the political status of the black population; fourthly, progress towards ending racial discrimination; fifthly, constitutional proposals that are acceptable to the people of Rhodesia as a whole; and, finally, no oppression of the majority by the minority or the minority by the majority.

By the end of 1977, however, the first seeds of a successful constitutional conference to finally resolve the Rhodesian crisis had already been planted. During the previous three years there had been a dramatic turn-around in Rhodesia's previously strong geo-strategic position. In 1974 the Portuguese revolution and subsequent rapid retreat from Angola and Mozambique left Rhodesia's northern and south-eastern borders dangerously exposed. Her sanction-busting outlets via Beira were now closed. The critical blow to Rhodesia's survival, however, had come from South Africa, her key ally to the south in terms of both military and economic support. With the Portuguese collapse, South Africa had been forced to reassess radically her policy towards a growing ring of hostile black states. In 1976, Smith was bluntly told to accept the principle of black majority rule. In his own words:

> We were placed in a situation where we virtually had no option. This was because of the actions of the South African Prime Minister John Vorster. As far as countries like Britain and America were concerned we could defy them as we had done over the years. We could not do that to the *one* country which controlled our life line. So, very reluctantly, we were forced to accept it.[6]

Rhodesia was to be sold out to facilitate a new détente. As Smith recalled, the South African Prime Minister, Vorster, was 'of the opinion that he could work with the black leaders to the north of us and help to solve the Rhodesian problem. He told me this. In return the black countries were going to accept South Africa and their philosophy. So, to a certain extent, we were to be used as a sacrificial lamb in helping to solve *South Africa's* problems.'[7]

As South Africa's military support receded in 1977–8, Rhodesia faced a new onslaught from the two guerrilla independence armies: ZIPRA led by Joshua Nkomo, and ZANLA led by Robert Mugabe.[8] Both had benefited from increased Chinese and Soviet military support with new bases being opened up in Mozambique. Within a year the cumulative effect of these military pressures was revealed in Rhodesian government security statistics. In 1977 a total of 1759 guerrillas and 197 members of the security forces died inside Rhodesia as well as 1055 civilians, of whom 56 were white. By the summer, casualties were running at the rate of 100 a week compared with the average of three a week in the first five years of hostilities. In the year preceding the Lancaster House meeting the fighting had been most intense. This year alone accounted for over one-third of the total casualties sustained since the guerrilla war proper had begun in December 1972.[9] All this affected a country of barely seven million blacks and a quarter of a million whites.

The economic impact of the war was equally devastating. Mining receipts had fallen because of the collapse in market prices. Tobacco and maize production fell, particularly in the increasingly deserted north-eastern war zones, while Rhodesia's other industries were costing more in foreign exchange than they earned. Consumer spending was being progressively eroded by the steady exodus of whites. By 1978 an estimated 600 to 1000 whites a month were 'taking the gap' (deserting the country) including a disproportionately large number of white males of military age. In 1977 Rhodesia's GNP fell in real terms by 7 per cent, 4 per cent more than the year before. The economy also needed to create 110 000 more jobs a year simply to absorb black unemployment, a problem only partially redressed by their recruitment into the guerrilla forces![10]

As Christopher Coker has observed, the real impact of the war could be measured by the 1978–9 budget which provided for a net increase in defence appropriation of only 2 per cent, 1 per cent less than 1977 if taken as a proportion of total public expenditure. In short, Rhodesia appeared 'to have deliberately budgeted for the war's de-escalation, a gesture less of confidence ... than of a belief that the economy could no longer keep pace with the war's escalation'. In Coker's words, 'the cost of the guerrilla war was becoming insupportable both in human and economic terms'.[11]

By December, 1977, Smith had bowed to the prospect of elections and an 'internal settlement', which he nevertheless hoped would still maintain the whites in power. As if to underline the precarious security situation the elections were held in the middle of a major guerrilla insurgency launched between 17 and 21 April 1979. Eighteen out of 932 polling stations were attacked. Bishop Abel Muzorewa, leader of the UANC,[12] emerged the victor with a 64 per cent majority of the votes cast and 51 out of the 72 black seats in parliament. Although 1 750 000 out of a possible 2 750 000 votes were cast the exclusion of the Patriotic Front and the terms of a new constitution designed to give the white minority a substantial controlling influence stopped short of the famous 'six principles' and of the British pledge of majority rule. Consequently, the new government of Zimbabwe-Rhodesia received no British or international recognition and sanctions remained firmly in place. While Zimbabwe-Rhodesia now faced a 'doomsday scenario' which could now only be resolved by a constitutional conference, other external politico-military factors were effectively laying the foundations for such a summit meeting. The Patriotic Front forces, while enjoying even greater success in their guerrilla war,[13] were facing severe pressure from the front line African states – principally Zambia and Tanzania, Mozambique and Botswana – to reach a political settlement. Repeated cross-border raids by Rhodesian special forces (mainly SAS and Selous Scouts) had caused severe damage to their infrastructures, especially to Zambia and Mozambique.[14] By 1979, the leaders of these latter countries, Kenneth Kaunda and Samora Machel, had become desperate for a peace settlement.

With Rhodesia politically and militarily prostrate and facing a growing crisis of morale (largely due to atrocities such as the Elim Mission massacre and the shooting down of two Rhodesian airliners)[15] by mid-1979 only two final pieces remained to complete the 'political jigsaw' for a major constitutional conference in London. The Conservative administration, led by Margaret Thatcher, which came to power in May 1979, had taken a strong stand over 'terrorism' and her pre-election statements suggested that she alone would be prepared both to lift sanctions and, in her own words, to meet 'wide expectations that we would recognise the new Muzorewa Government'.[16] Even during the post-election fact-finding tour by Lord Harlech, designed to consult the leaders of Zambia, Tanzania, Botswana, Malawi and Angola, Mozambique and Nigeria, Thatcher reconfirmed: 'I was not at all keen at this stage that he should even talk to the leaders of the Patriotic Front ... their forces had carried out atrocities which disgusted everyone and I was as keen to avoid dealing with terrorists abroad as I would be at home.'[17] Her strong antipathy towards the Patriotic Front was reconfirmed in a hardline speech made on a visit to Canberra, Australia on 1 July 1979. Clearly a reversal of Conservative policy was essential if an all-party solution to the Rhodesian problem including the PF was to be achieved. As with many of the post-war superpower summits the 'evolution' of political, military and economic pressures had reached a point where a summit had become 'both a diplomatic and a political necessity'.[18]

The opportunity for the 'conversion' of Mrs Thatcher came with the convening of the Commonwealth Heads of Government summit at Lusaka, in August 1979. It was here that the substantial obstacles to the convening of the Lancaster House conference later in the year were overcome. In the words of Charlton: 'The future of Britain's last colony in Africa was settled in Lusaka ... the understanding arrived at there proved strong enough to weather all the storms that followed.'[19] Lusaka presented the opportunity for interpersonal contact and 'signals' between the major players to lay the foundations and agenda for a major summit as well as sound out future negotiating positions. At Lusaka the 'conversion' of Thatcher was achieved, due not only to the influence of her Foreign Secretary, Lord Carrington, later to chair the Lancaster House conference, but also largely to a group of five Commonwealth leaders, namely Kenneth Kaunda of Zambia, Julius Nyere of Tanzania, Malcolm Fraser of Australia, President Zia of Bangladesh, and the Commonwealth Secretary General 'Sonny' Ramphal. As Kaunda put it: 'we did not capture her ... but ... when we began discussing these matters seriously, especially with the influence of Peter Carrington ... we began to see her start accepting the principle of a London conference on Zimbabwe. And this began to change things.'[20] The pre-conference role of Lord Peter Carrington proved to be crucial. In Thatcher's own words, 'unpleasant realities had to be faced. Peter Carrington's view was that it was essential to secure the widest possible recognition for a Rhodesian regime since that country held the key to the whole Southern African region. He turned out to be right.'[21] Her full confidence in Carrington was to prove a decisive factor in securing the success of the Lancaster House conference later in the year.

Of the Commonwealth leaders, Kaunda and Fraser's roles were particularly crucial, emphasizing the impact that individual participants can make on summit diplomacy. Earlier, at Canberra, Thatcher had been 'taken aback' by the 'trenchancy with which ... Fraser had maintained that Australia would line up with the front line states in the forthcoming meeting in Lusaka and against any concessions to Muzorewa or Smith'.[22] The fact that Fraser was himself a fellow Conservative leader could only increase the efficacy of his arguments at Lusaka.

Kaunda's role in Thatcher's 'volte-face' revealed a masterly handling of the diplomatic procedures at Lusaka, ranging from the skilful use of 'smoke-filled rooms' (usually Kaunda's personal study) and spectacular Commonwealth banquets, to the informal atmosphere of a dance floor where a great personal rapport was established with Thatcher in their famous 'duo waltz'. In Kaunda's own words, 'We were not really *fighting* her, we were putting ... reasonable points. The whole lot of us. We met in this room several times. Each time we discussed these matters we went back to the main "summit" and explained what was taking place.'[23] Again, these informal and 'ceremonial' procedures formed an integral part of the summit negotiations, procedures which, in the words of Weihmiller and Doder, 'often involve as much advance negotiation and preparation as the issues of the meetings themselves'.[24]

In fact Thatcher's conversion to the idea of a constitutional conference incorporating the Patriotic Front reflected the impact of a wide range of national, international, political and economic pressures.[25] Not least was the impact of the Commonwealth institution itself. In the words of Sir Michael Palliser, Head of the Foreign Office, 'I do think it [the Commonwealth] played some part in the change in *attitude* by the Prime Minister ... there was a great understanding of the value of the Commonwealth as an instrument and as an organization; therefore, of the desirability of keeping the Commonwealth in play; of supporting what we wanted to do in Africa – and in Rhodesia.'[26] A second major influence was that of the Queen. As President Kaunda pointed out, there were two very important ladies at Lusaka. At Commonwealth conferences the presence of the Queen undoubtedly had a 'cementing' effect and her crucial role at Lusaka as the Rhodesian issue was finally coming to a head in 1979 was confirmed by the Nigerian leader, Olusegun Obasanjo. 'As you know, all of us in the Commonwealth have a tremendous regard for the Queen. Her presence obviously gave hope. I don't know if she whispered in to any ears for the type of compromise which eventually came out at the Lusaka conference.'[27] Kaunda reinforced the point: 'Queen Elizabeth, as always at these conferences, was a tower of strength for us. In this case she played a major role in the whole thing ... leaders of the Commonwealth, of all sorts of political thought, are agreed on one thing, they can *trust* her.'[28] Indeed, this symbolic role of the Queen as a key political interlocutor underlined the unique nature of Commonwealth summitry when compared to the great post-war superpower, NATO and G-7 summits.

The final piece of the 'political jigsaw', namely the agreement of the Patriotic Front leaders to the principle of a negotiated political settlement in London, was also 'pre-cooked' at another crucial summit, that of the Non-Aligned Conference held in Cuba between 7 and 9 September 1979. Until that conference both the Patriotic Front leaders, Nkomo and Mugabe, had, despite Lusaka, advocated a purely military solution to the Rhodesian problem. Robert Mugabe had been particularly confident of a rapid military victory by his Zanla forces in 1979:

> Our liberation struggle had progressed to where we believe we had more than two thirds of the country ... we had the rural areas in our grip ... the end of 1979 with the coming of the rains was going to see the development of the *urban* guerrilla struggle ... we felt that we needed yet another thrust in order to bring the fight home to where the whites had their citadels.[29]

The final thrust never materialized. Despite the steady erosion of the Rhodesian internal security situation, Rhodesian special forces continued to launch daring cross-border raids against the guerrilla host states,

Zambia and Mozambique. Consequently at Havana, Mugabe and Nkomo were literally coerced into accepting the concept of a political settlement in London. In Mugabe's words, 'the Front Line states said we *had* to negotiate, *had* to go to this conference'.[30] Kaunda's words summarized the fraught atmosphere at this summit:

> We had a job to convince both Robert Mugabe and Joshua Nkomo to go to London. They were saying ... they were going to continue to fight. In fact ... we *turned* on the freedom fighters in Cuba ... we said 'give the British Government a chance to prove that they are sincere in what they are saying to us'.[31]

Thus, at two key summits held during the course of 1979, at Lusaka and Havana, the political foundations for the great constitutional conference to be held at Lancaster House had been laid. The attendance of all parties, from a right-wing Conservative government led by Thatcher to the Marxist-oriented Mugabe-led guerrilla movement, Zanu, had been effectively secured at both these conferences. At both summits deals were brokered, and formal and informal, domestic and international pressures were applied to ensure that all the leading players would be placed in a viable negotiating position at the major summit to be held at Lancaster House.

Moreover, it was a conference for which not only had full representation and participation been secured at previous meetings, but it was one that 'differed' from all earlier conferences in that discussions on the agenda, notably the constitution, were 'more or less academic'. As Ken Flower, Head of Rhodesian Intelligence has pointed out: 'The real argument was over the control of the instruments of power in the run-up to the elections.'[32] It was a conference, moreover, in which one party occupied a recognized, dominant position. This was a political reality strongly underlined in Lord Carrington's opening address to the conference:

> I would like to hope that there is a difference between this meeting and those which have preceded it. This is a constitutional conference, the purpose of which is to decide the proper basis for the granting of legal independence to the people of Rhodesia.... The agreement reached at Lusaka had made it possible for the British Government to convene the conference.... Britain has at times been ... described on the one side as choosing to stand with arms folded on the touch line and, on the other, as not being serious in its determination to de-colonise. Let me assure you today, if anyone is in any doubt, that we could not be more serious in our intention to achieve a satisfactory basis for the granting of legal

independence for the people of Rhodesia and in this attempt to bring about an end to the war.[33]

Mrs Thatcher herself recognized the key advantages of Britain's political position at the outset of the conference. The fact that 'nearly everyone considered that it was a British responsibility to solve the problem ... gave us a relatively free hand if we knew how to use it'.[34] In the words of Davidow, the conference presented the classic opportunity for the exercise of 'dominant third party mediation'.[35]

Fortunately for Mrs Thatcher the man she selected for conference Chairman, Lord Carrington, was a man who, as all parties later agreed, was endowed with an extremely deft hand at diplomacy. For much of his career he had been deeply involved in wide-ranging, often tortuous negotiations whether it be with service chiefs over defence cuts at the MOD, or tense confrontations with, for example, Maltese Prime Minister Dom Mintoff over the lease of British bases in Malta in 1971. As Davidow has pointed out, the Foreign Secretary

> possessed many of the qualities of a good negotiator, self assurance, tact, dignity, humour, ability to demonstrate anger, intelligence and personal magnetism variously described as lordly charisma or aristocratic bearing.... In addition to his qualities and training, Carrington's most important characteristics were his considerable capacity for hard work, his mastery of detail and his ubiquity. His continuous presence provided continuity in leadership and a personal manifestation of his government's commitment to a negotiated settlement.[36]

Lord Carrington not only had the full backing and confidence of the Prime Minister, but he also had, in his own words, 'an excellent team in the Foreign Office working on Rhodesia: Derek Day, who went out to Salisbury until our main conference started in London, Tony Duff, Robin Renwick, Charles Powell, all first class dedicated men – I know that no institution but the Foreign Office could have produced such support and such skill'.[37] Ken Flower, a prominent member of the Muzorewa delegation, suggested, however, that there was evidence of some bias:

> Carrington and his highly efficient team were intent on what they called a 'first class solution', into which all parties would be tied. We would have preferred a 'second class solution' where the Patriotic Front would have opted out, and there were many occasions when we had reason to believe that some members of the British team were helping towards that end.[38]

In his memoirs Lord Carrington claimed that he, personally, felt no such bias: 'I was already sadly convinced that the "internal settlement" was probably a fudge in terms of the domestic support it really commanded. It was widely seen as a device to perpetuate the white man's rule behind an amenable and unrepresentative black front and, although this was by no means completely fair, there was something in it.'[39] Indeed, such overt support for the Muzorewa delegation could have engendered severe ramifications for Britain's international position. 'To have recognised the "internal settlement" at that time would have led to embargoes on British goods around the world, rejection of British counsel and influence "because of Rhodesia"; and within Rhodesia Nkomo and Mugabe would have done all in their considerable power to step up the insurrection – with Soviet and Chinese assistance respectively. The "internal settlement" offered no solution. There had to be a better way.'[40] Thus intense international, political and economic pressures played a crucial role in ensuring that a successful settlement of the Rhodesian problem was an overriding foreign policy priority for the new Thatcher administration.

In the planning and conduct of the Lancaster House conference, Lord Carrington made full use of both Britain's and his own personally dominant position. One of his first acts was to restrict the number of negotiating parties. He recognized that 'one of the problems of all the other conferences, that all the other proposals had brought with them, was the involvement of other people in the negotiations'. Lord Carrington noted how David Owen's 1977–8 proposals had 'suffered very much from having the Americans there' as 'the more people you involved in this the more difficult it was to get a solution'. Again, 'it was the legacy of Lusaka which left us with that opportunity at the Lancaster House conference. We never allowed anybody beyond the front door there who was not either Rhodesian or British ... it did make it very much a "family affair".'[41] Thus, numerous other external 'actors' – notably the OAU, the Front Line States, the Commonwealth, the United Nations, and the USA – were left firmly in the wings. It was to be a summit meeting which would if necessary avoid 'regular channels' and therefore remain small, select, personal, and limited to countries which carried weight and influence.

Having secured significant control over participation at the conference, Lord Carrington also used his 'free hand' to dictate the order of the agenda to his advantage. As Mrs Thatcher observed, he deliberately 'arranged the agenda to take the most difficult questions last, so that the first item to be agreed was the new constitution; only then would come the question of the transitional arrangements; and finally the calling of a cease fire'.[42] Thus clarity of objective was achieved at the outset with the least controversial of issues dealt with first. As Lord Carrington recalled, 'I divided the agenda into different sections and I was adamant that the first of these must deal with a future constitution. I was not prepared to allow them to talk about other things until they had settled, with my approval, the constitution.'[43] This approach was reinforced by the continued use of deadlines to maintain maximum pressure on the participants. In the words of Mrs Thatcher, 'We reserved to ourselves the task of putting forward final proposals in each phase and we required the parties to respond, even if these proposals did not meet all their objectives.'[44] As at many of the US–Soviet summits, the actual holding of the summit and the widespread use of deadlines would help to 'force decisions on major policy issues – decisions that might otherwise be postponed'.[45]

Lord Carrington recalled that 'critical' to the success of the conference was 'my determination to take matters step by step. On each step some of the parties demurred, saying they could not climb further without seeing entirely and exactly what stood at the head of the stairs. I refused to accept this. I was sure that previous attempts had failed through attempting over-precision too early, through framing complex plans of ultimate order instead of coaxing minds towards the resolution of the next practical, intermediate step in debate. Each step might be imperfect in logic, or even in principle, but it must be realistic – in the sense of not being a clear outrage to one of the parties and thus unacceptable.'[46]

Lord Carrington was perhaps also able to exceed his chairman's brief by frequent use of both overt and covert pressure to encourage agreement. As Mrs Thatcher confirmed, 'at each stage we had to exert pressure – direct and indirect – on the two sides to reach a satisfactory compromise'.[47] These two tactics were only possible because both competing factions, the Muzorewa delegation and the Patriotic Front were, for varying reasons, in weak bargaining positions. It was the perfect setting for the exercise of coercive diplomacy by the British government. While both parties were understandably affected by a 'war weariness', of the two Zimbabwe-Rhodesia was in a particularly weak position. The country was clearly on its last military and political legs[48] and, with no international recognition and the continuation of sanctions, Zimbabwe-Rhodesia was now heavily dependent upon the Thatcher government to resolve these key conference issues. Indeed, it could be said that Zimbabwe-Rhodesia's domestic crisis almost totally undermined its negotiating position.[49]

Similarly, the Patriotic Front, while predicting military victory, had seen their room for political leverage severely curtailed as a result of the Cuba summit. Moreover, both factions were by no means united. The Muzorewa delegation was an uneasy coalition of parties ranging from liberal nationalist delegates such as Sithole, to extreme conservative Rhodesian Front representatives such as Ian Smith. In the words of Ken Flower, 'We were far less homogenous than the Patriotic Front, for our delegation comprised Muzorewa's UANC (United African National Congress), Sithole's ZANU, Smith's RF and a newly formed party led by Ndiweni.... Another result of this division in the Zimbabwe-Rhodesian delegation was that at the plenary sessions the Bishop, who had no hope of matching Nkomo and Mugabe in the cut and thrust of debate, could make little use of the ablest debaters in his delegation, the eloquent Nabaningi Sithole and the vastly experienced Ian Smith. He had to rely on the British Chairman to see fair play.' Indeed, 'back in his hotel the Bishop would lapse into fits of depression, realising that the Patriotic Front were too smart for him as he could not rely on his own delegation and that the British might let him down'.[50] Moreover, Ian Smith's previously prominent and powerful role was severely diminished as a result of the 1978 internal settlement. As a minister without a portfolio Smith, in the words of Miles Hudson, had 'virtually no power and gradually became an isolated figure with little impact on events'.[51] Half-way through the conference Smith went home. Similarly, the apparent unity within the Patriotic Front delegation hid thinly disguised domestic tension reflecting tribal, personal, and ideological differences between the 'father' of African nationalism, Joshua Nkomo, leading the majority Ndebele-dominated party (ZAPU) and the avowed Marxist, Mugabe, leading the Mashona-dominated party (ZANU).

Lord Carrington was able to exploit these divisions ruthlessly. Of the two Patriotic Front leaders Nkomo was seen as particularly vulnerable to persuasion. In the words of Lord Carrington, 'Nkomo wanted a settlement, and had a motive for participation. ... His own tribal following, the Ndebele, were less committed to the military struggle, the guerrilla war against Government forces, than were Mugabe's. Nkomo felt he would, in an independent country, enjoy prestige, a power base and a chance of ending up on top. He hadn't a great deal of time.'[52]

The settlement of one issue, that of the constitution, showed how all these different tactics were brought successfully to bear on the two delegations. Lord Carrington rapidly cajoled the weak Muzorewa delegation to accept the constitution by a vote of eleven to one. When, after accepting the principle of 20 white seats without a blocking mechanism in the new Zimbabwe parliament, the Patriotic Front later demanded an executive head of state combining the role of prime minister and president, Carrington simply announced that he would go ahead with Muzorewa, if necessary without the Patriotic Front, in discussion of the transitory arrangements (the next item on the agenda). It was a fruitful, constantly repeated pattern of negotiation underlining again the overall dominance of Britain at the conference. 'Proposals tabled by Carrington, agreement by Muzorewa, objection and all kinds of threats by the Patriotic Front, Carrington announcing that he would go ahead with Muzorewa alone; Patriotic Front agreement. It was an elegant and highly successful scenario.'[53]

Robert Mugabe, by far the most articulate delegate at the conference, was acutely aware of these subtle tactics albeit often powerless to combat them. 'I never trusted the British. Never at all .... Their strategy was to get Muzorewa in and perhaps to excise part of the Patriotic Front, the Zapu party led by Nkomo ... we never trusted the Conservative party ... we dreaded the fact that they were placed in such a strong position ... with what is more, the support of our own allies.'[54]

Joshua Nkomo, the co-leader of the Patriotic Front delegation, also lambasted Lord Carrington's

'Spider Tactics' ... it was a spider type of arrangement. It is easier to attract a victim if you can separate him from the rest and get him alone. What it meant really was that Carrington was sitting in the centre and darting to every side of his big round web, organising the conference and in a position to handle us all *separately* ... really getting us moving in *his* direction. Caught in the web.[55]

Carrington and his supporting team were also not averse to the exercise of 'low politics' in order to achieve their objectives. As at the Lusaka Summit there was a constant use of the 'smoke-filled room' scenario with numerous private dinner parties held with different members of delegations and organised by various government officials, notably Sir Anthony Duff, a leading Foreign Office delegate.[56] Ken Flower, Head of Rhodesian Intelligence, again recalled the importance of these informal behind-the-scene meetings in achieving conference goals.[57] It has also been alleged that the British 'bugged' the hotel and telephones of both the Patriotic Front and Muzorewa delegations. Flower claims that such covert tactics were even deployed by the Foreign Office to undermine Thatcher's natural tendency to support the Muzorewa faction. Flower recalled: 'I could only guess then at British double dealing behind the scenes and it was to be several years before something of the extent of their duplicity emerged, such as the revelation that a senior FO official was given the job of handling an FO press campaign to discredit the Bishop and push Thatcher towards Mugabe.'[58] Thus maximum use of the summit location was made by the British establishment to maintain dominance over the participants in the negotiation process.

Indeed, Carrington himself was able to use the press highly effectively. As Davidow has observed, 'journalists naturally gravitated to the FCO for authoritative information on the conference proceedings ... Ready access ... allowed the British to leak information in the support of their own tactical advantage and, as evidenced by repeated FCO-stimulated [newspaper] articles about the imminence of the "second class solution" or dissension within the PF's ranks'.[59] By contrast, Flower recalled how, in the propaganda battle between the two rival delegations, the Patriotic Front effectively won over the media. 'The Patriotic Front were ... getting infinitely more time on British television whereas most of our delegation kept away from the media although Ian Smith, who was lionised on arrival, continued to be popular with the London crowds.'[60]

Britain's negotiating position at the Lancaster House conference was further strengthened by both the presence and absence of other external actors. Key supporting players, notably the Commonwealth, USA and South Africa, while barred from negotiations, were allowed free range outside the conference rooms.

As at the earlier Lusaka summit, the role of the individual Commonwealth leaders, aligned with that of the monarchy, proved crucial toward resolving key issues at the Lancaster House conference, notably the hotly contested conditions for the cease-fire. In relation to the Commonwealth role, Michael Charlton has commented upon the skilful tactics deployed by the Secretary General Shridath Ramphal. He 'organised what amounted to a parallel conference in London while that at Lancaster House was in session. There were no less than 32 meetings of Commonwealth High Commissioners held in London in order to exert pressure.'[61] Ramphal himself acknowledged that he 'spent many nights with Nkomo and Mugabe in their London apartments talking them into postures of agreement'.[62] Again these tactics underlined the importance of the Commonwealth 'family' connection in resolving these summit differences, a unique factor clearly absent from other international summits of the post-war period.

Amongst the Front Line States, Mozambique, as the primary host to ZANLA forces, proved crucial in ensuring Mugabe's agreement, particularly to the cease-fire arrangements which formed the final issue on the conference agenda. The Foreign Office in particular 'identified Mozambique early as offering an opportunity to gain some leverage over events and also Mugabe's ambitions. It proceeded to conduct a remarkably successful diplomacy following which the President of Mozambique, Samora Machel, delivered more, perhaps, than Lord Carrington could have hoped.'[63] Mrs Thatcher, conscious of her inexperience in foreign policy and adopting a low profile role outside the conference rooms, also paid tribute to Mozambique's role. 'The heads of the Front Line States all sent in High Commissioners to see me for a progress report. President Machel ... was especially helpful in putting pressure on Robert Mugabe.'[64] Ken Flower took a more extreme view of the extent of Mozambique's pressure. 'Machel had virtually ordered Mugabe to sign, indicating that, if he did, not the most he could expect back in Mozambique was political asylum or a villa on the coast.'[65] Thatcher concluded: 'The Lancaster House proposals could not have got through without the support of the Presidents of the Front Line States and, indeed, many other Commonwealth countries.'[66] Again, this was a cogent example of how timing, and the build-up of domestic pressures upon interested parties could significantly influence the processes and resolution of international summits.

The Lancaster House conference also benefited from the absence and, indeed, lack of interference by the two superpowers, emphasizing how far it had become a British Commonwealth 'family affair'. Both Carrington and the bulk of the Foreign Office had always remained sceptical of the threat presented by Soviet and Chinese influence in the region. As Sir Michael Palliser pointed out, 'it is an interesting paradox that Mozambique which was regarded as a very Marxist and Soviet-influenced country played the most helpful part in due course towards a settlement in Rhodesia. I do not think for Russian purposes.'[67] The USA, however, despite being excluded from direct participation in the conference, did make one major contribution to the resolution of a key issue. When Mugabe seemed to be prepared to break up the conference on the issue of compensation to white farmers, 'faces were saved at the last moment by the setting up of an international fund for land development supported by the USA. A Beechers Brook had been jumped.'[68] Again, Thatcher paid fulsome tribute to American support on this issue and, indeed, other issues. 'Heavy pressure from the USA and the Front Line States finally led the Patriotic Front to accept our proposal for the cease fire on 17 December.'[69]

As at Lusaka, even the Royal Family were deployed at times to influence the two delegations, particularly the Zimbabwe-Rhodesia delegation. Julian Amery, a leading right-wing critic of the government, recalled 'how Muzorewa and a number of senior Rhodesian whites as well as blacks were ... "nobbled" by the skill of the Foreign Office .... Even the Royal Family were brought into play ... some of the senior military figures, the white establishment, were feted and ... were taken to see the Queen Mother. Things of that sort. The Queen Mother was known to be a great friend of Rhodesia. They were taken aside and told, you know, "we don't want you to break your friendship with the British establishment".'[70]

Finally, Lord Carrington's advisers skilfully used the summit's location, their 'home ground advantage', in order to ensure continued progress. Britain's political and legal institutions were used to secure many of the Conference decisions. In order to confirm agreement for the second major item on the conference agenda, that of the transfer of power, not only was Bishop Muzorewa forced to relinquish office as Prime Minister, but a new governor, Lord Soames, was rapidly installed on 27 October. Moreover his position was 'set in stone' by legislation passed in the form of an Enabling Bill in the House of Commons on the 7 November to allow the government to provide for the Governor's arrival in Rhodesia and to grant the new Independence Constitution. In Davidow's words, the 'sending of Soames to Rhodesia prior to the final agreement, was the most audacious piece of extra-conference pressuring but one which the British felt necessary to bring the proceedings to their end'.[71]

In conclusion, the Lancaster House agreement represented, in many ways, a complete novelty in terms of the preparation, format and conduct of other post-war international summits. This was due to several unusual political factors. Firstly, it was a summit which had been largely pre-empted or 'pre-cooked' by two other key summits – Lusaka and Cuba. At both of these two summits the intransigence of two of the three parties was considerably modified through political pressure and the acceptance of key aspects of the Lancaster House agenda was largely secured. Thatcher on the one hand, and Mugabe and Nkomo on the other, once sharing a deep mutual antipathy, were persuaded or cajoled into the principle of a settlement before the summit even met. Moreover, one key issue, the first issue on the conference agenda, the new Rhodesian constitution, was also tacitly agreed – only the transfer of power and cease-fire arrangements had to be negotiated (albeit tortuously). Furthermore, like other Commonwealth heads of government summits, the unique role of the Commonwealth as an institution and the 'healing role' of the British monarchy ensured that the summit remained an internal 'family affair' between leaders sharing a degree of common imperial heritage. Both at Lusaka and at Lancaster House the key actors had been directly pressurized and persuaded through the use of 'high' and 'low' political strategies by British, African and other Commonwealth leaders to gravitate towards a consensus agreement. Moreover, at Lancaster House, the two superpowers were carefully excluded from what had become a singularly 'Commonwealth affair'. Most important of all, Lancaster House was not a summit of equals: one party, Britain, was dominant from the outset. The British government enjoyed unchallenged authority and considerable 'home' advantages, both institutional and cultural. By contrast, the other two contending parties, the Muzorewa delegation and the Patriotic Front, had both been brutally forced out of their laagered political positions – the Zimbabwe-Rhodesian delegation by acute economic and political pressures, the Patriotic Front delegations by the overt pressure of neighbouring black states, notably Zambia and Mozambique, both of whom sought a rapid end to a war which was destroying the very infrastructure of their societies. Both the delegations were therefore left highly vulnerable to British manipulation. In the words of Peter Carrington, 'once the conference got going anyone who took an initiative to march out would have a progressively tougher time in explaining this to the world and to the UN. It was a card I could play with some confidence. They all – or almost all – had had an incentive to confer. And soon nobody wanted to be seen as the one to break things up.'[72] It was a classic scenario for the exercise of coercive diplomacy by the British government. This brings us to the final point, the importance of the role of individuals in this particular summit. The role of Mrs Thatcher behind the scenes, the role of Lord Carrington 'up-front' in the Chair and the external pressures exerted by, notably, President Machel of Mozambique, President Kaunda of Zambia and the Commonwealth Secretary General, also proved instrumental in accounting for the success of the Lancaster House conference. From beginning to end, the Lancaster House conference remained a Commonwealth 'family affair' in which a dominant 'mother country' successfully, and with the help of some of her progeny, solved one of the last great colonial problems of the twentieth century.

NOTES AND REFERENCES

The opinions expressed in this article are entirely my own and do not reflect the views of either the Royal Military Academy, Sandhurst, or the Ministry of Defence.

1. For details of the conference proceedings see: *Southern Rhodesia: Report of the Constitutional Conference Lancaster House, London Sept–Dec 1979.* Cmd paper 7802 (HMSO, 1980). For a comprehensive analysis of the Conference see also J. Davidow, *A Peace in Southern Africa: The Lancaster House Conference on Rhodesia 1979* (London, Westview Press, 1984).
2. For the historical background to the crisis, see especially, D. Martin and P. Johnson, *The Struggle for Zimbabwe* (London, Faber and Faber, 1981), J. Barber, *Rhodesia: The Road to Rebellion* (Oxford, OUP, 1967) and R. Blake, *A History of Rhodesia* (London, Eyre Methuen, 1977).

3. R. C. Good, *The International Politics of the Rhodesian Rebellion* (London, Faber and Faber, 1973), p. 165. See also H. Wilson, *The Labour Government 1964–70* (London, Weidenfeld and Nicolson, 1974), pp. 232–9.
4. See Wilson, *Labour Government*, pp. 195, 717–19, 726–9, 795 for the 'Fearless' talks and pp. 199, 194–413, 715–18, 729, 749, 795 and 967 for the 'Tiger' talks.
5. For a detailed discussion of these talks and the earlier, failed, Geneva summit, see D. Owen, *Time to Declare* (London, Penguin, 1991), chapter 13, pp. 219–318.
6. Ian Smith, Interview, in M. Charlton, *The Last Colony in Africa: Diplomacy and the Independence of Rhodesia* (Oxford, Blackwell, 1990), p. 2.
7. Ibid., p. 4.
8. ZIPRA (Zimbabwe People's Revolutionary Army) was the military wing of ZAPU (Zimbabwe African People's Union) led by Joshua Nkomo. ZANLA (Zimbabwe African Liberation Army) was, correspondingly, the military wing of ZANU (Zimbabwe African People's Union) led by Robert Mugabe which had broken away from ZAPU in 1963, two years after ZAPU's formation in 1961. In 1976, both guerilla armies allied together to form the Patriotic Front (PF).
9. C. Coker: 'Decolonisation in the Seventies: Rhodesia and the Dialectic of National Liberation', in *The Round Table*, vol. 69 (1979), p. 128.
10. Ibid. Martin Meredith provides even more startling evidence of the crisis of white morale. In December 1978, nearly 3000 whites left the country bringing the total number for 1978 to more than 18 000. Over a three year period – 1976–8 – the exodus amounted to nearly 50 000 whites or one fifth of the white population. Even allowing for the number of immigrants, the loss in three years was nearly 32 000. M. Meredith, *The Past is Another Country: Rhodesia 1890–1979* (London, Andre Deutsch, 1979), p. 353.
11. Coker, 'Decolonisation', p. 128.
12. Four black parties stood for election: Muzorewa's UANC (United African Nation Council); Sithole's wing of ZANU; Chirau's ZUPO (Zambabwe United People's Organization); and Ndiweni's UNFP (United National Federal Party). The Rhodesian Front (RF) easily won the 20 white seats required to keep a controlling influence over the new Zimbabwe-Rhodesia government. Meredith, *The Past is Another Country*, pp. 361–2.
13. For detailed analysis of the guerrilla war see, especially, L. H. Gann and T. H. Henriksen, *The Struggle for Zimbabwe: Battle in the Bush* (New York, Praeger, 1981), T. O. Ranger, *Peasant Consciousness and Guerrilla War in Zimbabwe* (London, Heinemann, 1985), and D. Lan, *Guns and Rain: Guerrillas and Spirit Mediums in Zimbabwe* (London, James Currey, 1985).
14. Meredith estimates that over the two years 1976–8 'at least 3500 guerrillas and their supporters were killed and hundreds of tons of supplies destroyed' in Mozambique alone by Rhodesian forces. Meredith, *The Past is Another Country*, p. 351.
15. For the deleterious impact upon white morale see, for instance, D. Hills, *The Last Days of White Rhodesia* (London, Allen and Unwin, 1981), especially chapters 2 and 4.

16. M. Thatcher, *The Downing Street Years* (London, Harper Collins, 1993) p. 72.
17. Ibid., pp. 72–3.
18. G. R. Weihmiller and D. Doder, *US–Soviet Summits: An Account of East–West Diplomacy at the Top 1955–1985* (London, University Press of America, 1986), pp. xii–xiii.
19. Charlton, *Last Colony in Africa*. p. 38. As Thatcher later confirmed, 'after Lusaka I believed that it [the Rhodesian settlement] could be done'. Thatcher, *The Downing Street Years*, p. 77
20. Interview with Kaunda in Charlton, *Last Colony in Africa* pp. 54–5.
21. Thatcher, *The Downing Street Years*, p. 73.
22. Charlton, *Last Colony in Africa*, p. 32.
23. Interview with Kaunda, ibid., pp. 55–6.
24. Weihmiller and Doder, *US–Soviet Summits*, p. xiv.
25. One of the most overt pressures was the announcement by the Nigerian government on the first day of the Lusaka Summit of their nationalization of BP, an announcement regarded as 'inexcusable' and greeted with 'fury' by Carrington. Interview with Lord Carrington in Charlton, *Last Colony in Africa*, p. 47. Carrington also faced pressure from the right wing of the Conservative Party but this was overcome at the October party conference.
26. Interview with Sir Michael Palliser, ibid., p. 57.
27. Interview with General Olusegun Obasanjo, ibid., p. 59.
28. Interview with Kenneth Kaunda, ibid., p. 59.
29. Interview with Robert Mugabe, ibid., pp. 52–3. Undoubtedly the PF's exclusion from the Lusaka summit reinforced the desire for a military solution.
30. Ibid., p. 69.
31. Interview with Kenneth Kaunda, ibid., p. 68.
32. K. Flower, *Serving Secretly, Rhodesia into Zimbabwe 1964–81* (London, John Murray, 1987), p. 232.
33. *Southern Rhodesia*, Cmd Paper 7802, pp. 3–5.
34. Thatcher, *The Downing Street Years*, p. 73.
35. Davidow, *Peace in Southern Africa*, chapter 9, pp. 115–21.
36. Ibid., p. 104.
37. Lord Carrington, *Reflect on Things Past* (London, Collins, 1988), p. 292.
38. Flower, *Serving Secretly*, p. 232. Flower was Head of Rhodesian Intelligence.
39. Carrington, *Reflect on Things Past*, p. 290.
40. Ibid., p. 291.
41. Charlton, *Last Colony in Africa*, p. 63. For an important post-war summit parallel (Rambouillet 1975), see R. D. Putnam and N. Bayne, *Hanging Together: Cooperation and Conflict in the Seven-Power Summits* (London, Sage, 1987), p. 29.
42. Thatcher, *The Downing Street Years*, p. 77.
43. Carrington, *Reflect on Things Past*, p. 299.
44. Thatcher, *The Downing Street Years*, p. 77. See also Davidow, *Peace in Southern Africa*, pp. 109–10.
45. Weihmiller and Doder, *US–Soviet Summits*, p. xiii.
46. Carrington, *Reflect on Things Past*, p. 301.
47. Thatcher, *The Downing Street Years*, p. 77.

48. On 20 December 1979, for instance, Ken Flower received a security briefing from the Rhodesian CIO (Central Intelligence Organization) admitting that 'the current situation is not good owing to the terrorist presence which has made itself felt ... throughout the country with the possible exception of the major urban areas'. Up to 15 000 ZANLA and ZIPRA guerrillas were deployed internally and over 45 000 externally. CIO to K. Flower in Flower, *Serving Secretly*, p. 248.

49. For a discussion of the impact of domestic politics upon the conduct of summitry see, especially, Putnam and Bayne, *Hanging Together*, pp. 276–8.

50. Flower, *Serving Secretly*, p. 234.

51. M. Hudson, *Triumph or Tragedy? Rhodesia to Zimbabwe* (London, Hamish Hamilton, 1981), pp. 168–9.

52. Carrington, *Reflect on Things Past*, p. 293.

53. Hudson, *Triumph or Tragedy? Rhodesia to Zimbabwe*, p. 171.

54. Interview with Mugabe in Charlton, *Last Colony of Africa*, p. 66.

55. Interview with Nkomo, ibid., pp. 77–8.

56. Flower, *Serving Secretly*, p. 235.

57. Ibid., pp. 235–6. See also Carrington, *Reflect on Things Past*, p. 297.

58. Flower, *Serving Secretly*, p. 239.

59. Davidow, *Peace in Southern Africa*, p. 105.

60. Flower, *Serving Secretly*, p. 235.

61. Charlton, *Last Colony in Africa*, p. 109.

62. Interview with Shridath Ramphal in Charlton, *Last Colony in Africa*, p. 109. Indeed, Carrington remembered 'having to keep Sonny Ramphal ... from interfering'. Carrington, *Reflect on Things Past*, p. 300.

63. Charlton, *Last Colony in Africa*, p. 119. As Carrington noted, Machel 'relied extensively on Rhodesian maize ... He was fed up, he had plenty of enemies at home and his internal problems gave him quite sufficient worries.' Carrington, *Reflect on Things Past*, p. 294. The 'maize weapon' was also used against Zambia by the Muzorewa government during the Conference with maize sales banned on 5 November. See Hudson, *Triumph or Tragedy?*, p. 172.

64. Thatcher, *The Downing Street Years*, p. 77.

65. Flower, *Serving Secretly*, p. 247.

66. Thatcher, *The Downing Street Years*, p. 77.

67. Interview with Sir Michael Palliser in Charlton, *Last Colony in Africa*, p. 9.

68. Charlton, *Last Colony in Africa*, p. 82. The USA's willingness to play a low profile role at Lancaster House may not only have reflected awareness that the problem was very much a Commonwealth 'internal' problem but also may have been symptomatic of its post-Vietnam political decline. See Putnam and Bayne, *Hanging Together*, pp. 16–18 and 272–3.

69. Thatcher, *The Downing Street Years*, p. 78.

70. Interview with Julian Amery in Charlton, *Last Colony in Africa*, p. 129.

71. Davidow, *Peace in Southern Africa*, p. 111.

72. Carrington, *Reflect on Things Past*, p. 298.

14 The Rio Earth Summit
John Lanchberry

INTRODUCTION

The Earth Summit was the biggest intergovernmental conference ever held. More correctly called the United Nations Conference on Environment and Development (UNCED), the summit was held in Rio de Janeiro between 3 and 14 June 1992. About forty thousand people attended either as delegates or observers. One hundred and eighty-three countries were represented. More than one hundred heads of state and government were present and publicity for the conference was assured by the attendance of about seven thousand representatives of the news media.

Although UNCED was certainly a big event, attended by many world leaders and although it was widely if often incorrectly reported, many scholars are sceptical as to whether it really achieved anything of substance. This chapter puts the opposite view.[1] Admittedly, the machinery of the UN system did grind exceedingly slowly both at the conference and during the preparatory negotiations for it. Also, the agreements concluded at the summit are rather thin on commitments which would oblige governments to take radical actions concerning the environment. Nevertheless, not only did UNCED briefly raise public awareness of the major issues in environment and development but, more significantly, it resulted in some potentially important agreements which were specifically designed to develop with time and which many states have been keen to implement since Rio. One can thus contend that UNCED was, in the words of the conference handouts, a 'good start' on the road to sustainable development.

The aim of this chapter is to outline what the summit did and did not achieve by seeking the answers to three questions. The first is, what was the UNCED for? In attempting to answer this question an examination is made of why the summit was held, what it was intended to achieve and the preparatory processes leading up to it. The next question is, how did the conference function? Here, an outline description is given of what happened during the two-week meeting, how the event was organized and who attended it. Finally, the question of what was achieved at Rio is

220

addressed by discussing what has happened to the agreements concluded at the meeting and what their impacts are likely to be on the behaviour of governments and peoples.

WHAT WAS THE PURPOSE OF THE EARTH SUMMIT?

Background

The Rio Earth Summit is often thought of simply as being the direct successor of the 1972 Stockholm Environmental Conference[2] but it was much more than that, certainly in terms of tangible results: two legally binding agreements were concluded at the summit together with a detailed 'agenda' for sustainable development in the twenty-first century. In contrast, the main outcome of the Stockholm Conference was a declaration which, although it laid down some environmentally sound principles, was not really a basis for action by governments and was certainly not legally binding. Also, while it is true that the Stockholm Conference was the first high-level intergovernmental meeting to take environmental issues seriously, these issues were primarily the concern of the northern, developed countries and not those of the southern, developing countries. The southern nations were mainly concerned with the problems of poverty, ignorance and disease. Indeed, they were prepared to accept a considerable degree of pollution and environmental degradation in order to develop their industry and agriculture (the prime causes of degradation and pollution). Consequently, many developing countries did not participate in the Stockholm Conference and it could not therefore be said to be a 'world summit' addressing global environmental issues.

UNCED was, in fact, inspired mainly by the Brundtland Report[3] of 1987 which linked the environmental concerns of the North with the development concerns of the South. Indeed, the Brundtland Report coined the term 'sustainable development', pointing to both the wasteful and environmentally damaging effects of 'over consumption' in the developed countries and the equally destructive effects of poverty in the developing ones.

Shortly after the publication of the report, Mrs Brundtland became Prime Minister of Norway and she promoted its findings at a high political level. Joined by some unlikely allies (amongst them Prime Minister Thatcher, President Gorbachev, President Mitterrand and Prime Minister Gandhi) she raised environment and development issues at the UN in the mid-1980s and, by the end of 1988, had rallied 50 world leaders in support of some sort of action based on the findings of the report. As a consequence, on 22 December 1989, the UN General Assembly adopted resolution number 44/228 which set up the UN Conference on Environment and Development which, at the 'highest possible level', was to:

> elaborate strategies and measures to halt and reverse the effects of environmental degradation in the context of increased national and international efforts to promote sustainable and environmentally sound development in all countries ... [recognizing] ... that the promotion of economic growth in developing countries is essential to address problems of environmental degradation.

Specifically, UNCED was intended to address the following environmental issues:[4]

1. Protection of the atmosphere by combating climate change, depletion of the ozone layer and transboundary air pollution;[5]
2. Protection of the quality and supply of freshwater resources;
3. Protection of the oceans and all kinds of seas (including their living resources);[6]
4. Protection and management of land resources by, *inter alia*, combating deforestation, desertification and drought;
5. Conservation of biological diversity;
6. Environmentally sound management of biotechnology;
7. Environmentally sound management of wastes, particularly hazardous wastes;
8. Improvement of the living and working environment through the eradication of poverty;
9. Protection of human health conditions and improvement of the quality of life.

On these general matters relating to environment and development, it was intended that a legally non-binding text called 'Agenda 21' would be agreed at the summit. It was hoped that this would serve as a blueprint for how the nations of the world could preserve the environment and achieve sustainable development in the twenty-first century. It was also anticipated that a non-binding statement of intent known as the 'Rio Declaration' (similar to the 1972 Stockholm Declaration) would be issued at UNCED.

In the late 1980s, at more or less the same time as it was agreed to hold the Earth Summit, the UN General Assembly also decided to address some specific issues of global concern with legally binding conventions. These issues were: i) the destruction of the world's forests; ii) the loss of genetic diversity amongst species of plants and animals (biodiversity); and iii) possible 'global warming' (more correctly called climate change). Desertification was also identified as a problem needing a legal instrument (a convention) to deal with it but negotiations on the topic were not begun until after UNCED, although the issue was raised at the conference together with the more contentious issue of population growth.[7]

The UN did not originally agree to negotiate all of the conventions to be signed at exactly the same time. The idea of a climate change convention, for example, arose from an initiative by the UN Environment Programme (UNEP), the World Meteorological Organization (WMO) and the International Council of Scientific Unions (ICSU),[8] and also from a General Assembly Resolution of December 1988 to protect the climate as a 'common heritage of mankind'. However, the negotiations on the three main issue areas became included under the general UNCED umbrella and all of the conventions were eventually due to be opened for signature at Rio, although each negotiating process remained separate.

Preparatory Processes for the Rio Summit

Each of the agreements due to be signed at the Rio Summit had its own negotiating process, except for the Rio Declaration which was essentially a summary of Agenda 21. The Conventions on Climate and Biodiversity were negotiated over the two-year period preceding the conference by Intergovernmental Negotiating Committees (INCs) each administered by its own secretariat. Agenda 21 was drafted during a similar series of lengthy Preparatory Committee meetings (Prepcoms) chaired by the Singapore Ambassador Tommy Koh and administered directly by the UNCED Secretariat under the Conference Secretary General, Maurice Strong. The Forests Convention was to have been agreed under the auspices of the UN Food and Agriculture Organization (FAO) but early discussions proved contentious and they were therefore shifted to the main UNCED Prepcoms. Preparation of all of the agreements was, of course, primarily undertaken by delegations from governments but there was also a significant input from both intergovernmental organizations (IGOs, such as the UN Development Programme, WMO and UNEP) and non-governmental organizations (NGOs), whose participation was actively solicited by the UN.

The preparatory processes leading up to the Earth Summit, and negotiations on international environmental agreements in general, are not typically the high-level political or diplomatic processes that they are popularly imagined to be. Indeed, few diplomats are usually fielded by states and direct involvement of politicians is usually reserved for summits. In most negotiations on environmental agreements, delegations and their leaders are normally from environment ministries or other specialist agencies, such as meteorological offices or development agencies. They thus tend to be technically competent but often lack legal or negotiating skills. Larger delegations from, say, the OECD (Organization of Economic Co-operation and Development) countries usually include lawyers and experts from foreign ministries but the representatives of smaller and poorer nations are often quite at sea in negotiating processes. Consequently, on the more contentious issues many delegations need to consult frequently with their political masters at home.

It should also be mentioned that UN negotiating processes are painfully slow, particularly when they involve many states, as in the case of the agreements due to be signed in Rio which, at least in theory, involved all of the states in the world. This slowness is due partly to negotiators often needing to seek advice from their domestic decision-makers on more contentious issues, partly to the complexity of many environmental issues and, especially, to the consensus mechanism which operates in all UN-sponsored negotiations. Although it is evidently desirable to reach agreement between as large a majority of states as possible on matters of global concern, absolute consensus is rarely necessary and achieving it can result both in delays reaching any agreement and in the agreements themselves being watered down as a consequence of their having to take into account all possible points of view. This tended to be the case for all of the 'Rio agreements' where there was considerable divergence of opinion between states on almost all matters of any importance to them. Some of the main areas of disagreement between states in particular negotiating processes are outlined below, together with brief descriptions of how the negotiations were instigated and how they developed.

The Framework Convention on Climate Change

High-level scientific and policy-related debate on possible changes to the climate of the world as a result of anthropogenic emissions of greenhouse gases[9] began in 1979 with the first World Climate Conference in Geneva, continued through a series of international conferences in Villach, Austria,[10] and culminated in the Toronto Conference of 1988[11] which concluded that:

> The Earth's atmosphere is being changed at an unprecedented rate by pollutants resulting from human activities, inefficient and wasteful fuel

use, and the effects of rapid population growth in many regions. These changes represent a major threat to international security and are already having harmful consequences in many parts of the globe.... Far reaching impacts will be caused by global warming and sea level rise which are becoming increasingly evident as a result of atmospheric concentrations of carbon dioxide and other greenhouse gases.

The Villach and Toronto conferences led to the WMO, UNEP and ICSU setting up the intergovernmental Panel on Climate Change (IPCC) in 1988 to establish what, if anything, was happening to the global climate and what the impacts of changing climate might be. Shortly after the publication of the IPCC's first scientific assessment[12] and the Second World Climate Conference in November 1990, the United Nations General Assembly established the Intergovernmental Negotiating Committee (INC) on the Framework Convention on Climate Change in December 1990. As its name implies, the job of the Committee was to negotiate a Climate Change Convention.

From its inception there was little agreement within the INC as to what action should be taken to avoid 'dangerous' climate change. Although the 1990 IPCC report stated that a cut in anthropogenic greenhouse gas emissions to less than 50 per cent of 1990 levels would be needed to stabilize greenhouse gas concentrations in the atmosphere, it did not say whether such a cut was necessary in order to avoid significant, adverse impacts on mankind or on the environment in general. Consequently, the key INC debates on what commitments the Convention should contain concerning emission limitations were less well informed than they might have been.[13]

By the end of 1991 most governments were agreed that they wanted a Climate Convention to sign in Rio but there was no agreement on the level of commitments that the agreement should contain. Amongst the industrialized nations, for example, Germany wanted substantial emission reduction in line with the Toronto Targets,[14] whereas the USA and UK were opposed to anything more than emission stabilization. (In essence, the UK and USA positions were that cutting emissions, other than by energy-saving measures, would be costly to their economies and that they would therefore only commit to substantial emission reductions if rapid and dangerous climate change was certain.) There was similar divergence amongst developing nations with India and China being opposed to emission reductions, except in northern countries, because they might impede their development, and the Alliance of Small Island States (AOSIS) being in favour of massive cuts.[15] Some oil-exporting nations, led by Saudi Arabia and Kuwait, which had a declared interest in promoting the burning of fossil fuels, were opposed to emission reductions of any sort. (Fossil fuel burning gives off carbon dioxide and accounts for well over half the global warming potential of all anthropogenically emitted greenhouse gases.)

By the time of the last INC meeting (in May 1992) before the Rio Summit there was no consensus on many matters of importance, particularly on the level of commitments that the convention should contain, and the draft treaty was a mass of square brackets.[16] Indeed, had it not been for the political imperative of the summit the agreement might well have foundered at this stage. By this time, negotiations on both of the other main treaties (Forests and Biological Diversity) looked like failing. (Indeed, those on the Forests Convention already had, for reasons which will be explained later.) The thought of turning up to a summit with no chance of an agreement to sign was not a prospect that many national leaders relished nor, indeed, was it a prospect that most negotiators wished to propose to their political masters. Moreover, a lot of political capital had been expended on starting negotiations on a climate treaty, notably by the EEC and particularly Germany, Holland and Britain. To have called off negotiations at such a late stage could have been very embarrassing to such states. Therefore, prior to the final week of the negotiations, the INC Bureau,[17] led by the Committee Chairman M. Ripert of France, redrafted the entire text so as to make many of the main features of the agreement ambiguous, or at best vague, but agreeable to most governments.[18] The text of the agreement was agreed on the last possible meeting day before the summit.

The Convention on Biological Diversity

Negotiations on the Convention on Biological Diversity began as an ambitious attempt to conserve all of the world's species of plants and animals. The agreement was intended to ensure that natural biodiversity was not lost by the actions of mankind and also to ensure the environmentally sound management of biotechnology. It could be, and was, said that there was little point in drafting a new international agreement on biological diversity. There were already numerous treaties covering the protection of plants and animals, including at least one which dealt specifically with biological diversity: the legally non-binding but widely implemented FAO Undertaking on Plant Genetic Resources. However many of the existing agreements had overlapping and sometimes conflicting objectives and it therefore made sense to attempt to draw them together and rationalize them. Also, it seemed to make sense to have a legally binding agreement specifically covering the exploitation of biological resources, because many developing countries felt strongly that the diversity of their species had been, and was being, unfairly exploited by developed countries.

This feeling of injustice was particularly keenly felt by developing countries, such as Brazil, that are home to a wide range of biological species. Many of these species had been used to make highly profitable products in northern countries, with little or no payment being made to the country of origin. Many modern drugs, for example, derive from natural biological products, often from tropical forests, but once the key compounds of medical importance are isolated, they can often be artificially synthesized in developed countries. The same increasingly applies to products made by genetic engineering, where developing countries feel strongly that if biological material originated in their countries then they should have a share of the profits of any sales of genetically manipulated material. To try to mitigate this type of dispute, many drugs companies have now set up significant research facilities in countries such as Brazil.

The talks on the Convention quickly focused on the question of biotechnology and the use of biological resources, rather than on the protection of biodiversity *per se*, and consequently ran into trouble at the outset. Arguments centred on the ownership of genetic resources and particularly on the rights of the pharmaceutical industry and the budding genetic technology companies in developed countries to exploit genetic resources at what the developing countries regarded as a fairly low or even negligible cost. As in the case of the climate talks, the INC on Biodiversity eventually reached an impasse. The developed nations, led by the USA and backed by the others including the UK, were unwilling to commit themselves to making significant compensation payments[19] for the use of genetic resources from other nations, and the developing countries were generally insistent on such payments.

At the final INC (Nairobi, 11–19 May 1992) the commitments section of the draft convention was scrapped in order to reach consensus, primarily at the instigation of the USA, which subsequently refused to sign the Treaty in Rio.[20] The draft Article 4 (General Obligations) was removed altogether and most remaining paragraphs which could be interpreted as containing important obligations were preceded by the words 'as far as possible and as appropriate' or 'in accordance with its [the States'] particular conditions and capabilities'. As with the Climate Convention, the Biodiversity Treaty might have been expected to founder at this stage but, again, it survived, albeit in a watered-down form, because of the political imperative of the impending summit.

The Forests Convention

Perhaps surprisingly, there is no international agreement specifically concerning the world's forests. There are several agreements which incidentally include forests in addition to the International Tropical Timber Agreement (ITTA), which, as its name implies, is concerned solely with tropical timber (and is really a resource management agreement rather than a conservation agreement). A convention on forest conservation was thus, perhaps, overdue. Moreover the ITTA was due to expire in 1992 and it was hoped that its successor might be included in a global agreement.[21]

The idea of a convention on forests was first mooted seriously in May 1990 by a committee chaired by Swedish Prime Minister Olsen, which was reviewing the Tropical Forestry Action Plan (TFAP) for the FAO. The concept was taken up by the G-7[22] economic summit meeting in Houston, Texas, in June 1990 after which the heads of government called for a treaty to be negotiated in time for signing at UNCED.

First the FAO Forestry Committee and then the FAO Council (its supreme decision-making body) discussed a proposal for the Convention on Forests drafted by the FAO Director General, Edouard Saouma. Initially the idea was to develop the agreement within the framework of the FAO, as nearly all treaties on flora and fauna have been since the Second World War. However, from the outset of the negotiations in late 1990 it was clear that few nations with substantial forests were prepared to agree to a treaty which would curtail their rights to exploit their forests as they wished. This was particularly so for some developing countries, notably Malaysia. Negotiations were also made more difficult by some developed nations, such as the USA and the UK, which were unwilling to have the FAO play a leading role in either the negotiations or in the operation of the agreement. It was therefore decided to try to negotiate the treaty within the framework of the UNCED preparatory process. The UNCED Preparatory Committees debated the forests issue but Malaysia expressed the same reservations as before and was joined in its objections by India, which also opposed a binding agreement. India's opposition had a different motivation from that of Malaysia: the Indian government suspected that the G-7, at the instigation of the USA, had proposed and supported a Forests Convention as a way of avoiding taking significant action to reduce their greenhouse gas emissions.[23]

Eventually, under pressure from the G-77,[24] the concept of having a treaty was abandoned and the Forests Convention was replaced by a non-binding agreement called the 'Declaration of Forest Principles' which, as its name suggests, lays down some important principles but is no substitute for a legally binding agreement. Even in this form, however, the UNCED negotiators were unable to agree a text by the time that the Earth Summit began.

Agenda 21

Agenda 21 was intended to be a set of guidelines on environment and development issues for states to follow in the twenty-first century: a sort of guiding principles of sustainable development. Drafting the Agenda was a massive undertaking, verging on the unmanageable. Each nation was invited to submit plans for inclusion in the document and these were drafted not only by national governments but also by the 'Major Groups' within each country.[25] The job of the four Prepcoms was then to amalgamate these plans into a single, coherent plan – which they did! The details of how this was achieved and, indeed, the contents of the resulting 500-page agreement are the subject of a separate book.[26] Suffice it to say that the first Prepcom was held in Nairobi in August 1990, and by the fourth and final Prepcom in New York in 1992, 85 per cent of Agenda 21 was complete. The main chapter headings in the Agenda are as follows:

Part I: Social and Economic Dimensions
1. Preamble
2. International cooperation to accelerate sustainable development in developing countries
3. Combating poverty
4. Changing consumption patterns
5. Demographic dynamics and sustainability
6. Protecting and promoting human health conditions
7. Promoting sustainable human settlement
8. Integrating environment and development in decision-making

Part II: Conservation and Management of Resources for Development
9. Protection of the atmosphere
10. Integrated approach to planning and management of land resources
11. Combating deforestation
12. Managing fragile ecosystems: combating desertification and drought
13. Managing fragile ecosystems: sustainable mountain development
14. Promoting sustainable agriculture and rural development
15. Conservation of biological diversity

16. Environmentally sound management of biotechnology
17. Protection of the oceans, all kinds of seas, including enclosed and semi-enclosed seas, and coastal areas
18. Protection of the quality and supply of freshwater resources
19. Environmentally sound management of toxic chemicals
20. Environmentally sound management of hazardous wastes
21. Environmentally sound management of solid wastes and sewage-related issues
22. Safe and environmentally sound management of radioactive wastes

Part III: Strengthening the Role of Major Groups
23. Preamble
24. Global action for women towards sustainable and equable development
25. Children and youth in sustainable development
26. Recognizing and strengthening the role of indigenous people
27. Strengthening the role of non-governmental organizations
28. Local authorities' initiatives in support of Agenda 21
29. Strengthening the role of workers and their trade unions
30. Strengthening the role of business and industry
31. Scientific and technological community
32. Strengthening the role of farmers

Part IV: Means of Implementation
33. Financial resources and mechanisms
34. Technology transfer
35. Science for sustainable development
36. Promoting education, public awareness and training
37. National mechanisms and international cooperation for capacity-building in developing countries
38. International institutional arrangements
39. International legal instruments and mechanisms
40. Information for decision-making

The Results of the Preparatory Process

By the time the Earth Summit began the Conventions on Climate Change and Biodiversity were agreed and only needed signing. The Convention on Forests had been abandoned and the non-binding Declaration of Forest Principles had been prepared instead, although it was not fully agreed by the time that the summit started. The Rio Declaration had, likewise, been largely agreed in advance. The bulk of Agenda 21 (500 pages) had also been agreed, leaving only really contentious matters such as finance, institutions and technology transfer for the conference to tackle.

The main purposes of the conference were thus to present the two Conventions for signature, to thrash out final details on the two nonbinding Declarations, and to reach agreement on Agenda 21 so that it could be submitted to the UN General Assembly for final approval in the autumn of 1992. Getting to this stage represented the completion of a massive organizational task and involved many thousands of working hours. Again, it should be stressed that without the political imperative of the Earth Summit this effort would probably not have been forthcoming and agreement on such a diverse range of documents would, almost certainly, not have been reached. Indeed, given that many Western developed countries were entering into economic recession and the Soviet bloc had recently fragmented, it is very unlikely that either of the conventions, which are potentially costly to implement, would have been agreed at all.

HOW DID THE EARTH SUMMIT FUNCTION?

The Summit Venue and Attendance

The Earth Summit was held at Riocentro Conference Centre, a set of very large, interconnected structures resembling an oversized space-age tented camp. Dating from 1977, its location in a swampy area some 35 kilometres south of the hotels in Copacabana and Ipanema,[27] where most of the delegates stayed, made it an excellent venue from the point of view of security but the choice of site was not immediately appreciated by those delegates taking the bus to the conference, which took 80 minutes on a good day. However, once past the rings of armed guards and tanks, most attendees agreed that Riocentro was more than adequate for the task of housing the vast conference,[28] and that the Brazilian and regional government had done a good job in organizing the meeting.

The bulk of the people attending UNCED were, of course, delegates, with probably the next most numerous grouping comprising UN officials. Apart from the UNCED Secretariat and the two INC Secretariats, large numbers of staff, including guards, were brought in from the UN offices in New York, Geneva and Nairobi, as well as from UN agencies and intergovernmental organizations in other locations. The number of accredited press representatives grew to over 7000 by the end of the conference and the number of accredited non-governmental organizations was 1500, usually with at least two people attending from each organization. As a consequence of the vast numbers of people present, access to many meetings was very restricted and all groups, including delegations, were 'ticketed' (particularly the section of the conference attended by heads of government). Indeed, much to their disgust, the press were excluded from most meetings of any importance, including the summit itself, although the NGOs were allowed almost unrestricted access (except in terms of numbers) to all meetings except a very brief 'mini-summit' attended only by heads of government with one adviser each.

The Conference

UNCED was divided into two main parts: the conference proper and the 'summit segment', although there were also pre-conference sessions on 1 and 2 June at which the agenda and rules of the conference were agreed. The work needed to complete Agenda 21, the Declaration of Forest Principles and the Rio Declaration was done in the earlier part of the conference, between 3 and 11 June. The summit segment (12 and 13 June) was mainly taken up by national policy statements by heads of government and state. UNCED concluded on 14 June with a meeting at which the texts were formally adopted.

The first section of the conference (3 to 11 June) was conducted in two separate parts. First, there were plenary debates at which policy speeches were given by delegates. As the summit segment approached it was increasingly the senior delegates who gave speeches; in the early days of the plenary debates most of the speeches were given by officials but later on nearly all were given by environment or development ministers.[29] The debates were authoritatively chaired by the President of the Conference, President Fernando Collor de Mello of Brazil. Concurrently with the plenary debates, 'Main Committee' meetings were held at which the final details of Agenda 21 were negotiated. These meetings were usually attended by at least one delegate from each nation and were chaired by the Singaporean Ambassador, Tommy Koh, who had also run the Prepcoms. Because of the inevitable difficulties in reaching agreement on some topics (such as finance) several sub-committees were formed from the Main Committee. The principle, long-standing, sub-committees were on Finance and Technology Transfer but there were typically about eight sub-committees meeting on any particular day and, as the summit segment loomed, night.[30] Koh was a highly skilled chairman, steering the more contentious passages through to agreement with a bravura display of wit and humour.[31] It should again be stressed that political imperative was extremely important in hastening the negotiations and in getting things decided. Many national leaders were attending the conference and they usually wanted to be perceived as making meaningful contributions to the summit. Few were prepared to let their negotiators appear obstructive during the final negotiations. There were, however, exceptions to this general rule, notably the USA. Widely publicized differences of opinion on the US stance at the summit broke out between the head of the US delegation, Reilly, and the US administration. These arguments boiled down to the question of whether the US administration might allow the delegation to adopt a more conciliatory position on some issues which were not really of central policy importance to the US.[32] The fact that the conference was a summit meeting undoubtedly persuaded the US administration to shift its position on some minor policy matters but on major issues they were unyielding.

The sorts of problems encountered in the US delegation were far from unique at UNCED; they were merely more visible and more widely reported because the USA was perceived to be playing the leading role in the conference. Indeed, it is worth noting that in many ways the Earth Summit was held at almost exactly the wrong time for many nations. For example, the US economy was in recession and President Bush was coming up for re-election, facing not only Democratic opposition but also right-wing opposition in the form of Ross Perot. Bush was therefore in a double bind. He felt that he could not risk committing himself to any course of action which might lead to further loss of American jobs, for fear of both the Democrats and his own party. Neither could he do anything that might cost either the government or industry too much money, for fear of losing his wealthier right-wing supporters to Perot. So he did very little, which was unfortunate because, particularly following the break-up of the Soviet Union, many countries were looking for a firm lead from the USA and they did not get it. Russia and the former Eastern bloc countries were in no position to commit themselves to any action at all and had other, more pressing, priorities. The European Community (EC) could have tried to take a lead, instead of the USA, but amongst its larger member states only Germany was keen to make fairly substantial commitments. Like the USA the UK was well into economic recession, Italy was entering a period of political turmoil and France generally considered that it was already doing enough on many major issues.[33] In the rather unhappy position of having no positive leadership UNCED perhaps failed to achieve all that it might have in less economically troubled times.

During the first week of the conference the two Conventions were opened for signing and representatives of more than 150 states had signed each of them by 14 June. This was a major achievement but was rather soured by the USA failing to sign the Convention on Biological Diversity. The US had reasonable reservations concerning ambiguities in the agreement, as did the UK. However, the UK signed the agreement with a caveat, or rather a statement of what it understood by the agreement. A more conciliatory US administration could have done the same and received substantial praise for doing so, particularly from developing nations. In a similarly politically inept way Malaysia also failed to sign the Convention.

By the time that the summit segment began, the sub-committees had completed their business and, in the plenary session, the environment and development ministers were replaced by their heads of state or government, all of whom wished to speak at length and most of whom usually got their own way. However, because 102 notables wished to speak at the summit, they were limited to seven minutes each – a severe test of President Collor's chairmanship. On the first day only President Museveni (Uganda) and President Castro Ruz (Cuba) kept to time.[34] Very few leaders gave speeches of any substance, perhaps because many had more pressing problems at home, although some did commit their states to more substantial actions than were agreed in the Conventions or Agenda 21. For example, Chancellor Kohl re-committed Germany to the Toronto Targets rather than the greenhouse gas stabilization targets mentioned in the Climate Convention. Very few, with the notable exception of Castro, demonstrated any oratorical prowess.

Running concurrently with the Summit Plenary there was a Main Committee meeting at ministerial level at which final agreement on Agenda 21 was worked out. In addition, a very brief mini-plenary was held in which all of the heads of state and government met around a very large table, which, as many NGOs contended, contained a substantial amount of newly harvested tropical hardwood. This meeting was conceived mainly as a photo opportunity and received a lot of publicity but, because it was so short (half a day), achieved nothing of any consequence. In fact, the success of the summit in bringing together so many world leaders was also, in some ways, its greatest failing. Although the presence of the leaders pushed negotiators to do more than they might otherwise have done in the preparatory negotiations and lent momentum and authority to the follow-up processes, there was insufficient time for the presidents and prime ministers to get together for any meaningful discussions. Old friends and political allies met informally but there was no real chance for discussions on new or contentious issues or for new initiatives to be taken.

The most important single meeting, in terms of achievements, was the final session of the plenary discussions on Sunday 14 June, at which

Agenda 21, the Rio Declaration and the Declaration of Forest Principles were formally agreed. Nearly all heads of government and state had by that time gone home, although by then there was perhaps little for them to do.

It was easy to be cynical about the achievements of the summit in its immediate aftermath, and many observers were. This disillusionment arose partly because the two Conventions were widely perceived to contain minimal commitments and Agenda 21 was a non-binding agreement and could not therefore be 'enforced'. (Legally binding international agreements can rarely be enforced either but the popular perception is that they can.[35]) Certainly, fairly little was achieved actually at the summit. However, if viewed as part of a continuing process, then the summit was important. It highlighted significant environmental and developmental issues in an international forum attended by many world leaders and thereby ensured that the process of negotiating and implementing agreements on these issues would continue at a lower intergovernmental level – a process which is described briefly in the following outline of what has happened to the Rio agreements since Rio.

THE SUBSEQUENT DEVELOPMENT OF THE RIO AGREEMENTS

Since the Earth Summit the main agreements have been ratified and have entered into force with great speed compared to most other international environmental agreements. Within three years of the summit, the Biodiversity and Climate Conventions had come into force, the Commission on Sustainable Development had had three major review meetings, negotiations on the Desertification Convention had been concluded and the first World Population Conference had been held. This section explains how each of the agreements has begun to be implemented and examines their potential impact and future development. The population issue is not considered in any detail because, although high-level talks on the problem were instigated at Rio, they were not really part of the Rio process as it was originally conceived. Moreover, in assessing the efficacy of the summit it is probably more valuable to examine how well the UNCED and its related processes met their original objectives; and the population issue was never really on the agenda for Rio.

Agenda 21

The key feature of Agenda 21 is that it establishes both a process for reviewing its implementation and a body whose main task is to ensure that the review functions effectively, which makes it far more than a simple declaration of intent. This body is the United Nations Commission on Sustainable Development (CSD) which was set up as part of the Agenda when it was approved by the United Nations General Assembly in November 1992. The CSD reviews and reports on the implementation of the Agenda at national, regional and international levels and also serves as a forum for debate on sustainable development issues. It comes under the auspices of the Economic and Social Council (ECOSOC) of the UN but has a reasonable degree of independence from it.

The first substantive meeting of the CSD was held in May and June 1993, the second was held in May 1994, the third in April 1995, and it will continue to meet annually in the future. It is perhaps encouraging for the success of the Commission that most nations were represented at its first meetings at a fairly senior level – by environment or development ministers, or both. Another indication of the importance which states appear to attach to the CSD is the decision at the first session to form a review body of workable proportions comprising representatives of 50 nations each elected to serve a limited term. This arrangement should help the Commission to arrive at decisions much more rapidly than if it had comprised all of the states which are parties to the agreement. Most interested observers would contend that the parties to the agreement would probably not have made such a sensible institutional arrangement had they not been concerned with the effective operation of the review process.

Agenda 21 has very ambitious aims and it is too early to tell whether the CSD will be effective in helping to reach its objectives. So far though, the Commission has received considerable political support and has established the types of organizational structures which are likely to lead to it being reviewed effectively. This may, in turn, lead to the effective implementation of the agreement. It is almost certain that without the political 'push' given by the Earth Summit, the CSD and Agenda 21 would not have progressed so far or so fast.

The Climate Convention

By early 1994 the Climate Convention had been ratified by more than 50 states and it therefore came into force in March 1994. The first Conference of the Parties (CoP) to the Convention was held in March and April 1995 in Berlin by which time the agreement had about 120 parties. The Convention contains no substantial commitments concerning anthropogenic emissions other than, loosely, for those parties listed in Annex 1 of the agreement[36] to limit their greenhouse gas emissions to 1990 levels by the year 2000. (Because of the ambiguities and, indeed, omissions which were built in order to obtain consensus on the treaty exact interpretation of the meaning of the commitments is contentious.)

After the summit, climate negotiations resumed in the INC in December 1992 on the principle that although the Convention was legally complete the negotiators could work through issues which had not been fully addressed by the agreement and which would need to be resolved if the Convention was to get off to a prompt start. By the time of the first Conference of the Parties in March 1995 as many Negotiating Committee meetings had been held since Rio as were held before it. The post-Rio meetings have been productive in elaborating articles in the agreement which were left deliberately vague in order to get the Convention ready for signature at UNCED. For example, although the treaty mentions reporting and review processes these are not specified in any detail and much work was needed before the first CoP on exactly how to implement them.[37]

In the INC some governments wanted to move quickly to negotiating protocols to limit greenhouse gas emissions more severely. In September 1994 the Association of Small Island States (AOSIS) and Germany tabled proposals for protocols to be discussed at the first CoP. These were not, in fact, taken up by the conference but it did decide to begin negotiations on a protocol to cut emissions within specified timescales, and the negotiations were to be completed within two years. Considering all of the problems which arose in negotiating the Convention in the first place, and initial opposition to discussions on a protocol on cuts in emissions in the INC, this is a remarkable outcome. It is very difficult to be sure how much of this change of heart was brought about by changing domestic policies and how much was due to the negotiating process in general, and the Earth Summit in particular. Certainly, within the INC and CoP, there was a lot of international pressure for some states, notably the members of OPEC, to change their positions but it is doubtful whether UNCED had any direct influence. However, the Earth Summit may have helped to provide the impetus for the parties to proceed faster than they might otherwise have done, and the presence of many senior politicians at the Berlin CoP (which was in many ways a sort of mini–follow-up to the Earth Summit) undoubtedly had an effect on the final outcome.

The Convention on Biological Diversity

By the end of 1993 more than 30 countries had ratified the Convention on Biological Diversity and it came into force on 29 December 1993. As in the case of the Climate Convention, details of the agreement were elaborated in the period prior to the first meeting of the Conference of the Parties, which was held in November 1994 in the Bahamas, by the same negotiating committee as originally drafted the agreement: the Intergovernmental Committee (INC) on the Biodiversity Convention, which last met in June 1994. There have, however, been fewer meetings than for the Climate Convention and they have been generally less constructive. However, they did achieve consensus on a number of potentially important actions; for example, one of the main outcomes of the INC meeting in October 1993 was an agreement that a scientific meeting should be convened to report on research aimed at finding out how to implement the Convention, including how to perform scientific and technical assessments of biodiversity.

Reviewing implementation of the Biodiversity Convention has proved to be a difficult task, in part because the agreement is based on a concept rather than a specific set of goals, and in part because it has no firm commitments to review. Nevertheless the CoP has begun to set up a framework for evaluation of implementation and has also begun to consider how the treaty provisions on technology cooperation and capacity-building might be put into effect. As in the case of the Climate Change Convention, there is provision for a Subsidiary Body on Scientific, Technical and Technological Advice. The role of this body is, as its name suggests, to advise the CoP on technical matters and developments relating to the Convention. But, as in the case of Agenda 21 and the Climate Convention, it is still too early to assess whether the Biodiversity Convention will establish effective implementation review mechanisms. At present this does not seem likely because the Convention is still dogged by the same arguments which adversely affected it at, and before, Rio. However, there is currently a move towards separating out the contentious issue of ownership of genetic resources by negotiating a protocol on the subject. If this succeeds, progress on the rest of the Convention may become more rapid.

Overall, the Earth Summit processes may not have helped the cause of the Convention on Biological Diversity. Most states were not really prepared to debate the subject prior to the Earth Summit and the negotiating process for it was too short for such a complex and underdiscussed subject. In many ways UNCED thus tended merely to highlight problems associated with the topic, rather than solve them. Summits require a lot of preparation if they are to succeed and neither the Biodiversity nor the Forests Convention had enough preparation.

The Convention on Desertification

Negotiations on the United Nations Convention on Desertification, which began immediately after UNCED, were concluded on 18 June 1994 in Paris. The Convention was opened for signature, also in Paris, on 14 October 1994. Progress in the negotiations was thus extremely rapid. In many ways the Convention is a very advanced agreement, particularly considering that it was concluded between some of the world's least developed and poorest states, and that it addresses one of the key environmental and development issues of today. Sadly, it is doubtful if it will be implemented fully because of lack of funds, unless it manages to attract more interest from developed countries.

CONCLUSIONS: THE CONSEQUENCES OF THE EARTH SUMMIT

If viewed as part of an ongoing process, the Earth Summit achieved considerable success, specifically in what it originally set out to do, which was to draft and then review implementation of an agenda for sustainable development in the twenty-first century. Agenda 21 is a remarkably radical document for most of the world's governments to have negotiated and then signed. In spite of the fact that it is not legally binding, it is treated with a reasonable degree of seriousness by most states and its implementation is reviewed each year by fairly senior groups of politicians. Without the political imperative of the Earth Summit it is doubtful whether such an agreement would have been reached or whether its implementation would have been undertaken so rapidly and with such high-level political involvement. Moreover, the publicity surrounding the summit helped to raise public awareness of sustainable development issues which has, in turn, helped to keep the level of interest by politicians higher than it might otherwise be.

The effect of the summit on the legal agreements which were tacked onto it (the Climate Convention, the Biodiversity Convention, the Forests Convention and, belatedly, the Desertification Convention) are less clear cut. The Climate Convention was negotiated, and has progressed, relatively rapidly but it may well have done so anyway, given the rather obvious consequences of doing nothing about possible climate change.[38] Likewise, negotiations on the linked issue of desertification progressed speedily although the Convention suffers from a lack of support from developed countries. Negotiations on the Convention on Biological

Diversity did not run smoothly and the agreement has not fared very well since Rio, largely because of a fundamental rift between northern and southern states over rights to genetic resources. It is difficult to see how this issue could have been resolved at the Earth Summit and it remains difficult to see how the issues might be resolved now, unless a protocol can be negotiated which in effect hives off the contentious parts of the agreement to another forum, leaving the parties to concentrate on potentially more important issues. The negotiations on the Forests Convention, of course, failed, as was probably inevitable from the outset.

In retrospect, it was probably not a good idea to link negotiations on the Conventions, other than perhaps the Climate Convention, to the summit as they tended to distract attention from the main business (Agenda 21) and most were insufficiently well prepared to stand much chance of being successfully concluded in a limited timescale. Moreover, because the Conventions had separate negotiating committees (except for the Forests Convention) they were never really part of the UNCED process anyway. Using the summit to force the pace on the negotiations on the Climate Convention may have helped in its rapid development, but trying to do the same in the cases of the Biodiversity and Forests Conventions, which needed more preliminary – even informal – negotiations beforehand, probably impeded progress on them as fundamental policy rifts were revealed and highlighted, making subsequent progress more difficult. There was a fairly widespread view at Rio that having some sort of convention on biological diversity was better than having none at all but, so far, progress in the Conferences of the Parties to the Convention has not supported this view.

Another failing of the Earth Summit was that it did not provide a forum for discussion between world leaders. Admittedly, this was not its main intent and their presence was only really useful in stimulating prior and subsequent negotiations. Nevertheless, the fact that they did not have time to talk together meant that they had no chance of overcoming any significant policy differences (even given that there were probably too many heads of government present for any significant progress to have been made anyway). In this sense, the Earth Summit was unusual amongst summits, where the aim is primarily to enable discussion between heads of government. Overall, however, the summit did succeed in its main aims of getting an agreement on sustainable development off to a good start and of raising public awareness of the topic.

NOTES AND REFERENCES

1. For an elaboration of the author's views, see J. Lanchberry, 'The Earth Summit Conference', in J. B. Poole and R. Guthrie (eds), *Verification 1993* (Brassey's/VERTIC, 1993), pp. 229–38.
2. The United Nations Conference on Human Environment held in Stockholm in June 1972.
3. The Brundtland Report is properly called the Report of the World Commission on Environment and Development and was published in 1987.
4. This list is taken verbatim from UNGA Resolution 44/228, part 1, paragraph 12.
5. Of these, only climate change needed to be covered by a legally binding convention, ozone depletion and transboundary air pollution having been dealt with respectively by the Vienna Convention on Substances that Deplete the Ozone Layer (and protocols) and the UN-ECE Convention on Long Range Transboundary Air Pollution (and protocols).
6. These were already largely protected, as far as legally binding conventions were concerned, by the International Convention for the Prevention of Pollution from Ships (MARPOL), the Oslo and Paris Conventions, and the UNEP Regional Seas Agreements (and by the UN Law of the Sea which had not then come into force).
7. The problems of desertification and population growth were mentioned many times at UNCED by senior conference and UN officials, such as the conference Secretary General, Maurice Strong, the UN Secretary General Boutros Boutros Ghali and the Main Committee Chairman Tommy Koh. Prior to the conference, talking about population problems had been taboo in the UN and one of the positive outcomes of UNCED was that it put 'population' on the political agenda and led directly to the UN Population Conference in Cairo in September 1994.
8. UNEP, WMO and ICSU set up the Intergovernmental Panel on Climate Change (IPCC) in 1988.
9. Greenhouse gases absorb energy in the infra-red region of the electromagnetic spectrum. Many exist naturally as trace gases in the atmosphere and keep the mean surface temperature of the world about 33°C warmer than it otherwise would be. However, emissions due to the activities of mankind (anthropogenic emissions) are adding to the concentration of greenhouse gases in the atmosphere and may therefore be causing it to warm up. For a full description of this phenomenon see J. T. Houghton, J. J. Jenkins and J. J. Ephraums (eds), *Climate Change: The IPCC Scientific Assessment* (Cambridge, Cambridge University Press, 1990).
10. The Villach Conferences were held in 1980, 1983, 1985 and 1987. The latter was in two parts, the second part being held in Bellagio, Italy. The conferences were sponsored by the WMO, UNEP and ICSU.
11. The World Conference on the Changing Atmosphere: Implications for Global Security.
12. This concluded that 'emissions from human activities are substantially increasing the atmospheric concentrations of the greenhouse gases.... These increases will enhance the greenhouse effect, resulting on average in additional warming of the Earth's surface.'

13.   For a fuller discussion of this topic, see John Lanchberry and David Victor, 'The Role of Science in the Global Climate Negotiations' in Helge Ole Bergessen and Georg Parman (eds), *Green Globe Yearbook* (Oxford, Oxford University Press, 1995).

14.   The Toronto Targets derive from the Toronto Conference which called for a return to 1988 emission levels by the year 2000 and a 20 per cent cut by 2005.

15.   The Small Island States risk inundation if significant climate change (and concomitant sea level rise) occurs. For a fuller discussion of the negotiations see D. Bodanski, 'The United Nations Framework Convention on Climate Change: A Commentary', *Yale Journal of International Law*, vol. 18, no. 2 (Summer 1993).

16.   Square brackets indicate that the text contained therein has not been agreed by all parties.

17.   The Bureau consisted of the Chairman and Executive Secretary of the Committee, representatives of the main UN regions (Southern America, and so forth) and important interested groupings, such as AOSIS.

18.   Last minute redrafting of treaty texts by chairmen is a fairly common feature of UN negotiations but this redraft was extreme by any standards. In this case, there is a fairly well substantiated rumour that the contentious parts of the text were, in fact, agreed between the US head of delegation (Bob Reinstein) and the UK delegation head (Tony Brenton), who was mandated to speak for the EU.

19.   In practice, most developed states were willing to pay for the exploitation of resources but they were unwilling to commit themselves legally to having to do so invariably.

20.   The USA signed the agreement only when the new Democratic administration of President Clinton replaced the Republican administration of President Bush, who was in office at the time of the summit and during most of the negotiations which led up to it.

21.   The ITTA has since been renewed for a further ten years.

22.   The Group of Seven supposedly richest democratic nations.

23.   The Indian case was complex but basically they thought that the USA was proposing to preserve and enhance forests because they are a major sink for carbon dioxide (plants convert carbon dioxide first into sugars and then into starches and cellulose); the idea being that the USA could avoid reducing its carbon dioxide emissions by planting trees to mop them up.

24.   The G-77 is the main negotiating bloc for the developing countries. It has far more than 77 members, and always has had. The name derives from a sort of parody of the G-7 group of most prosperous nations.

25.   'Major Groups' include those concerned with environment, development, youth, women, farmers, trade unions, science, religion, indigenous peoples, business and industry and local government.

26.   For such a book, see Stanley P. Johnson (ed.), *The Earth Summit: The United Nations Conference on Environment and Development (UNCED)* (Graham and Trotman/Martinus Nijhoff, 1993).

27.   Copacabana and Ipanema are the more salubrious southern suburbs of Rio.

28.   The NGO parallel conference, the Global Forum, was sited in the centre of Rio in a beautiful location with views of the bay and Sugar Loaf.

Unfortunately, it was so far from the UN Conference that the Forum was sparsely attended by UNCED delegates and observers.

29. The arrival of ever more senior representatives led to some interesting games of musical chairs in the conference hall. Each state had only one desk with three seats in file behind it, with the most senior representative taking the front seat. Thus, whenever a more senior person arrived, all of the others moved back one seat with the person at the back losing their seat and having to leave. By the time that the summit proper started, very few officials had seats because all were taken by ministers or other VIPs.

30. Sub-committees also worked on the Declaration of Forest Principles and on the Rio Declaration.

31. Agenda 21 would have been agreed without Koh but probably not in quite such a radical form. Koh had a genuine sympathy for the poorer nations and his consummate skill as a chairman enabled him to achieve a lot for them. His humour was particularly effective in getting round contentious issues. A typical remark was (referring to a phrase in square brackets), 'Does anyone disagree with the words "fair and equitable" ... USA?' The USA did object on this occasion, to much laughter, but did so thereafter with decreased frequency.

32. Reilly was head of the US Environmental Protection Agency (and ex-head of the World Wildlife Fund, USA) and was generally perceived to be 'green'. President Bush's administration was generally perceived not to be.

33. For example, after the oil crisis of the 1970s the French adopted the policy of trying to ensure their independence from fossil fuel suppliers by embarking on a programme of building nuclear power stations. Because a very large proportion of greenhouse gases and other atmospheric pollution comes from fossil fuel power stations, the French policy resulted in their having the lowest emissions per capita in Europe. The government did not therefore see why they should commit themselves to substantial emission reductions, either in the Climate Convention or in Agenda 21. French policy in other areas related to the environment placed them in a similarly atypical position compared to other European states.

34. Scurrilous rumours circulated at the conference suggested that President Castro's speech was the shortest that he had ever made. Possibly as a consequence of this, his was the most warmly received speech of the summit and brought him a standing ovation from a sizeable minority of the delegates.

35. Public perception of events such as the Earth Summit are, of course, influenced by press reports. Unfortunately, the news media covering the summit generally did a very poor job of reporting it: few journalists seemed to understand what was going on and many press reports were wildly inaccurate.

36. These countries are developed countries.

37. For an account of the INC negotiations since the summit see David Victor and Julian Salt, 'Climate since Rio', *Environment* (November 1994).

38. The development of the agreements for the protection of the ozone layer (the Vienna Convention, Montreal Protocol and London and Copenhagen Amendments) were similarly rapid and had no summit to help to propel them forward, although they did attract a lot of high-level political attention.

Part IV
Conclusions

15 How Useful is Summitry?
David H. Dunn

The analysis in the preceding chapters has thus far sought to define summitry, explain its evolution and growth, and evaluate its uses and abuses in
specific institutional and *ad hoc* environments. From this analysis, it is
clear that summitry is a multifaceted phenomenon, utilized in a variety of
different circumstances. From its early origins summitry has become a
global reality of modern diplomacy. This much is evident from the examination of summitry in the specific political contexts above. Whether or
not the evolution of summitry is a useful development in a general sense,
however, remains controversial. For James Der Derian, for example, 'at
the level of great power politics, perhaps our best hope – and the best ele-
vation – for understanding the other at the highest reaches remains the
much maligned "summit"'.[1] By contrast Domenico Bartoli's judgement is
that 'a summit conference combines the risk of misunderstandings ... with
the most sensational publicity. It is a cross between secret and open diplomacy, and ends by accumulating the drawbacks of both.'[2] In order to
understand and evaluate the impact and usefulness of summit diplomacy
more generally, therefore, it is necessary to look at its advantages and disadvantages more explicitly and thematically.

THE ADVANTAGES OF SUMMIT DIPLOMACY

The rationale most often cited for these meetings is that they provide an
opportunity for political leaders to get a measure of their opposite number
in order to be better able to gauge their conduct. In a sense this function is
the classic information-gathering role of the diplomat, conducted at first
hand by the political leader. Many memoirs of senior politicians are
replete with comments about the indispensability of meeting their opposite
numbers. Typically, every autobiography of a head of government or
foreign minister details the first impressions made on them by political
allies and adversaries alike. Some of these impressions reach the public
realm immediately, such as Thatcher's 1984 statement that Gorbachev was
a man 'with whom she could do business'. More typical in form, however,

is Thatcher's observation in her memoirs that the French President Giscard d'Estaing 'was never someone to whom I warmed'.[3]

Getting to know other heads of government also serves the purpose of breaking down the barriers of mutual suspicion which inevitably exist between two parties who are unfamiliar with each other. Overcoming such barriers is useful both in subsequent negotiations at the summit, and in the context of their broader relationship. In this way confidence in a relationship, so essential to routine diplomacy, can be established at the highest working level. Another motivation for this kind of meeting is that politicians, especially those democratically elected who have attained high office by successful application of their interpersonal skills, often believe that they can 'charm' their foreign counterparts to their own advantage. On occasions when a genuine rapport is established, as between Prime Minister Thatcher and President Reagan, tangible diplomatic benefits can result.

At the other end of the diplomatic spectrum, summits have been most valued by politicians for their symbolic importance. This has been manipulated in various ways, ranging from the state visit to reassure an ally – exemplified by Kennedy's trip to Berlin in 1961 symbolizing US commitment to the defence of the city – to the way in which the outcome of superpower summits was presented as a barometer of East–West relations and comparative political advantage. The importance attached to the 'spirit' of Geneva and Camp David in the public's perception of the state of the cold war relationship has already been mentioned. Similarly, and self-consciously, the Moscow summit of 1972 was orchestrated as a central symbol of the new relationship of superpower détente. The Vienna summit of 1979 was also viewed by both superpowers as a symbol of improved relations which marked the end of a protracted period of mistrust.[4] Meetings at summit level are also of value in symbolizing a change in the relationship between the parties resulting from the agreement of a new policy. The visits by German Chancellor Willy Brandt to Moscow and Warsaw, and his meeting with East German Prime Minister Willi Stoph in 1970 are examples where meetings at summit level were used to signal the change in policy adopted by the new Chancellor and to underscore symbolically the FRG's commitment to its new Ostpolitik. The handshake on the White House lawn between Yasser Arafat and Yitzhak Rabin in 1993 was equally important as an attempt to symbolize the new era of relations between Israel and the Palestinian people. The importance of symbolism at summit meetings can be taken to excess, however, as demonstrated by President Carter's reaction to criticism that his trip to Vienna to sign the SALT II Treaty was following in the footsteps of Neville Chamberlain. So obsessed was Carter with not looking like Chamberlain at the airport that he ordered that there should be no umbrellas at Vienna, despite the rain, declaring, 'I'd rather drown than carry an umbrella.'[5]

An associated advantage of the symbolic role of summitry is the propaganda value that such meetings represent for both the countries and the individuals concerned. The desire for summit meetings between the cold war antagonists, for example, was exploited in their public diplomacy as evidence of their willingness to advance world peace. Similarly, the willingness of so many heads of government, including George Bush, to attend the Earth Summit in Rio in 1992 is testimony to their desire to be seen to be taking environmental concerns seriously, even if this commitment was not matched by their willingness to accept or act upon an agreed agenda. Participation in international dialogue is seen by many politicians as of advantage in itself. It gives the impression to domestic audiences, especially at crucial points in the electoral cycle, both that they are 'doing something', and that what they are doing matters. Nor is this desire limited to world leaders. Common is the desire among politicians for meetings with important world leaders in the expectation that their own status will be enhanced by association, for as Hamilton and Langhorne observe, 'air travel and television cameras have made world statesmen of the humblest party hacks'.[6]

The propaganda value of a state or official visit can be for the benefit of one of two audiences. Its main focus may be the domestic audience of the visitor, playing on the importance that the host state attaches to its relationship with the official guest or state represented. A variation of this is where the host's intention is that the prestige of the official visitor, such as the President of the United States, will enhance the domestic standing of the visited regime. Alternatively, an official visit may serve the purpose of providing a foreign leader with the opportunity to appeal to the government and citizens of another country, and persuade them to view his or her home country in more positive, or even less negative, terms. It was the latter purpose which lay behind President Gorbachev's impromptu walkabouts in Washington in December 1987. Pakistani Prime Minister Benazir Bhutto's visit to the US in June 1989 was another example of an official visit used for propaganda purposes. This visit, however, was meticulously planned to maximize its public diplomacy impact, with a public relations firm hired to gain the best media access, frame the right strategic message, and even draft the six keynote speeches.[7]

In addition to their symbolic role, summit meetings are useful for a number of important substantive diplomatic tasks. For example, they play an educative role in several ways. At the most fundamental level they force political leaders to focus on the international rather than the domestic

implications of their policies, and require them to master their briefs in the
foreign policy area in order to give a competent performance. The summit
meetings themselves then constitute an opportunity for them to explain
their policy positions to their foreign counterparts, and to be briefed in turn
by the latter on the other party's position. Face to face meetings of this
nature leave little room for ambiguity, as Thatcher indicated after her first
meeting with the Chinese leadership over Hong Kong in 1982: 'We each
knew where the other stood.'[8] Summit meetings are also educational in a
more general sense in that they allow leaders to discuss issues and to be
briefed on subjects to which they would otherwise devote little time.
Regular, serial summit meetings such as the G-7, and CHOGM summits
where the pace is less urgent and the agenda less packed, are particularly
suited to this role.[9] Summit meetings also allow leaders to learn how well
their opposite numbers have thought through their positions on certain
issues, as opposed to how well their officials would have this view conveyed. Similarly, they afford an opportunity to learn the passion with which
certain positions may be held at the highest levels. Meetings of this nature
also allow the transfer of political wisdom between leaders with great experience of office and their newer counterparts. Thus during their meeting in
Aspen in August 1990 in the wake of the Iraqi invasion of Kuwait Thatcher
was able to offer counsel to President Bush in the light of her Falklands
War experience, advising him that 'this was no time to go wobbly' in an
attempt to strengthen his resolve.[10] In such circumstances summit meetings
offer the opportunity to construct and pronounce an agreed position of solidarity on a given issue or issues.

Summit meetings are also useful in imposing deadlines on a negotiation
process. In many bargaining situations the last points conceded are often
the most bitterly disputed. A set date for either the signing of a treaty or
the issuing of a final communiqué is often a useful discipline against a
more protracted negotiating process. The desire for the political leadership to conclude an agreement in order that the summit is seen to have
been a success often forces those concerned with the detailed negotiations
to clear away any remaining deadlocks in advance of the summit and to
identify any problems which remain truly intractable at their level. This
allows the summit itself to focus on these issues and to resolve them by
virtue of the political authority vested in those present. The influence of
the deadline is obviously more acute for 'one-off' or *ad hoc* summit meetings, since there is no prospect of the issues being deferred to the next
round of a serial summit. Indeed the September 1978 Camp David Summit
between Egypt, Israel and the United States was deliberately described by
President Carter as a last-chance effort to breathe new life into the failing

Middle East peace process which had started so dramatically with the initial meeting between Sadat and Begin.[11] The singularity of this opportunity undoubtedly contributed to its final success.

Meetings at summit level are also useful for elevating issues to the top of the international agenda and for dealing with problems with a speed and authority lacking in the established diplomatic channels. They also provide the opportunity to make progress in a number of different issue areas by allowing for bargaining across the agenda, or 'on a broad front' of issues. This 'linkage' of different issues, given its name by the diplomacy of Kissinger, is one of the most obvious advantages of this type of diplomatic activity. Not only does the summit provide the opportunity to pull together bureaucratically separate strands of diplomatic endeavour, but it does so in a way which allows compromises and deals in specific areas which would not be possible without counterbalancing concessions elsewhere. This function is particularly important when the diplomatic relationship between the parties is characterized at the lower level by bureaucratically separate officials limited by their departmental capacities.[12] In addition to this linking role for bargaining purposes summits are also valuable in that they allow issues to be considered in a holistic framework, allowing for policy coordination and integration at the international level. The G-7 summit meetings and the deliberations of the European Council are particularly suited to this type of activity. Indeed the rise to the top of the foreign policy agenda of instabilities in the financial markets and soaring energy and raw material prices promoted the development of these two international fora.

Summits also provide the opportunity for bold acts of international leadership capable of producing results which could not be accomplished at a lower level. Such breakthroughs can occur by virtue of the very act of meeting in itself, such as President Sadat's visit to Jerusalem in 1977 and Brandt's Ostpolitik summit meetings, or they can result from bold initiatives undertaken as part of a meeting which was not expected to produce dramatic results, such as the Reagan–Gorbachev summit of November 1986.[13] The common factor in this summit activity is the willingness of political leaders to exercise executive authority in an attempt to make a radical breakthrough on a particular issue area. While successful to a greater or lesser extent in all the cases cited above, this is by no means always the case. Chamberlain's flight to Munich in 1938 was a summit meeting of this nature with disastrous consequences. One should also not overlook the fact that Reagan's putative willingness to abandon all nuclear weapons at the Reykjavik summit, without reference to or regard for his allies, rocked the NATO alliance.

A similar function is fulfilled when a political leader acts as a mediator between disputing parties in order to resolve a crisis or overcome some diplomatic impasse. Already mentioned is the key role played by President Carter in the negotiation of the Camp David Accords. Several advantages follow from providing the services of a neutral interlocutor, who is at the same time an important actor on the world stage, if not an ally to the disputing parties. The summit is able to progress by virtue of the political authority of the parties involved, with the intermediary acting as a catalyst in the equation, being in a position to table compromises which the disputants might feel able to accept, but could not have proposed themselves. Whether this role need be fulfilled by a head of government, however, is open to question. Indeed one aspect of the 'political leader as mediator' role was exemplified by Henry Kissinger between November 1973 and January 1974 in his mediation of the Middle East conflict whilst he was National Security Adviser. Flying repeatedly between Arab capitals and Jerusalem in an attempt to bring about agreements on military disengagement, Kissinger set a pattern of 'shuttle diplomacy' which was to be repeated by successive politicians at levels below that of the summit.[14] For example, as an intermediary in the Falklands crisis in 1982, US Secretary of State Alexander Haig travelled 34 000 miles in five days in his attempt to broker a peaceful settlement to this conflict. While ultimately unsuccessful in avoiding further bloodshed this diplomacy was useful, at least from the British point of view, in demonstrating the intractability of the Argentine Junta and in filling the diplomatic vacuum until the Royal Navy was able to arrive to expel the invaders. As Ambassador Henderson records, 'Without Haig's toing and froing Argentinian intransigence would not have been exposed, and if this had not happened America might not have been so ready to back us in the way they did.'[15] Thus where political leaders are unable or unwilling to meet, mediation is best left to emissaries.

Finally, the involvement of political leaders dealing directly with one another can be useful for the promotion of exports and, indeed, the national image. This is particularly important for countries such as the Gulf states, which like to conclude export deals, such as major arms purchases, at the highest political level.

THE DISADVANTAGES OF SUMMIT DIPLOMACY

As has been demonstrated, elevating diplomatic interaction to the level of the summit can benefit from the greater degree of authority and publicity which these meetings enjoy. With these advantages, however, comes a set of corresponding disadvantages. An early critic of meetings between political principals was Harold Nicolson. Writing in 1919, and inflamed by what he regarded as the failures of the Versailles Conference, Nicolson lamented that

> Nothing could be more fateful than the habit (the at present fatal and pernicious habit) of personal contact between the statesmen of the world. It is argued, in defence of this pastime, that the foreign secretaries of the nations 'get to know each other.' This is an extremely dangerous cognisance. Personal contact breeds, inevitably, personal acquaintance and that in turn, leads in many cases to friendliness: there is nothing more damaging to precision in international relations than friendliness between contracting parties.... Diplomacy is the art of negotiating documents in a ratifiable and therefore dependable form. It is by no means the art of conversation. The affability inseparable from any conversation ... produces allusiveness, compromises, and high intentions.[16]

Nor is this criticism absent from commentaries of contemporary summit meetings. With the collapse of the Soviet Union both Presidents Bush and Clinton have been accused of supporting the leadership of first Gorbachev and then Yeltsin at the expense of their country's overall relationship with Moscow. While both American leaders defended their approach on the grounds that Russia's democratic future was inextricably bound up with the fortunes of these two individuals, others criticized them for being over supportive of personalities with whom they felt that they could work. President Clinton was criticized, for example, for being 'oddly protective of his counterpart' at the May 1995 Moscow summit, an approach which critics argued 'reinforces the impression that the administration has a pro-Yeltsin policy, not a pro-democracy policy'.[17]

As well as the danger of getting to know, like and depend on their opposite numbers there is also the danger that leaders will form judgements on insufficient or ideologically motivated grounds at summits. David Owen indicated this tension in negotiating with what he regarded as the 'corrupt' and 'totalitarian' Soviet leadership, when he remarked that 'I had to deal with these people within the diplomatic niceties but I despised and distrusted them.'[18] More famous was the conclusion which Khrushchev drew from his 1961 summit meeting with President Kennedy in Vienna that, 'I know for certain that Kennedy doesn't have a strong backbone, nor, generally speaking, does he have the courage to stand up to a serious challenge.'[19] Even between allies personal relationships at the summit may influence the diplomatic relationship. For example, as Ball argues, in the 1960s 'Anglo-American relations were seriously impeded by the fact that President Johnson and Prime Minister Wilson were temperamentally poles apart and did not basically like one another'.[20] On the other hand, the positive personal relationship between President Kennedy and Prime Minister Macmillan at the Nassau summit was, according to Ball, instrumental in securing Britain's purchase of the Polaris missile system against the advice of both the American State Department and the Pentagon. Ball's conclusion about the dangers of summitry are very clear, that 'when leaders have disparate backgrounds, customs, and language and, in many cases, ethical attitudes and ideologies, summitry is more likely to produce mistaken and misleading impressions than a clear meeting of minds'.[21]

As well as the potential for clashes of personality there is also the risk in summit diplomacy that the politician's lack of diplomatic expertise may actually impede the negotiation of an agreement or indeed lead to a misunderstanding. Again this disadvantage is not restricted to the involvement of leaders, as some of the following examples illustrate. Alexander Haig's failure as a mediator in the Falklands crisis, according to Freedman and Gamba-Stonehouse, may in part have 'reflected personal limitations; tact, patience and calm temper were not his strengths ... he did not always appreciate the nuances of the dispute and the symbolic baggage carried by words such as "interests" and "wishes" when considering the views of the islanders'.[22] Ambassador Henderson was no less revealing in his description of Haig's 'characteristic way of saying two contradictory things in succession'.[23] Another example is provided by the summit meeting on British entry to the European Economic Community between Prime Minister Macmillan and President de Gaulle at Rambouillet in 1962. There was speculation within the British Foreign Office at the time as to whether Macmillan's decision to conduct this meeting in French had 'materially altered the course of history' given the Prime Minister's linguistic limitations.[24] This mixture of lack of technical competence with supreme self-confidence has also proved damaging to the negotiation of arms control agreements by politicians. In his personal 'back channel' contacts with Soviet Ambassador Dobrynin as part of the SALT I negotiations Kissinger gratuitously conceded an important point to the Soviet Union by excluding Submarine Launched Ballistic Missiles (SLBMs) from their discussion of 'offensive weapons', with disastrous diplomatic consequences and to the detriment of the final agreement and SALT process. As chief US SALT negotiator Gerard Smith explains,

Here, in one sentence, the position on which the United States had pressed for almost a year was changed. There is no evidence to indicate that this major change in SALT policy was ever considered in advance by anybody except Kissinger – and perhaps not even by him. It may well have been a random answer of a fatigued and overextended man who did not realise the immense significance of his words. It was to take a lot of effort and expenditure of bargaining power to redeem those words and restore the earlier US position that SLBMs must be included in any SALT agreement. Dobrynin pocketed the offer diplomatically....[25]

Kissinger exacerbated his mistake by failing to admit his error to the official SALT negotiators with the result that they were at a disadvantage in trying to negotiate a point which had already been conceded at a higher level.[26] As this example shows, this disadvantage is not limited to the involvement of leaders in diplomacy. It is an example which nevertheless illustrates the dangers of this sort of activity whether engaged in by political principals or senior politicians more generally. For the most part, however, such instances are rare since many political leaders know their limitations and conclude, as did President Kennedy in 1961, that 'a summit is not a place to carry on negotiations which involve details'.[27] When detailed discussions are attempted this can lead politicians into areas beyond their competence, with unfruitful results. Ambassador Henderson describes one such encounter between Thatcher and Reagan in which a disagreement over the trans-Siberian pipeline 'led to a muddled discussion in which neither side knew the facts'.[28] Chancellor Kohl even admitted after the 1991 London G-7 summit that the details of the economic declaration were best left to the sherpas since 'only they really understand what it means'.[29] But if the participants' comprehension of the issue is limited then is this not a further disadvantage of summitry? This must certainly be the case if the lack of grasp of the issues is due to a lack of diligence on the part of the political leader. President Reagan was one head of state whose interest in and grasp of even rudimentary concepts in arms control is well documented.[30] His failure to prepare for the 1983 Colonial Williamsburg G-7 summit, however, was due only to indolence. Cannon gives an account of how White House Chief of Staff James Baker made a point of personally delivering a slimmed-down briefing-book to the President to ensure that he had mastered the material.

But when Baker returned ... the next morning, he found the briefing book unopened on the table where he had deposited it. He knew immediately that Reagan hadn't even glanced at it, and he couldn't believe it.

In an hour Reagan would be presiding over the first meeting of the economic summit, the only one held in the United States during his presidency. Uncharacteristically, Baker asked Reagan why he hadn't cracked the briefing book. 'Well, Jim, *The Sound of Music* was on last night', Reagan replied calmly.[31]

As well as being capable of incompetence or indolence there is also the danger that politicians will allow their vanity and penchant for badinage to lead them to score points from their opposite numbers at the summit. Such instances may be disruptive to the smooth running of a summit meeting and can be extremely destructive if aimed at a carefully worded compromise resulting from the meeting. At all levels of diplomacy, for a compromise position to be the basis of further harmonious interaction it is imperative that the conclusion not be hailed as a victory for either side, and instead that it be presented as the common ground of good sense. This is especially important following a summit meeting where such conclusions are in the media spotlight. For politicians eager to present the evidence of their negotiating victory to their domestic audiences, however, there is often a temptation to violate this diplomatic rule. Mrs Thatcher, for example, severely damaged her credibility in the eyes of the Commonwealth after her smug press conference immediately following the conclusion of a delicately formulated position. As Howe explains,

> Margaret set out to present not the successful achievement of a concerted Commonwealth policy for change in South Africa but only the triumphant insignificance of the concession *she* had had to make to achieve it.... [She] proclaimed that she had moved 'a tiny little bit'. With four little words she had at one and the same time humiliated three dozen other heads of government, devalued the policy on which they had just agreed – and demeaned herself. She had certainly ensured that they would be a good deal less easy at any future such meeting. Even I could scarcely believe my ears.[32]

Even when politicians refrain from such point-scoring immediately after a summit, the media attention which results from their involvement in diplomatic negotiations can still be an obstacle to good relations. Inevitably politicians will feel the need to justify their concessions to their domestic audiences as trivial and slight, while in the negotiating room they were described as painful and difficult to grant. With the media attention which political involvement brings, however, adversary and constituency each hear the message intended only for one set of ears.[33] The repercussions of these messages can help unravel hard-fought deals, and further complicate future negotiations.

The level at which summit negotiations are conducted also means that proposals made, deals struck, or arguments advanced are more difficult to disavow since they can not be dismissed as the unauthorized musings of a mere official. As Dean Rusk observed, 'the direct confrontation of the chiefs of government of the great powers involves an extra tension because the court of last resort is in session'.[34] A similar sentiment, if more dramatically expressed, is Dean Acheson's comment: 'When a chief of state or head of government makes a fumble, the goal line is open behind him.'[35] While this was obviously more important for crisis diplomacy between the superpowers than for other meetings in which the stakes were not so high, the point is generally applicable. Thus detailed caveats omitted, misleading impressions given and unsustainable concessions suggested are difficult to renegotiate after the political authority of the leader has been associated with them. This disadvantage of summit diplomacy can be compounded when leaders decide to conduct this 'court of last resort' unaided by their specialist advisers, or worse still, their own interpreters. Without their advisers they are less likely to conclude detailed negotiations which reflect the complexities of the issues concerned. Without their own interpreters leaders become totally dependent on the accuracy and integrity of the other side's officials and have no way of knowing if theirs or their interlocutor's words are being faithfully translated. In the absence of this safeguard their message may be mangled in translation because the interpreter either misunderstands, or misrepresents them for fear of offending the leader with candid language.[36] Furthermore, without their own interpreters there is no official observer's account of the negotiations apart from the version of events represented by the leader, whose account may be biased by the way he or she would have liked the talks to have gone, rather than being an accurate reflection of the actual discussion. Thus any embarrassing gaffes made by political leaders in such situations, or technical or linguistic subtleties missed by their inexpert eyes and ears, are likely to be lost forever from the official record.[37] Both Nixon and Kissinger at times relied solely on their interlocutor's interpreters with disadvantageous and embarrassing results. As chief US SALT negotiator Gerard Smith recalls of the May 1971 joint statement negotiated in secret by Kissinger: 'I was embarrassed by the obvious Russian origin of some of the language. No American would have proposed [such syntax]. That looked to me like transliteration of a Soviet text.'[38] While not a situation exclusive to summit meetings, as this example illustrates, the involvement of non-experts in diplomacy has disadvantages which are compounded when perpetrated by political leaders.

Another potential pitfall of summitry, which may be the consequence of a failure to consult expert advice, is the possibility that broader political messages can be conveyed inadvertently during such meetings. Nixon's surprise visit to China in 1972 is a classic example of a visit intended primarily for domestic electoral advantage which was interpreted in Beijing and the surrounding region as the US 'kowtowing' to the Chinese and an act of recognition of their pre-eminence in Asia.[39] This visit was also deeply damaging to America's relations with Japan in general and to Prime Minister Sato's authority in particular. The latter, who had resisted internal pressure for a *rapprochement* with China in deference to Washington, was humiliated not only by the visit but by the fact that he was given no prior warning of the President's plans. The symbolism of Nixon's visit to Asia and the loss of face which he had inflicted on Sato were cultural considerations which the President had failed to consider, since they did not form part of his own decision-making processes and he had failed to take expert advice.[40] For Nixon, the most important symbolic aspect of the visit was that it marked the end of the isolation of China, and the thaw in hostility in relations between Washington and the communist regime in Beijing. His own cultural perspective blinded him to the other meaning which his visit held for China, Japan and Asia more generally.

Negotiations across cultural divides have long been a problematic feature of diplomacy and international business alike which can only be overcome through detailed knowledge of the other party's perspective. By its very nature summit diplomacy can run into difficulties in this area if insufficient attention is paid to the values which different cultures attribute to both the form and substance of negotiation. Where leaders ignore local advice and act as if they are dealing with individuals who share their cultural perspectives, misunderstanding may well result. Indeed the very idea of the summit meeting may possess features which make it less suitable for conducting negotiations across cultures than the established diplomatic channels. This may be especially so in negotiations between Westerners, whose individualistic approach places little importance on the context of their talks, and those from 'high-context' societies such as those in Asia, Latin America and Egypt, where the context is regarded as crucial.[41] Whereas the approach of the Western 'low-context' culture is results-orientated, problem-solving and analogous to a Western business meeting, 'briskly cutting out the cackle for a necessary quick return' this approach is often antithetical to the 'high-context' cultural tradition.[42] For the latter, negotiation is less about problem-solving than about attending to a relationship. These cultures show great discomfort with a 'let's not beat about the bush' approach. As Cohen explains, 'for the smooth conduct of affairs in these societies, partners need to establish warm, personal ties'.[43] More specifically, as Solomon explains with reference to the Chinese, they

> attempt to identify foreign officials who are sympathetic to their cause, to cultivate a sense of friendship and obligation in their official counterparts, and then to pursue their objectives through a variety of stratagems designed to manipulate feelings of friendship, obligation, guilt or dependence.[44]

Thus when summit meetings take place between leaders from two different cultural groups problems may result unless these factors have been taken into account. One of the principle ways of overcoming these difficulties is to ensure that all points of substance have been agreed in advance and that the preparations for the summit have been cognizant of the cultural requirements and have accordingly included a substantial pre-negotiation phase. Even in these circumstances, however, cultural misunderstandings may result. The importance of not losing 'face' to individuals from 'high-context' societies, for example, has as one of its features the reluctance to deliver a blunt 'no' in negotiations. For individuals from 'low-context' societies the absence of a blunt refusal may lead to an exaggerated belief that a 'yes' remains possible. Thus during Prime Minister Sato's visit to Washington in 1969 when the Japanese leader replied to Nixon's question by saying 'Zenshosoru' which, literally translated, means 'I will do my best', the President took it to mean that he had his guest's agreement.[45] In fact, however, the expression is a classic Japanese circumlocution implying 'it can't be done'. Only after Sato's return to Japan did it become apparent to Washington that no agreement had been reached. It was a misunderstanding which outraged Nixon who denounced Sato, in private, as a 'liar', and which caused distrust in their subsequent relationship.[46]

An associated disadvantage of summitry is the cultural expectation that the participant at a summit meeting is always 'in charge' and 'can deliver' on any promises made. In a sense this is cultural mirror-imaging in which the leadership role within other countries' decision-making processes are assumed to be the same as one's own. Where this is not the case misunderstandings may well result. At least part of Prime Minister Sato's inability to deliver what President Nixon wanted and believed he had been promised in November 1969 was the fact that the Japanese leader did not have the authority to make such an agreement on textile exports. Thus, for reasons of cultural differences, Cohen concludes of Sato's Washington visit: 'The summit conference was not the best forum for making negotiating progress; the hard sell was not the way to treat Japanese ministers; and domestic officials could not be railroaded or bypassed.'[47]

In cross-cultural negotiations, then, it should not be assumed that participants in summit meetings are able to act with executive authority. But this situation is not only limited to summits between leaders of different cultures. Indeed many prime ministers are effectively limited by their need for subsequent cabinet or parliamentary approval of policies which may prove contentious domestically. This is especially the case where the leader is the head of a coalition government, and the backing of the minority parties cannot be taken for granted. This is not only the case for prime ministers. Even the signature of the US President on the SALT II Treaty in 1979 was not enough to see that agreement enacted into law. As with Woodrow Wilson's attempt to take America into the League of Nations in 1920, President Carter was unable to muster enough support for his treaty to secure its ratification by the US Senate.

Summit meetings also have the disadvantage for modern leaders of being enormous consumers of time and energy. The effect of jet lag on the performance of politicians is one such consumer of energy which tends to be overlooked in most accounts of summit meetings, but its impact is unlikely to be negligible. According to experts, the body's natural clock, once in the air, is no longer fully synchronized with the world outside, with the result that travellers become disoriented, and judgement can be impaired. As a consequence, according to Horne, 'statesmen are likely to be less flexible in their thinking, more irritable and more forgetful. They tend to think in more rigid ways. If someone comes up with a good idea, they would have trouble assimilating it.'[48] For those who spend prolonged periods travelling, such as those engaged in episodes of shuttle diplomacy, there must be a corresponding cost to the quality of the negotiations.[49] That said, however, politicians, especially those who owe their office to the gruelling schedules of the campaign trail, are generally individuals of exceptional stamina. Thatcher's account of her preparation for her address before the joint Houses of Congress in 1985 illustrates this point perfectly.

> Ignoring any jet lag I practised [with the Autocue] until 4 am. I did not go to bed, beginning the new working day with my usual black coffee and vitamin pill, then gave television interviews from 6.45 am, had my hair done and was ready at 10.30 to leave for the Capitol.... I had a terrific reception.[50]

This is facilitated by the fact that for some leaders, at any rate, the aircraft on which they fly do not resemble ordinary scheduled airliners in anything other than their outward appearance. Instead, beds, office space and communications equipment make the internal environment of these aircraft much more comfortable than the flying experience of the general public.[51] However, the problem remains a salient factor in summit diplomacy and its influence should not be underestimated.

Even if politicians are able to minimize the effects of jet lag, the time taken in getting to and participating in summit meetings is time unavailable for other things in a busy schedule. This is especially so for those parts of summit meetings occupied by ceremonial wreath-laying, inspections of the guard and by official banquets. Added to this is the fact that half of all the time set aside for actually talking is usually taken up with translation of the other leaders' words, including the pleasantries required by protocol and the digressions indulged in by the participants. At the US–Soviet summit in Geneva in 1985, for example, Reagan digressed in his discussion with Gorbachev onto the subject of earthquakes, delivering a long monologue on their effects on California since AD 500. As one observer remarked, 'I tried to estimate how much time was consumed by Reagan's delivery and the interpreter's translation of his San Andreas Fault gig while the world wondered what momentous issues the two most important people on earth were wrestling over during their initial encounter.'[52]

Participation in summit meetings also has its share of personal dangers for those involved. Most obvious are the risks associated with long-distance travel. In the early days of air travel these risks were graver than they are now, with half the British delegation to the Yalta conference dying in a plane crash *en route*, and a similar fate befalling some of the UK delegates returning from the first UN conference in San Francisco in 1945.[53] While thankfully the deaths of leaders in transit are rare the risks exist and the loss of 'sherpas' would not be without cost to either the substance or the atmosphere of a summit. In a slightly different vein, Brezhnev was forced to admit to his physical ill health before his summit meeting with Carter in 1979, insisting that the summit not be held in the US as planned for fear that the transatlantic journey would be too much for him.[54] More commonly, however, frequent attendance at overseas meetings leads to the political ill health of the participants domestically. This applies equally to foreign ministers as well as leaders themselves. As Howe recounts, 'I was probably airborne for at least ten hours a week and overseas for much longer than that. This was bound to have an effect on my personal position in the political spectrum – on the Westminster stage, in the public eye, in my relations with colleagues.'[55] President Bush was certainly perceived by his critics and by the presidential electorate in 1992 as having spent a disproportionate amount of energy on international affairs, including summit meetings of one sort or another.[56] Attendance at summit meetings at key times resulting in important absences from the domestic scene can also be politically fatal. British Prime Minister Callaghan returned from a G-7 summit in Guadeloupe in the winter of 1978–9 to be represented in the popular press as unaware of and uncaring about the domestic political turmoil which he had left behind. The newspaper headline 'Crisis, what crisis?' alongside a picture of the sun-tanned Premier probably contributed to his electoral defeat the following spring. Similarly, Thatcher was attending a summit meeting in Paris in November 1990 when the mortal blow was struck to her leadership. Eager to participate in the summit celebrating the end of the cold war, Thatcher had miscalculated in assuming that her presence was not required in Westminster.

With so many disadvantages it is little wonder that professional diplomats should be so scathing in their lamentations about the growth of summitry. The worst dangers of summitry, however, are usually avoided by the caution of the participants and the measures taken as part of the preparatory process to minimize the risks. Central to the success of summitry is the role of advance preparation. Indeed steps are usually taken long in advance of the actual summit to ensure that a treaty will be ready for signature, or at the very least a communiqué can be agreed upon with which all parties are happy. As Kissinger observes, 'Nixon never left summit meetings to chance; all his were settled in their main parts before he arrived. He would not participate in one – until his desperate last months – without having a reasonable idea of its outcome.'[57] Nor was the insistence on caution and advance preparation true only for the major substance of Nixon's superpower summits. It was also true of the official communiqués which followed summit meetings. As Kissinger continues,

> The outside observer tends to believe, and is encouraged to do so by heads of government, that these joint pronouncements grow spontaneously out of the discussions they purport to summarize. The opposite is usually true. The discussions of heads of government are framed by a communiqué usually drafted beforehand. To leave communiqué drafting for the actual visit is to court disaster.[58]

Nor was Nixon exceptional in insisting upon this level of advance preparation to guard against failure. While this degree of attention to detail is obviously crucial for summits such as those between the superpowers in which the level of agreement was important symbolically, other circumstances also require such safeguards. Summits of short duration, such as European Council meetings, or those involving many parties, such as NATO summits, routinely prepare their final communiqués in advance. Indeed, at the 1995 G-7 summit in Halifax great embarrassment was caused when a draft of the final communiqué was leaked to the press ten days before the meeting.[59]

Summit meetings are usually prepared well in advance by both the relevant technical departments, such as the arms control or economics departments, and by the foreign ministry officials. It is these individuals, by and large, who will determine how successful a summit will be. As well as the preparation of the communiqués, detailed consultation is also conducted on the nature and substance of media contact and the public diplomacy aspects of the encounter, such as 'walkabouts', wreath-laying, visits, speeches and joint press statements.[60] Though these aspects of summit meetings appear relatively innocuous, if insufficient thought is given to their preparation they can overshadow the meeting itself. This was the case with the 1985 G-7 summit in Bonn where Reagan's decision to visit a war cemetery at Bitburg, at Chancellor Kohl's invitation, esca-lated into a major incident when it was discovered that 49 SS soldiers, some decorated for killing American servicemen, were buried there.[61] Rather than change Reagan's published itinerary, further preparations were made to offset the Bitburg ceremony with a visit to the Bergen-Belsen concentration camp. By this stage, however, the damage had already been done to Reagan's reputation in Germany and the US.

Advanced preparation of agreement in principle can often be the condition under which summit meetings actually take place. Some parties, rather than risk the failure of a summit, will postpone the meeting if insufficient progress is made in advance, if need be indefinitely. Such were judged to be the risks of a 'failed' summit for the Northern Ireland peace process by the Irish government in September 1995 that it unilaterally cancelled its summit meeting in London at less than one day's notice.[62] A more common way of trying to guard against the political consequences of a failure to achieve tangible success at summit meetings is to try to play down public expectations of the encounter. Thus summit meetings may be described as 'preparatory meetings' as was the case with the Vladivostok meeting between Brezhnev and Ford in 1974, or as merely a 'pre-summit', 'base camp', or 'talks about talks', as with the Reykjavik meeting between Reagan and Gorbachev in 1986. Another means of damping down expectations at a summit meeting is to stress the informality of the occasion. By removing the pomp and thus reducing the symbolism of a summit, leaders can insist that the purpose of their meeting is merely for background consultation. Thus at the Halifax G-7 summit in 1995 there were no state dinners, all meetings were working meetings and the location was chosen for its remoteness. Such preparations, however, are no guarantee against failure, as the many examples above illustrate.

CONCLUSIONS

As has been demonstrated, summitry is a risky business. It may create misunderstanding, cause unintended offence and sow the seeds of mistrust. What is more, its accomplishments may only be of political benefit for the individuals involved, and these achievements may be at the expense of longer-term diplomatic relationships. These risks, however, may only be magnified by summit meetings and would probably exist whether or not the leaders involved actually met. For this reason, one needs to be careful to differentiate between opposition to summit meetings as such and opposition to the involvement of politicians in international politics.

Because summitry does involve high stakes, however, it can also produce positive results. The political risks involved in meeting at this high-profile level can be very useful in galvanizing the bureaucracies of international institutions and domestic governments alike into finalizing the last details of an agreement. The meetings themselves can also act as pockets of urgency to ensure that remaining obstacles can be overcome. Providing there has been sufficient preparation, particularly in serial summits such as the European Council, summit meetings can indeed be the venue for substantive dialogue. Even if the main purpose is symbolic, this function of the summit should not be underestimated in its contribution to the dialogue between states. Nor should an overly cynical approach be taken to summit meetings which are largely 'pre-cooked'. Preparation is the key to success at summit meetings and the fact that agreement has been substantially reached before the meeting does not necessarily imply that this situation could have been achieved without the pressure of the forthcoming event itself. While largely a function of the international organization or relationship involved, the degree to which summit meetings are in fact 'pre-cooked' can vary enormously from issue to issue. Even in those fora, such as NATO summits, where the conclusions have been substantially predetermined, the 'pre-cooked' agenda needs the 'quick blast in the microwave' that its discussion and approval at the summit meeting bestows upon the final declaration.[63]

After falling into decline in the fifteenth century with the development of the resident ambassador, the summit meeting has re-established itself in the second half of the twentieth century, and shows no sign of decline. Summitry has evolved considerably in the post-war period. From being an exceptional and therefore high-profile event, summitry has developed to become a frequent and routine instrument of international diplomacy. As summits occurred more frequently, however, so too did the alarm of observers that this new development would seek to replace the established channels of diplomacy. Thus commentators like Jackson warned that 'with nothing but summit diplomacy the nations risk exchanging marriage for a mere mating, an intermittent rut in which a frenzied collision of the parties briefly and single-mindedly interrupts long intervals of mutual aversion'.[64] Such alarm, however, is misplaced since summitry has taken its place alongside the traditional channels of diplomatic discourse in a way which complements the pre-existing system. For serial summits at least, as meetings have become more institutionalized many of the dangers associated with this exceptional type of diplomatic encounter have disappeared. With fixed agendas, detailed advanced planning and the ease of conversation which results from the frequency with which leaders meet in one forum or another, summits have become an established part of the dialogue between states. While the growth of this new institution has been at the expense of the ambassador and the professional diplomatic service, it is far from clear that this has been to the general detriment of effective dialogue between states. As has been demonstrated above, summitry, while not without its risks, can bestow considerable benefits if employed judiciously and with caution. What is more, the temptation for politicians to become involved in this activity shows no sign of abating. Despite its critics, summitry has become the preferred means of international dialogue: diplomacy at the highest level.

NOTES AND REFERENCES

1. James Der Derian, *Antidiplomacy: Spies, Terror, Speed, and War* (Oxford, Blackwell, 1992), p. 34.
2. Cited by Chas W. Freeman, *The Diplomat's Dictionary* (Washington DC, National Defence University Press, 1994), p. 373.
3. Margaret Thatcher, *The Downing Street Years* (London, Harper Collins, 1993), pp. 463 and 71.
4. Strobe Talbott, *Endgame: The Inside Story of SALT II* (London, Harper and Row, 1979), p. 1.

5. Ibid., p. 7.
6. Keith Hamilton and Richard Langhorne, *The Practice of Diplomacy* (London, Routledge, 1995), p. 221.
7. Bhutto paid $400,000 to International Public Strategies, Inc. to market her themed visit of 'democratic partnership' which succeeded in improving her own and Pakistan's support ratings in the United States. See Jarol B. Manheim, *Strategic Public Diplomacy and American Foreign Policy* (Oxford, Oxford University Press, 1994), chapter 5. It is also interesting to contrast this example with the very different visit to Washington made by Korea's President Roh, which was low-key and made little impact in the US capital. Roh, however, was concentrating on domestic Korean opinion, and in these terms the visit was a great success. See chapter 4.
8. Thatcher, *The Downing Street Years*, p. 262.
9. Geoffrey Howe describes how the Commonwealth summits served as 'a useful coalescing of ideas', observing, 'what a pity it is ... that American leaders have no opportunity to enjoy such relaxed exchanges'. Geoffrey Howe, *Conflict of Loyalty* (London, Macmillan, 1994), pp. 350–1.
10. Thatcher, *The Downing Street Years*, p. 824.
11. See G. R. Berridge, *Diplomacy: Theory and Practice* (London, Prentice Hall/Harvester Wheatsheaf, 1995), p. 89.
12. Abba Eban, *The New Diplomacy: International Affairs in the Modern Age* (New York, Random House, 1983), p. 362.
13. Of Sadat's visit to Israel in November 1977 and the Middle East Peace process that led to the Camp David Accords, David Owen observes that 'it could only be the personal chemistry between the Right-wing leader of the Likud Party, Prime Minister Menachem Begin, and President Anwar Sadat, the former air force officer and member of Nasser's military committee that overthrew King Farouk, which would provide a breakthrough'. David Owen, *Time to Declare* (London, Michael Joseph, 1991), p. 341.
14. See Sir Geoffrey Jackson, *Concord Diplomacy: The Ambassador's Role in the World Today* (London, Hamish Hamilton, 1981), p. 16.
15. Nicholas Henderson, *Mandarin: The Diaries of an Ambassador* (London, Weidenfeld and Nicolson, 1994), pp. 474–5.
16. Harold Nicolson cited by Charles Thayer, *Diplomat* (New York, Harper and Brothers, 1959), p. 109. Nicolson was actually talking about foreign ministers here but the point is equally applicable to summit meetings.
17. Michael McFaul of the Carnegie Endowment in Moscow, cited in *Newsweek*, 22 May 1995, p. 25.
18. Owen, *Time to Declare*, p. 337.
19. Khrushchev, cited by Arkady N. Shevchenko, *Breaking with Moscow* (New York, Alfred A. Knopf, 1985), p. 117. Cited by Gordon R. Weihmiller and Dusko Doder, *US–Soviet Summits* (London, University Press of America, 1986), p. 48.
20. George Ball, *Diplomacy for a Crowded World* (Boston, Little, Brown and Company, 1976), p. 32. See also Alan P. Dobson, *Anglo-American Relations in the Twentieth Century* (London, Routledge, 1995), p. 131.
21. Ball, *Diplomacy for a Crowded World*, p. 32.
22. Lawrence Freedman and Virginia Gamba-Stonehouse, *Signals of War: The Falklands Conflict of 1982* (London, Faber and Faber, 1990), p. 239.

23. Henderson, *Mandarin*, p. 467.
24. Ball, *Diplomacy for a Crowded World*, p. 39.
25. Gerard Smith, *Double Talk: The Story of SALT I* (London, University Press of America, 1985), pp. 228–9.
26. See Raymond L. Garthoff, *Détente and Confrontation: American–Soviet Relations from Nixon to Reagan*, revised edition (Washington DC, Brookings Institution, 1994), chapter 5. As Garthoff notes, the diplomatic record on this episode 'has remained shrouded in secrecy and subject to confusion for a very good reason: Kissinger came to realise that he had not negotiated the substance of the offensive limitations advantageously, or even satisfactorily, and sought to conceal the fact' (p. 179). See also Smith, *Double Talk*, chapter 7.
27. Theodore C. Sorenson, *Kennedy* (New York, Harper and Row, 1965), pp. 541–2. Cited by Gordon R. Weihmiller and Dusko Doder, *US–Soviet Summits* (London, University Press of America, 1986), p. 44.
28. Henderson, *Mandarin*, p. 479.
29. Nicholas Bayne, 'The Course of Summitry', *The World Today*, vol. 48, no. 2 (February 1992), p. 28.
30. Reagan developed his own simplistic terminology for the different types of offensive systems under discussion, referring to them as 'slow flyers' and 'fast flyers'. Strobe Talbott, *Deadly Gambits* (London, Picador, 1984), p. 132. See also Robert, Scheer, *With Enough Shovels: Reagan, Bush and Nuclear War* (New York, Vintage Books, 1981).
31. Lou Cannon, *President Reagan: The Role of a Lifetime* (New York, Simon and Schuster, 1991), p. 41.
32. Howe, *Conflict of Loyalty*, p. 482.
33. Eban, *The New Diplomacy*, p. 556.
34. Cited by Freeman, *The Diplomat's Dictionary*, p. 371.
35. Dean Acheson, *Present at the Creation: My Years in the State Department* (New York, Norton & Company, 1969), p. 480.
36. See Ball, *Diplomacy for a Crowded World*, p. 38.
37. Ibid.
38. Smith, *Double Talk*, pp. 224–5.
39. As Ball explains, 'for the Chinese leadership the symbolism and excitement of the spectacle clearly meant a Great Leap Forward in world politics. The fact that the chief of state of the world's most powerful nation came five thousand miles and was content to spend most of his visit with the second in command, Prime Minister Chou, rather than the chief of state, Chairman Mao, was an unprecedented gesture of respect, verging on subservience, which the Chinese have not seen necessary or fitting to reciprocate.' *Diplomacy for a Crowded World*, p. 26.
40. Raymond Cohen, *Negotiating Across Cultures: Communication Obstacles in International Diplomacy* (Washington DC, United States Institute for Peace Press, 1991), p. 37.
41. The 'high-context'/'low-context' dichotomy was described by Edward T. Hall, *Beyond Culture* (New York, Anchor Books, 1973), p. 157; cited by Cohen, *Negotiating Across Cultures*, p. 25.
42. Jackson, *Concord Diplomacy*, p. 7.
43. Cohen, *Negotiating Across Cultures*, p. 53.

44. Richard H. Solomon, *Chinese Political Negotiating Behaviour: A Briefing Analysis* (Santa Monica, The RAND Corporation, 1985), p. 2; cited by Cohen, *Negotiating Across Cultures*, p. 53.

45. Raymond Cohen, 'Cross-Cultural Dimension of International Negotiation', unpublished paper, delivered at BISA Conference, Newcastle University, 17–19 December 1990, p. 11.

46. C. Haberman, 'The Japanese Have a Way (out) With Words', *International Herald Tribune*, 26–27 March 1988, pp. 1, 4; cited by Cohen, 'Cross-Cultural', p. 9.

47. Cohen, 'Cross-Cultural', p. 11.

48. Professor Jim Horne, Director of the Sleep Research Laboratory at Loughborough University. Cited by Marcus Warren, 'Politicians pay penalty for jet set high life', *Sunday Telegraph*, 15 January 1995. Other reports tell how accidents and injuries account for 25 times more deaths of travellers abroad than do infections or tropical diseases due to the disorientation caused by jet lag. See Lois Rogers, 'UK scientists find a wonder cure for jet lag', *The Sunday Times*, 20 July 1995.

49. Jackson, *Concord Diplomacy*, p. 18.

50. Thatcher, *The Downing Street Years*, p. 469.

51. George Shultz's memoirs, *Turmoil and Triumph: My Years as Secretary of State* (New York, Scribners, 1993) even includes a photograph of him playing golf on board Air Force One. See p. 594, plate 12.

52. Kenneth L. Adelman, *The Great Universal Embrace: Arms Summitry – A Skeptic's Account* (New York, Simon and Schuster, 1989), p. 124.

53. Jackson, *Concord Diplomacy*, p. 178.

54. Talbott, *Endgame*, p. 11.

55. Howe, *Conflict of Loyalty*, p. 397.

56. See Wyn Bowen and David H. Dunn, *American Security Policy in the 1990s: Beyond Containment* (Aldershot, Dartmouth Press, 1996), chapter 1.

57. Henry Kissinger, *White House Years* (Boston, Little, Brown and Company, 1979), p. 769.

58. Ibid., p. 781.

59. Reginald Dale, 'The G-7 Emperors Have No Clothes', *International Herald Tribune*, 13 June 1995.

60. Berridge, *Diplomacy*, p. 93.

61. See Lou Cannon, *President Reagan*, pp. 573–84. The Bitburg incident lost Reagan considerable domestic support, and 53 senators protested, but once announced could not easily be abandoned without damaging US–German relations.

62. *The Times*, 6 September 1995.

63. I am grateful to David Nicholls for this apt analogy.

64. Jackson, *Concord Diplomacy*, p. 7.

Index